Information Technology and Law Series

Volume 36

More information about this series at https://link.springer.com/bookseries/8857

Alessandro Mantelero

Beyond Data

Human Rights, Ethical and Social Impact Assessment in AI

ASSER PRESS

Springer

Alessandro Mantelero
DIGEP
Politecnico di Torino
Torino, Italy

ISSN 1570-2782 ISSN 2215-1966 (electronic)
Information Technology and Law Series
ISBN 978-94-6265-530-0 ISBN 978-94-6265-531-7 (eBook)
https://doi.org/10.1007/978-94-6265-531-7

Published by T.M.C. ASSER PRESS, The Hague, The Netherlands www.asserpress.nl
Produced and distributed for T.M.C. ASSER PRESS by Springer-Verlag Berlin Heidelberg

This T.M.C. ASSER PRESS imprint is published by the registered company Springer-Verlag GmbH, DE part of Springer Nature.
The registered company address is: Heidelberger Platz 3, 14197 Berlin, Germany

To Bruna and Giuseppe

Foreword

It is probably safe to say that at the time of writing[1] more than 99% of the world's population do not yet understand what a game-changer AI can be…or is already proving to be. Much news coverage, for example, is still given to efforts which aim to prevent states like Iran or North Korea from developing nuclear weapons and increasingly sophisticated means of delivering them. Yet relatively little news coverage is given to the fact that, in reality, AI has made nuclear weapons obsolete. Why would a state—or indeed a terrorist—wish to deploy or acquire a very expensive and relatively unstable nuclear weapon when it can instead deploy much cheaper AI-controlled devices which do not create a radioactive crater or destroy so many valuable assets in a target zone?

In one of the saddest unintentional puns to emerge about the endemic inability of the world's nations to agree and deploy sufficient safeguards and remedies in international law, AI powers LAWs—Lethal Autonomous Weapons. These can take many shapes and sizes but perhaps none more sinister than "killer drones" capable of facial recognition thus being able to single out human targets to which they can deliver an explosive device. These drones can not only be easily and cheaply mass produced to the extent that a million of them can be transported in a standard shipping container but they can be released in swarms so numerous which make it well nigh impossible for air defense systems to shoot down enough of them to make adequate defence a plausible option. In this way these cheap[2] devices, all capable of individually or collectively using AI to select and identify individual human beings as their targets, are well on the way to becoming weapons of mass destruction.

Killer drones and drone swarms do not only exist in the fertile imagination of some or in science fiction. They have been deployed in combat for at least the best part of two years. A panel of UN experts in March 2020 reporting about the conflict

[1]November 2021-January 2022.

[2]Current best estimates for costs of killer-drone LAWs range from between 10–30 dollars each if produced in sufficient quantities though those already available such as the Turkish-made Karga 2 understandably command a higher premium.

in Libya stated that "Logistics convoys and retreating [Haftar-affiliated forces] were subsequently hunted down and remotely engaged by the unmanned combat aerial vehicles or the lethal autonomous weapons systems such as the STM Kargu-2 ... and other loitering munitions,".[3] The U.N. report goes on: "The lethal autonomous weapons systems were programmed to attack targets without requiring data connectivity between the operator and the munition: in effect, a true 'fire, forget and find' capability."[4] This was not an isolated incident. More recently, during operations in Gaza in mid-May 2021, "the Israel Defense Forces (IDF) used a swarm of small drones to locate, identify and attack Hamas militants. This is thought to be the first time a drone swarm has been used in combat."[5]

The potential for harm in a device which can take actions which can infringe human rights by, e.g. discriminating on grounds of gender, age, ethnicity or political opinion should be immediately apparent. The fact that we already have devices such as AI-driven drones that could be programmed to identify a given individual off a list of politically inconvenient people and seek out and destroy such a person or be instructed to seek out and kill all people who look like Jews or dark-skinned people or all males in a city who are between the ages of 12 and 65 should have alarm bells ringing across all sectors of society. That they are not is a serious cause for concern in itself.

One of the many problems with LAWs is that the world currently does not have the right type of international law to cover this type of AI-driven technology. While, over the past 50 years, progress had been made on arms control in the form of the Treaty on the Non-Proliferation of Nuclear Weapons (1968–1970), the Chemical Weapons Convention (1997) and, most recently, the Biological Weapons Convention, the development and deployment of LAWs is characterised by lawlessness. Governments such as that of New Zealand have, in November 2021, taken a clear policy stance moving for a new international treaty to be made on the issue but these latest efforts were stunted during the 6th Review Conference of the Conventional on Conventional Weapons (CCW). Although, States agreed to continue the work of the Group of Governmental Experts related to emerging technologies in the area of lethal autonomous weapon systems for another year, with a renewed mandate for the group agreed to hold ten days of meetings in 2022, there is no guarantee that this will produce results better than those of 2021.

LAWs is just one example of why Alessandro Mantelero's study is an important book about an important subject. Although formally titled *Beyond Data: Human Rights, Ethical and Social Impact Assessment in AI*, it could equally have been titled *Beyond Law: Human Rights, Ethical and Social Impact Assessment in AI.* For although Mantelero is a legal scholar with a growing pedigree in Technology Law, his book is an explicit plea to go beyond law and instead embrace a more holistic approach to Artificial Intelligence. There can be no doubting Mantelero's

[3] https://undocs.org/S/2021/229.

[4] Ibid.

[5] https://www.newscientist.com/article/2282656-israel-used-worlds-first-ai-guided-combat-drone-swarm-in-gaza-attacks/.

commitment to human rights law, but he is fundamentally right in his position that a legal approach alone is not enough. Instead he advocates adoption of the HRESIA model. Today, especially with the advent of the GDPR, a growing number of people are familiar with the need to carry out an impact assessment in many of those cases where one intends to introduce a technology which deals with personal data. But, as Mantelero points out, HRESIA—Human Rights Ethical Social Impact Assessment—is a hybrid model taking into account the ethical as well as the social impact of a technology together with the legal dimensions such as those of human rights.

Mantelero is, through HRESIA, offering us a conceptual framework within which we can think about AI and also decide what to do about it from a policy point of view. The main components of HRESIA are the analysis of relevant human rights, the definition of relevant ethical and social values and the targeted application to given AI cases, thus combining the universality of human rights with the local dimension of societal values. In doing so Mantelero advocates a multi-stakeholder and human-centred approach to AI design. Participation and transparency form part of the mix promoted by HRESIA while retaining elements of more traditional risk management models such as the circular product development models.

Building on his knowledge of the most recent developments in data protection law, Mantelero walks the reader through the advantages and disadvantages of impact-assessment solutions in the field of data-centred systems such PIA/DPIA. SIA and EtIA. He is at pains to point out that "the recent requirements of the GDPR—according to the models offered by the DPAs fail to offer a more satisfactory answer—by explaining that "Despite specific references in the GDPR to the safeguarding of rights and freedoms in general as well as to societal issues, the new assessment models do nothing to pay greater attention to the societal consequences than the existing PIAs." Mantelero makes the point that "HRESIA fills this gap, providing an assessment model focused on the rights and freedoms that may be assessed by data use offering a more appropriate contextualisation of the various rights and freedoms that are relevant to data-intensive systems. The latter are no longer limited to data protection and should therefore be considered separately rather than absorbed in a broad notion of data protection". Mantelero's advocacy of HRESIA is part of his apparent agreement with the mood of those legal scholars who have highlighted "how the application of human rights is necessarily affected by social and political influences that are not explicitly formalised in court decisions" in a perspective wherein "HRESIA may be used to unveil the existing interplay between the legal and societal dimensions".

Much as I deem privacy to be important, I am delighted that the HRESIA methodology extends to all human rights and not just privacy. This is very much in line with the approach I explicitly advocated as UN Special Rapporteur on Privacy in my report to the UN' Human Rights Council in March 2016 as reflected in the HRC's resolution of March 2017 *Recognizing the right to privacy also as an enabling right to the free development of personality and, in this regard, noting with concern that any violation to the right to privacy might affect other human rights, including the right to freedom of expression and to hold opinions without interference, the right to freedom of peaceful assembly and association*. While also holding out the promise of significant benefits, AI has the potential to infringe or otherwise interfere with many or all of these human rights, hence the need for in-depth and constant detailed evaluation such as that inherent to a proper implementation of HRESIA.

Now, it is impossible in a work of relatively modest length to go in-depth through a comprehensive list of examples which would demonstrate beyond reasonable doubt that HRESIA is useful in all cases related to AI technology but it certainly promises to be a better start than most. Indeed, this is why I opened this preface with reference to just one example of AI-driven technology, i.e. LAWs. For the latter is clearly yet another instance where looking to existing rules or legal precedent may be helpful but certainly not enough. The societal impact of LAWs—including the potential use of such technologies against one's own civilian population and not exclusively against a foreign enemy—as well as the multifarious ethical dimensions should provide a perfect case-study for the advantages—and practical difficulties—involved in applying HRESIA.

Indeed I look forward to other scholars—and possibly even Mantelero himself—rising to the challenge and methodically applying the HRESIA approach to the catalogue of problems that AI brings with it. For the use of AI in weaponry such as LAWs is just one of many issues we should be paying attention to. The misuse of AI, including racial and gender bias, disinformation, deepfakes and cybercrime is as much a part of a long TO DO LIST as the very standard programming that goes into AI itself. Given that AI involves specifying a fixed objective' and since the programmer cannot always specify objectives completely and correctly, this results in a situation where having fixed but imperfect objectives could lead to an uncontrollable AI that stops at nothing to achieve its aim. What novel or useful solutions would HRESIA produce in Stuart Russell's oft repeated and now classic "children and the cat"[6] example? Likewise, what can HRESIA offer to an analysis of the impact that AI will have on jobs, making many obsolete and many workers redundant? What real benefits would the policy maker obtain from using HRESIA when faced with the decision of supporting, regulating or banning AI-powered robots designed to provide care to the elderly? How would HRESIA help resolve "privacy by design, privacy by default" issues in such cases not to mention the ethical and legally correct approaches to euthanasia, dementia, terminal illness, etc.?

Some analysts will no doubt spend much time over the coming years trying to pick holes in HRESIA. Eventually somebody may possibly also come up with an even better way of solving problems related to AI but, until that happens, Mantelero's work offers some of the insights into the theoretical underpinnings of why it could be a useful approach when doing so. It is also a sign of the times. For

[6]Wherein a domestic robot programmed to look after children, tries to feed the children but sees nothing in the fridge. "And then... the robot sees the cat... Unfortunately, the robot lacks the understanding that the cat's sentimental value is far more important than its nutritional value. So, you can imagine what happens next!".

the best part of forty years, we have been gradually moving away from a mono-disciplinary approach in problem-solving to a multi-disciplinary approach, often coupled with an inter-disciplinary approach. The perspective obtained at the intersection of several disciplines can also be one which is profoundly more accurate and more practical/pragmatic than one which is constrained by the knowledge and practices of any single discipline. Indeed, the very notion of HRESIA implies taking into account the perspective of other disciplines outside Human Rights Law, ethics and social impact. Computer science, applied technologies, economics and social psychology are only a few of the other disciplines that immediately come to mind which need to be deeply and constantly involved in the way that society needs to think about AI. Speaking of " a holistic approach" has become something of a cliché yet it is difficult to think of a context which requires it more than AI…and that basically is the nub of the message in Mantelero's current work. It is also an encouraging start on the fiendishly difficult task of regulating AI and producing sensible policy decisions outside the field of law which are however required to ensure that mankind reaps more benefits from AI and avoids the serious dangers inherent in the uncontrolled development and deployment of such technologies.

Tal-Qroqq, Malta Joe Cannataci
January 2022

Joe Cannataci was appointed as the first ever UN Special Rapporteur on Privacy in 2015, following the Snowden revelations about mass surveillance. His UN mandate was renewed in 2018 (until August 2021). He is head of the Department of Information Policy & Governance at the Faculty of Media & Knowledge Sciences of the University of Malta. He also co-founded and continues as Co-director (on a part-time basis) of STeP, the Security, Technology & e-Privacy Research Group at the University of Groningen in the Netherlands, where he is Full Professor, holding the Chair of European Information Policy & Technology Law. A Fellow of the British Computer Society (FBCS) and UK Chartered Information Technology Professional (CITP), his law background meets his techie side as a Senior Fellow and Associate Researcher at the CNAM Security-Defense-Intelligence Department in Paris, France and the Centre for Health, Law and Emerging Technologies at the University of Oxford. His past roles include Vice-Chairman/Chairman of Council of Europe's (CoE) Commmittee of Experts on Data Protection 1992–1998, Working Parties on: Data Protection and New Technologies (1995–2000); Data Protection & Insurance (1994–1998); CoE Rapporteur on Data Protection and Police (1993; 2010; 2012).

Preface

As you set out for Ithaka
Hope the journey may be long,
Full of adventures, full of discovery
Κωνσταντίνος Π. Καβάφης
Constantine Cavafy, Edmund Keeley, and Philip Sherrard, Voices of Modern Greece: Selected Poems (Princeton University Press 1981).

As in Cavafy's poem, this is the story of a journey lasting several years. It began in 2012, when, after several studies on data protection, my first investigation of the impact of large-scale data-intensive systems appeared in an article on Big Data and the risks of digital information power concentration published in an Italian law review.[7]

A few years after the Aspen Institute's report on The Promise and Peril of Big Data[8] and several months after the provocative paper presented by danah boyd and Kate Crawford at the Oxford Internet Institute,[9] Big Data became my new field of enquiry for two spring terms as a visiting fellow there in 2013 and 2014.

As a privacy scholar, I was concerned about the imbalance of power created by large-scale concentration of data and predictive power in the hands of a limited number of big players. Recognising the limits of the traditional individual

[7]Mantelero A (2012) Big Data: i rischi della concentrazione del potere informativo digitale e gli strumenti di controllo [Big Data: the risks of digital information power concentration and oversight tools]. Il diritto dell'informazione e dell'informatica 2012 (1), 135–144.

[8]Bollier D (2010) The Promise and Peril of Big Data. Aspen Institute, Washington, DC http://www.aspeninstitute.org/sites/default/files/content/docs/pubs/The_Promise_and_Peril_of_Big_Data.pdf. Accessed 27 February 2014.

[9]boyd d and Crawford K (2011) Six Provocations for Big Data. A Decade in Internet Time: Symposium on the Dynamics of the Internet and Society, Oxford Internet Institute, 21 September 2011 https://papers.ssrn.com/abstract=1926431. Accessed 3 August 2021; boyd d and Crawford K (2012) Critical Questions for Big Data: Provocations for a Cultural, Technological, and Scholarly Phenomenon. 15 Information, Communication & Society 662.

consent-based model,[10] I began to explore the collective dimension of data protection.[11]

Antoinette Rouvroy was working at the time on her report on Big Data for the Council of Europe[12] and the peculiar circumstances of new scientific research practices in the digital era brought an unexpected consequence. After reading the draft of her report online, I posted several comments that led to my involvement as an adviser to the Council of Europe's Consultative Committee of the Convention for the Protection of Individuals with regard to Automatic Processing of Personal Data, a collaboration that remains ongoing, first on Big Data,[13] and later on AI regulation.[14]

These brief autobiographical notes, at a time when a concurrence of social and technological factors gave rise to a wave of AI development, explain the genesis of this book.

An interest in the theoretical limits of the existing legal framework—centred on data protection law and models established in the 1970s and early 1990s—plus my direct experience of the international regulatory demands and dynamics were the two driving forces behind extending the initial scope of my research to cover the new algorithmic society.

[10] Mantelero A (2014) The future of consumer data protection in the EU Re-thinking the "notice and consent" paradigm in the new era of predictive analytics. 30(6) Computer Law & Security Review 643–660; Mantelero A (2014) Toward a New Approach to Data Protection in the Big Data Era. In Urs Gasser, Jonathan Zittrain, Robert Faris, Rebekah Heacock Jones (eds) Internet Monitor 2014: Reflections on the Digital World (Berkman Center for Internet and Society, Harvard University 2014) https://dash.harvard.edu/handle/1/13632937. Accessed 13 August 2021.

[11] Mantelero A (2017) From Group Privacy to Collective Privacy: Towards a New Dimension of Privacy and Data Protection in the Big Data Era. In Taylor L., Floridi L., and van der Sloot, B. Group Privacy New Challenges of Data Technologies. Springer International Publishing, Chm, pp. 139–158.

[12] Rouvroy A (2015) "Of data and men". Fundamental rights and freedoms in a world of Big Data. Council of Europe–Consultative Committee of the Convention for the Protection of Individuals with regard to Automatic Processing of Personal Data, T-PD-BUR(2015)09REV, Strasbourg, 11 January 2016 https://rm.coe.int/16806a6020. Accessed 4 August 2021.

[13] Council of Europe, Consultative Committee of the Convention for the Protection of Individuals with regard to Automatic Processing of Personal Data (2017) Guidelines on the protection of individuals with regard to the processing of personal data in a world of Big Data, T-PD(2017)01, Strasbourg, 23 January 2017 https://rm.coe.int/16806ebe7a. Accessed 4 February 2017.

[14] Council of Europe, Consultative Committee of the Convention for the Protection of Individuals with regard to Automatic Processing of Personal Data (2019) Guidelines on Artificial Intelligence and Data Protection, Strasbourg, 25 January 2019, T-PD(2019)01 https://rm.coe.int/guidelines-on-artificial-intelligence-and-data-protection/168091f9d8. Accessed 13 February 2019; Council of Europe, Consultative Committee of the Convention for the Protection of Individuals with regard to Automatic Processing of Personal Data (2019) Report on Artificial Intelligence Artificial Intelligence and Data Protection: Challenges and Possible Remedies, T-PD(2018)09Rev. Rapporteur: Alessandro Mantelero https://rm.coe.int/artificial-intelligence-and-data-protection-challenges-and-possible-re/168091f8a6. Accessed 13 February 2019.

In 2017, with the launch of the H2020 Virt-EU project on Values and Ethics in Innovation for Responsible Technology in Europe,[15] a more structured examination of the impact of Big Data yielded an assessment model that looked beyond data protection, including its collective dimension. This was the PESIA (Privacy, Ethical and Social Impact Assessment) model, which broadened the traditional privacy impact assessment to include ethical issues for society raised by the new data-intensive applications.[16]

The legal component of the PESIA, however, remained largely focused on data protection. A turning point in my research came in 2018 when I presented my work on PESIA at an Expert Workshop on the Right to Privacy in the Digital Age organised by the Office of the UN High Commissioner for Human Rights in Geneva, where Joe Cannataci encouraged me to look beyond data protection and consider the broader human rights scenario. This suggestion together with discussions during an EU Agency for Fundamental Rights expert meeting a few days later altered my perspective, spawning the idea of the HRESIA (Human Rights, Ethical and Social Impact Assessment) which is the focus of this book.

As is customary in academia, this initial seed was subsequently refined in conferences and seminars around Europe, as well as publications. It was also fed by my direct field experience in various ERC Executive Agency ethics committees, the Ada Lovelace Institute Rethinking Data Regulation Working Group (2019–21) and not least in the work of the Council of Europe's Ad hoc Committee on Artificial Intelligence (CAHAI).[17]

After three years' investigation of the topic—plus several periods of research in Spain, at the Universitat Oberta de Catalunya and the Universidad de Murcia, free of daily academic commitments—I hope in this book to provide a theoretical and concrete contribution to the debate on the impact of AI on society from a legal and regulatory point of view.

---

[15] Values and ethics in Innovation for Responsible Technology in Europe (IT University of Copenhagen, London School of Economics and Political Science, Uppsala Universitet, Politecnico di Torino, Copenhagen Institute of Interaction Design, and Open Rights), project information available at https://cordis.europa.eu/project/id/732027. Accessed 15 August 2021.

[16] Virt-EU Values and ethics in Innovation for Responsible Technology in Europe (2018) Deliverable 4.3. Second Report: Report to the internal members of the consortium on the PESIA methodology and initial guidelines https://ec.europa.eu/research/participants/documents/downloadPublic?documentIds=080166e5c0587e55&appId=PPGMS. Accessed 15 August 2021. See also Council of Europe, Consultative Committee of the Convention for the Protection of Individuals with regard to Automatic Processing of Personal Data 2017 ("2.3 Since the use of Big Data may affect not only individual privacy and data protection, but also the collective dimension of these rights, preventive policies and risk-assessment shall consider the legal, social and ethical impact of the use of Big Data").

[17] Council of Europe (2020) Towards regulation of AI systems. Global perspectives on the development of a legal framework on Artificial Intelligence systems based on the Council of Europe's standards on human rights, democracy and the rule of law. DGI (2020)16 https://rm.coe.int/prems-107320-gbr-2018-compli-cahai-couv-texte-a4-bat-web/1680a0c17a. Accessed 4 January 2021. See also Chap. 4.

While interest in the impact of AI on human rights and society has grown in recent years and is now explicitly mentioned in several hard and soft law AI proposals, some approaches remain focused on data protection even at the cost of stretching its boundaries. Examples include an extended interpretation of fairness, and the call for a broad use of the data protection impact assessment, reshaped as a human rights impact assessment.

Against this background, Chap. 1 looks at the limitations of data protection law in addressing the challenges of data-intensive AI, stressing how a genuinely human-oriented development of AI requires that the risks associated with AI applications be managed and regulated.

Following this recognition of the limitations and challenges, Chap. 2 develops the human rights impact assessment (HRIA),[18] the central component of the HRESIA model. Although HRIAs are already in place in several contexts, the chapter emphasises the peculiarity of AI applications and the need to rethink the traditional human rights assessment.

It also aims to close the existing gap in the current regulatory proposals that recommend the introduction of HRIA but fail to furnish a methodology in line with their demands, since the quantification of potential impact that risk thresholds entail is either lacking or not fully developed in HRIA models.

Chapter 3 builds on the initial idea of the PESIA model, focusing on the ethical and societal impacts of AI, but without taking a questionnaire-based approach. The new assessment model is centred on the role of expert committees building on experience in the field of biomedicine and research.[19] Such expert assessment is key to an evaluation that is necessarily contextual in the case of ethical and social issues.

Having outlined all the components of the HRESIA and their interaction, Chap. 4 compares the proposed model with the chief risk management provisions of the two European AI proposals from the Council of Europe and the European Commission. Highlighting their differences and weaknesses with respect to standard impact-assessment models, the chapter shows how the HRESIA can complement these proposals and act as an effective tool in their implementation.

The novelty of the issues at stake, the continuing debate on AI regulation, and the range of possible tools (sandboxes, auditing, certifications, etc.), as well as the recent theoretical contributions in the fields of human rights and digital technology, inevitably leave open questions on future implementations, which are discussed in the concluding chapter.

---

[18] An early version of this model appeared in Mantelero A and Esposito MS (2021) An Evidence-Based Methodology for Human Rights Impact Assessment (HRIA) in the Development of AI Data-Intensive Systems. Computer Law & Sec. Rev. 41, doi:10.1016/j.clsr.2021.105561, Sections 1–3, 5, and 6 (all authored by Alessandro Mantelero).

[19] I am grateful to Maria Belén Andreu Martínez (Universidad de Murcia) for comments on medical ethics provided to the draft of this chapter.

With its focus on *ex ante* risk analysis and human rights-oriented design, the book does not discuss the *ex post* remedies to harms caused by AI based on product liability and liability allocation.[20]

As in Cavafy's poem, my research has taken me on a long journey of varied experiences, combining academic work, drafting policy and empirical analysis. I have had many travelling companions within the international community of privacy scholars. Growing year by year, it is still a small and close-knit community made up of research centres across Europe, formal and informal meetings, and leading law journals.

The book has involved me in a marvellous voyage into the global dimension of data regulation and human rights. The reader will be the judge of this work, but the closing stanzas of Cavafy's poem reflect my feelings of gratitude to all those who made some contribution, however small, to the journey and shared the experience with me:

Without her you wouldn't have set out.
She has nothing left to give you now.

And if you find her poor, Ithaka won't have fooled you.
Wise as you will have become, so full of experience,
you'll have understood by then what these Ithakas mean.

Turin, Italy
October 2021

Alessandro Mantelero

[20]European Parliament, Policy Department for Citizens' Rights and Constitutional Affairs and Directorate-General for Internal Policies, 'Artificial Intelligence and Civil Liability' (2020) https://www.europarl.europa.eu/RegData/etudes/STUD/2020/621926/IPOL_STU(2020)621926_EN.pdf. Accessed 24 July 2021; European Commission (2020) Report on the Safety and Liability Implications of Artificial Intelligence, the Internet of Things and Robotics https://ec.europa.eu/info/publications/commission-report-safety-and-liability-implications-ai-internet-things-and-robotics-0_en. Accessed 5 May 2020; European Parliament–Directorate General for Parliamentary Research Services (2020) Civil Liability Regime for Artificial Intelligence: European Added Value Assessment https://data.europa.eu/doi/10.2861/737677. Accessed 3 July 2021; Council of Europe, Expert Committee on human rights dimensions of automated data processing and different forms of artificial intelligence (MSI-AUT) (2019) Responsibility and AI. A Study of the Implications of Advanced Digital Technologies (Including AI Systems) for the Concept of Responsibility within a Human Rights Framework. Rapporteur: Karen Yeung https://rm.coe.int/responsability-and-ai-en/168097d9c5. Accessed 11 July 2021; European Commission–Expert Group on Liability and New Technologies and New Technologies Formation (2019) Liability for Artificial Intelligence and Other Emerging Digital Technologies https://www.europarl.europa.eu/meetdocs/2014_2019/plmrep/COMMITTEES/JURI/DV/2020/01-09/AI-report_EN.pdf. Accessed 3 July 2021; Lohsse S, Schulze R, and Staudenmayer D (eds) (2019) Liability for Artificial Intelligence and the Internet of Things: Münster Colloquia on EU Law and the Digital Economy IV. Baden-Baden, Nomos, Hart Publishing.

Contents

About the Author

Alessandro Mantelero is Associate Professor of Private Law and Law & Technology at the Polytechnic University of Turin, Italy, where he holds the Jean Monnet Chair in Mediterranean Digital Societies and Law. He is Council of Europe scientific expert on AI, data protection and human rights and has served as an expert on data regulation for several national and international organizations, including the United Nations, the EU Agency for Fundamental Rights, and the European Commission. He is Associate Editor of Computer Law & Security Review and member of the Editorial Board of European Data Protection Law Review.

Chapter 1
Beyond Data

Contents

Abstract In a technology context dominated by data-intensive AI systems, the consequences of data processing are no longer restricted to the well-known privacy and data protection issues but encompass prejudices against a broader array of fundamental rights. Moreover, the tension between the extensive use of these systems, on the one hand, and the growing demand for ethically and socially responsible data use on the other, reveals the lack of a framework that can fully address the societal issues raised by AI.

Against this background, neither traditional data protection impact assessment models nor the broader social or ethical impact assessment procedures appear to provide an adequate answer to the challenges of our algorithmic society. In contrast, a human rights-centred assessment may offer a better answer to the demand for a more comprehensive assessment, including not only data protection, but also the effects of data use on other fundamental rights and freedoms.

Given the changes to society brought by technology and datafication, when applied to the field of AI the Human Rights Impact Assessment must then be

A. Mantelero, *Beyond Data*, Information Technology and Law Series 36,
https://doi.org/10.1007/978-94-6265-531-7_1

enriched to consider ethical and societal issues, evolving into a more holistic Human Rights, Ethical and Social Impact Assessment (HRESIA), whose rationale and key elements are outlined in this chapter.

Keywords AI · Data protection · Ethical Impact Assessment · Human rights · Privacy Impact Assessment · Risk-based approach · Self-determination · Social Impact Assessment

1.1 Introduction

All AI applications rely on large datasets, to create algorithmic models, to train them, to run them over huge amounts of collected information and extract inferences, correlations, and new information for decision-making processes or other operations that, to some extent, replicate human cognitive abilities.

These results can be achieved using a variety of different mathematical and computer-based solutions, which are included under the umbrella term of AI.[1] Although they differ in their technicalities, they are all data-intensive systems and it is this factor that seems to be the most characteristic, rather than their human-like results.

We already have calculators, computers and many other devices that perform typical human tasks, in some cases reproducing our way of thinking or acting, as demonstrated by the spread of machine automation over the decades. The revolution is not so much the 'intelligent' machine, which we had already (e.g. expert systems), but the huge of information these machines can now use to achieve their results.[2] No human being is able to process such an amount of information in the same way or so quickly, reach the same conclusions (e.g. disease detection through diagnostic imaging) with the same accuracy (e.g. image detection and recognition) as AI.

These data-intensive AI systems thus undermine a core component of the individual's 'sovereignty' over information:[3] the human ability to control, manage and use information in a clear, understandable and ex post verifiable way.

This is the most challenging aspect of these applications, often summed up with the metaphor of the black box.[4] Neither the large amounts of data – we have always

---

[1] Several documents have tried to provide a definition of Artificial Intelligence. See *inter alia* UNESCO 2021; Council of Europe, Committee of Ministers 2020; Council of Europe, Consultative Committee of the Convention for the Protection of Individuals with regard to Automatic Processing of Personal Data (Convention 108) 2019; OECD 2019; The European Commission's High-level Expert Group on Artificial Intelligence 2018.

[2] Bellagio Big Data Workshop Participants 2014; Mayer-Schönberger and Cukier 2013; McKinsey Global Institute 2011; Bollier 2010.

[3] Westin 1970.

[4] Pasquale 2015.

had large datasets[5] – nor data automation for human-like behaviour are the most significant new developments. It is the intensive nature of the processing, the size of the datasets, and the knowledge extraction power and complexity of the process that is truly different.

If data are at the core of these systems, to address the challenges they pose and draft some initial guidelines for their regulation, we have to turn to the field of law that most specifically deals with data and control over information, namely data protection.

Of course, some AI applications do not concern personal data, but the provisions set forth in much data protection law on data quality, data security and data management in general go beyond personal data processing and can be extended to all types of information. Moreover, the AI applications that raise the biggest concerns are those that answer societal needs (e.g. selective access to welfare or managing smart cities), which are largely based on the processing of personal data.

This correlation with data protection legislation can also be found in the ongoing debate on the regulation of AI where, both in the literature and the policy documents,[6] fair use of data,[7] right to explanation,[8] and transparent data processing[9] are put forward as barriers to potential misuse of AI.

Here we need to ask whether the existing data protection legislation with its long and successful history[10] can also provide an effective framework for these data-intensive AI systems and mitigate their possible adverse consequences.

1.2 Rise and Fall of Individual Sovereignty Over Data Use

When in 1983 the German Constitutional Court recognised the right to self-determination with regard to data processing,[11] the judges adopted an approach that had its roots in an earlier theoretical vision outlined in the 1960s. This was the idea of individual control as a key element in respect for human personality.

This idea was framed in different ways depending on the cultural context[12] and legal framework.[13] It also extended beyond the realm of data protection as it could relate to general personality rights however they are qualified in different legal

[5] An example is the Library of Alexandria with half a million scrolls.

[6] European Parliamentary Research Service 2020.

[7] Clifford and Ausloos 2018; Kuner et al. 2018. On fairness and AI, see also Selbst et al. 2019.

[8] Wachter et al. 2018.

[9] Zarsky 2016; Felzmann et al. 2019.

[10] Lynskey 2015; Gonzalez Fuster 2014; Bygrave 2002; Mayer-Schönberger 1997.

[11] Federal German Constitutional Court (Bundesverfassungsgericht), 15 December 1983, Neue Juristische Wochenschrift, 1984, p. 419; Rouvroy and Poullet 2009.

[12] Whitman 2004.

[13] Strömholm 1967.

contexts.[14] Regardless of the underpinning cultural values of data protection, the idea of an individual's power to counter potential data misuse is in line with the European tradition of personality rights.

As with personal names, image, and privacy, for personal data too, the theoretical legal framework aims to give individuals a certain degree of sovereignty regarding the perceivable manifestation of their physical, moral and relational identity. The forms and degree in which this sovereignty is recognised will differ over time and may follow different patterns.[15]

Individual sovereignty contains two components: the inside/outside boundary and the need to protect these boundaries. In personality rights and data protection, these boundaries concern the interaction between the individual and society (control) and the need for protection concerns the potential misuse of individual attributes outside the individual sphere (risk). While this does not rule out the coexistence of a collective dimension, the structure of individual rights is based on the complementary notions of control and risk.[16]

This has been evident since the earliest generations of data protection regulation, which were based on the idea of control over information[17] as a response to the risk of social control relating to the migration from dusty paper archives to computer memories.[18] Their purpose was not to spread and democratise power over information, but to increase the level of transparency about data processing and guarantee the right to access to information, providing a sort of counter-control over the collected data to the citizen.[19]

In these first data protection laws we can see the context-dependent nature of this idea of control, where the prevalence of data processing in public hands and the complexity of data processing for ordinary people led regulators to focus on notification, licencing,[20] right to access and the role of independent authorities. There was no space for individual consent in this socio-technical context.

The current idea of control as mainly centred on individual consent, already common in the context of personality rights, emerges in data protection as the result of the advent of personal computers and the economic exploitation of personal

---

[14] Brüggemeier et al. 2010. See also Cannataci 2008.

[15] Westin 1970; Samuelson 2000; Rodotà 2009. See also Hummel et al. 2021.

[16] Solove 2008, p. 24.

[17] Westin 1970, pp. 158–168 and 298–326; Breckenridge 1970, pp. 1–3. See also Solove 2008, pp. 4–5; Mahieu 2021.

[18] Secretary's Advisory Committee on Automated Personal Data Systems 1973; Miller 1971, pp. 54–67, Chaps. 1 and 2; Mayer-Schönberger 1997, pp. 221–225; Bennett 1992, pp. 29–33 and 47; Brenton 1964; Packard 1964.

[19] Secretary's Advisory Committee on Automated Personal Data Systems 1973; Mayer-Schönberger 1997, p. 223.

[20] Bygrave 2002, pp. 75–77.

information, no longer merely functional data but a core element of profiling and competitive commercial strategies.[21]

These changes in the technological and business frameworks created new demands on legislators by society as citizens wished to negotiate their personal data and gain something in return.

Although the later generations of European data protection law placed personal information in the context of fundamental rights,[22] the main goal of these regulations was to pursue economic interests relating to the free flow of personal data. This is also affirmed by Directive 95/46/EC,[23] which represented both the general framework and the synthesis of this second wave of data protection laws.[24] Nevertheless, the roots of data protection still remained in the context of personality rights making the European approach less market-oriented[25] than other legal systems. The Directive also recognised the fundamental role of public authorities in protecting data subjects against unwanted or unfair exploitation of their personal information for marketing purposes.

Both the theoretical model of fundamental rights, based on self-determination, and the rising data-driven economy highlighted the importance of user consent in consumer data processing.[26] Consent was not only an expression of choice with regard to the use of personality rights by third parties, but became a means of negotiating the economic value of personal information.[27]

---

[21] Although direct marketing has its roots in mail order services, which were based on personalised letters (e.g. using the name and surname of addressees) and general group profiling (e.g. using census information to group addressees into social and economic classes), the use of computer equipment increased the level of processing of consumer information and generated detailed consumer profiles. See Petrison et al. 1997, pp. 115–119; Solove 2001, pp. 1405–1407.

[22] Council of Europe, Convention for the Protection of Individuals with regard to Automatic Processing of Personal Data, opened for signature on 28 January 1981 and entered into force on 1 October 1985. http://conventions.coe.int/Treaty/Commun/QueVoulezVous.asp?NT=108&CL=ENG. Accessed 27 February 2014; OECD 1980.

[23] Directive 95/46/EC of the European Parliament and of the Council of 24 October 1995 on the protection of individuals with regard to the processing of personal data and on the free movement of such data [1995] OJ L281/31.

[24] EU Directive 95/46/EC has a dual nature. It was based on the existing national data protection laws, and designed to harmonize them, but at the same time it also provided a new set of rules. See the recitals in the preamble to Directive 95/46/EC. See also Poullet 2006, p. 207; Simitis 1995.

[25] On the different approach based on granting individual property rights in personal information, Schwartz 2004; Samuelson 2000; Lessig 1999. For criticism, see Cohen 2000.

[26] See Charter of Fundamental Rights of the European Union (2010/C 83/02), Article 8 [2010] C83/389. See also Productores de Música de España (Promusicae) v Telefónica de España SAU, C-275/06, para 63–64. http://curia.europa.eu/juris/liste.jsf?language=en&jur=C,T,F&num=C-275/06&td=ALL. Accessed 27 February 2014; Federal German Constitutional Court (Bundesverfassungsgericht), 15 December 1983 (fn 11). Among the legal scholars, see also Schwartz 2013; Tzanou 2013; Solove 2013.

[27] But see Acquisti and Grossklags 2005.

With the advent of the digital society,[28] data could no longer be exploited for business purposes without any involvement of the data subject. Data subjects had to become part of the negotiation, since data was no longer used mainly by government agencies for public purposes, but also by private companies with monetary revenues.[29]

Effective self-determination in data processing, both in terms of protection and economic exploitation of personality rights, could not be achieved without adequate awareness about data use.[30] The notice and consent model[31] was therefore a new layer added to the existing paradigm based on transparency and access in data processing.

In the 1980s and 1990s data analysis increased in quality, but its level of complexity remained limited. Consumers understood the general correlation between data collection and the purposes of data processing (e.g. miles and points to earn free flights for airlines or nights and points for hotels) and informed consent and self-determination were largely considered synonyms.

This changed with the advent of data-intensive systems based on Big Data analytics and the new wave of AI applications which make data processing more complicated and often obscure. In addition, today's data-intensive techniques and applications have multiplied in a new economic and technological world which raises questions about the adequacy of the legal framework – established at the end of the last millennium and having its roots in the 1970s – to safeguard individuals' rights in the field of information technology.

The current social environment is characterised by a pervasive presence of digital technologies and an increasing concentration of information in the hands of just a few entities, both public and private. The main reason for this concentration is the central role played by specific subjects in the generation of data flows. Governments and big private companies (e.g. large retailers, telecommunication companies, etc.) collect huge amounts of data in the course of their daily activities. This mass of information represents a strategic and economically significant asset, since these large datasets enables these entities to act as gatekeepers to the information that can be extracted from datasets. They can choose to restrict access to the data to specific subjects or to circumscribed parts of the information.

Governments and big private companies are not alone in having this power, but the information intermediaries (e.g. search engines,[32] Internet providers, data

---

[28] Negroponte 1994; Castells 1996.

[29] OECD 2013; European Data Protection Supervisor 2014.

[30] The notice describes in detail how the data is processed and the purposes of the processing.

[31] See Articles 2(h), 7(a) and 10, Directive 95/46/EC. See also Article 29 Data Protection Working Party 2011, pp. 5–6; Article 29 Data Protection Working Party 2014a. With regard to personal information collected by public entities, the Directive 95/45/EC permits the data collection without the consent of data subject in various cases; however, the notice to data subjects is necessary in these cases. See Articles 7, 8 and 10, Directive 95/46/EC. See also Alsenoy et al. 2014; Kuner 2012, p. 5; Brownsword 2009.

[32] See also Sparrow et al. 2011.

brokers,[33] marketing companies), which do not themselves generate information, do play a key role in circulating it.[34]

Even where the information is accessible to the public, both in raw and processed form,[35] the concurrent effect of all these different sources only apparently diminishes the concentration of power. Access to information is not equivalent to knowledge. A large amount of data creates knowledge only when the holders have the appropriate tools to select relevant information, reorganise it, place it in a systematic context and the people with the skills to design the research and interpret the results of analytics.[36]

Without this, data only produces confusion and ultimately results in less knowledge, when information is subject to incomplete or biased interpretation. The mere availability of data is not sufficient in AI,[37] it is also necessary to have the adequate human[38] and computing resources to handle it.

Control over information therefore not only regards limited access data, but can also concern open data,[39] over which the information intermediaries create added value with their analytical tools.

Given that only a few entities are able to invest heavily in equipment and research, the above dynamics sharpen the concentration of power, which has increased with the latest wave of AI.[40]

In many respects, this new environment resembles the origins of data processing, the mainframe era, when technologies were held by a few entities and data processing was too complex to be understood by data subjects. Might this suggest that the future will see a sort of distributed AI, as happened with computers in the mid 1970s?[41]

The position of the dominant players in AI and data-intensive systems is not only based on expensive hardware and software, which may get cheaper in the future. Nor does it depend on the growing number of staff with specific skills and knowledge, capable of interpreting the results provided by AI applications.

The fundamental basis of their power is represented by the huge datasets they possess. These data silos, considered the goldmine of the 21st century, are not freely accessible, but represent the main or collateral result of their owners' business, creating, collecting, or managing information. Access to these databases is

---

[33] Federal Trade Commission 2014; Committee on Commerce, Science, and Transportation 2013.

[34] Cannataci et al. 2016, pp. 25–29.

[35] This is true of open data sets made available by government agencies, information held in public registries, data contained in reports, studies and other communications made by private companies and, finally, online user-generated content.

[36] Bollier 2010 ("As a large mass of raw information, Big Data is not self-explanatory"); boyd and Crawford 2012; Cohen 2013, pp. 1924–1925; The White House 2014, p. 7.

[37] Mayer-Schonberger and Cukier 2013; Dwork and Mulligan 2013.

[38] Science and Technology Options Assessment 2014, p. 95; Cohen 2013, pp. 1922–1923.

[39] Federal Trade Commission 2014, p. 13.

[40] Mantelero 2014a.

[41] On the risks related to "democratized big data", Hartzog and Selinger 2013, pp. 84–85.

therefore not only protected by law, but is also strictly related to the data holders' peculiar market positions and the presence of entry barriers.[42]

This makes it hard to imagine the same process of 'democratisation' as occurred with computer equipment in the 1980s repeating itself today.

Another aspect that characterises and distinguishes this new concentration of control over information is the nature of the purposes of data use: data processing is no longer focused on single users (profiling), but has increased in scale to cover attitudes and behaviours of large groups[43] and communities, even entire countries.[44]

The consequence of this large-scale approach is the return of fears about social surveillance and the lack of control over important decision-making processes, which characterised the mainframe era.

At the same time, this new potentially extensive and pervasive social surveillance differs from the past, since today's surveillance is no longer largely performed by the intelligence apparatus, which independently collects a huge amount of information through pervasive monitoring systems. It is the result of the interplay between private and public sectors,[45] based on a collaborative model made possible by mandatory disclosure orders, issued by courts or administrative bodies, and extended to an undefined pool of voluntary or proactive collaborations by big companies.[46]

In this way, governments may obtain information with the indirect "co-operation" of consumers who quite probably would not have given the same information to public entities if requested. Service providers, for example, collect personal data on the basis of private agreements (privacy policies) with the consent of the user and for specific purposes,[47] but governments exploit this practice by using mandatory orders to obtain the disclosure of this information.[48] This dual mechanism hides from citizens the risk and extent of social control that can be achieved by monitoring social media or other services using data-intensive technologies.[49]

---

[42] Mayer-Schönberger and Ramge 2022; Cohen 2019.

[43] Taylor et al. 2017; Floridi 2014; boyd 2012; Bloustein 1977.

[44] E.g., Taylor and Schroeder 2015.

[45] Bennett et al. 2014, pp. 55–69; Richards 2013, pp. 1940–1941; Michaels 2008; Hoofnagle 2003, pp. 595–597; Simitis 1987, p. 726. See also Mantelero and Vaciago 2013.

[46] See also Council of Europe 2008.

[47] On the current relationship between data retention and access to personal information by government agencies or law enforcement authorities, Reidenberg 2014.

[48] Rubinstein et al. 2014; Kuner et al. 2014; Cate et al. 2012; Swire 2012; Brown 2012; Pell 2012; Brown 2013; European Parliament, Directorate General for Internal Policies, Policy Department C: Citizens' Rights and Constitutional Affairs, Civil Liberties, Justice and Home Affairs 2013a.

[49] European Parliament 2013; European Parliament, Directorate General for Internal Policies, Policy Department C: Citizens' Rights and Constitutional Affairs, Civil Liberties, Justice and Home Affairs 2013b, pp. 14–16; European Parliament, Directorate General for Internal Policies, Policy Department C: Citizens' Rights and Constitutional Affairs, Civil Liberties, Justice and Home Affairs 2013a, pp. 12–16. See also DARPA 2002; National Research Council 2008; Congressional Research Service 2008.

In addition, the current role played by private online platforms and the environment they create, which also include traditional state activities,[50] raise further issues concerning the possibility of them having an influence on individual and collective behaviour.[51]

In this scenario, the legal framework established in the 1990s to regulate data use[52] has gone to crisis, since the new technological and economic contexts (i.e. market concentration, social and technological lock-ins) have undermined its fundamental pillars,[53] which revolve around the purpose specification principle, the prior limitation of possible uses,[54] and an idea of individual self-determination mainly based on the notice and consent model.

The purpose specification and use limitation principles have their roots in the first generation of data protection regulation, introduced to avoiding extensive and indiscriminate data collection that might entail risks in terms of social surveillance and control.

In the 1980s and 1990s, with the advent of a new generation of data protection regulation, these principles not only put a limit on data processing, but also became key elements of the notice and consent model. They define the use of personal data made by data controllers, which represents important information impacting users' choice. Nevertheless, the advent of AI applications makes it difficult to provide detailed information about the purposes of data processing and the expected outputs.

Since data-intensive systems based on AI are designed to extract hidden or unpredictable inferences and correlations from datasets, the description of these purposes is becoming more and more generic and approximate. This is a consequence of the "transformative"[55] use of data made by these systems, which often makes it impossible to explain all the possible uses of data at the time of its initial collection.[56]

These critical aspects concerning the purpose specification limitation have a negative impact on the effectiveness of the idea of informational self-determination as framed by the notion of informed consent.

---

[50] This is the case with virtual currency (Facebook Libra), public health purposes (the role of Google and Apple in contact tracing in the Covid pandemic), education (e-learning platforms).

[51] This is the case with disinformation and its impact on the political arena. See e.g., Marsden et al. 2020; European Commission, Directorate General for Communication Networks, Content and Technology 2018.

[52] See Sect. 1.1.

[53] Cate 2006, pp. 343–345; Cate and Mayer-Schönberger 2013b; Rubinstein 2013; Solove 2013, pp. 1880–1903; Crawford and Schultz 2014, p. 108.

[54] See also Schwartz 2011, pp. 19–21; Hildebrandt 2013.

[55] Tene and Polonetsky 2012. Big Data analytics make it possible to collect a large amount of information from different sources and to analyse it in order to identify new trends and correlations in data sets. This analysis can be conducted to pursue purposes not defined in advance, depending on emerging correlations and different from the initial collection purposes.

[56] See also Article 29 Data Protection Working Party 2013a, pp. 23–27, pp. 45–47; Article 29 Data Protection Working Party 2013b.

First, the difficulty of defining the expected results of data use leads to the introduction of vague generic statements about the purposes of data processing. Second, even where notices are long and detailed, the complexity of the AI-based environment makes it impossible for users to really understand it and make informed choices.[57]

Moreover, the situation is made worse by economic, social, and technological constraints, which completely undermine the idea of self-determination with regard to personal information which represented the core principle of the generation of data protection regulation passed in the 1980s and 1990s.[58]

Finally, as mentioned before, we have seen an increasing concentration of informational assets, partly due to the multinational or global nature of a few big players in the new economy, but also due to mergers and acquisitions that created large online and offline companies. In many cases, especially in IT-based services, these large-scale trends dramatically limit the number of the companies that provide certain services and which consequently have hundreds of millions of users. The size of these dominant players produces social and technological lock-in effects that accentuate data concentration and represent further direct and indirect limitations to the consumer's self-determination and choice.[59]

1.3 Reconsidering Self-determination: Towards a Safe Environment

In the above scenario, characterised by data-intensive applications and concentration of control over information, the decision to stick with a model based largely on an idea of informational self-determination centred on informed consent is critical to the effective protection of individuals and their rights.[60]

This leads us to reconsider the role of user self-determination in situations where individuals are unable to understand data processing and its purposes fully[61] or are not in a position to decide.[62] In these cases, the focus cannot be primarily on the user and self-determination but must shift to the environment. A broader view is

---

[57] Brandimarte et al. 2010; Turow et al. 2007; Federal Trade Commission 2014, p. 42. On the limits of the traditional notices, see also Calo 2013, pp. 1050–1055; Solove 2013, pp. 1883–1888; World Economic Forum 2013, p. 18; Pasquale 2015.

[58] See Sect. 1.2.

[59] See above Sect. 1.2.

[60] Solove 2013, p. 1899.

[61] The Boston Consulting Group 2012, p. 4.

[62] See also Recital No. 43, GDPR ("In order to ensure that consent is freely given, consent should not provide a valid legal ground for the processing of personal data in a specific case where there is a clear imbalance between the data subject and the controller, in particular where the controller is a public authority and it is therefore unlikely that consent was freely given in all the circumstances of that specific situation").

needed, with human-centred solutions and applications where the burden of assessing the potential benefits and risks for individual rights and freedoms does not fall mainly on the shoulders of the impacted individuals or groups.

Without limiting the freedom of individuals not to be subject to AI-systems – with the exception of cases of prevailing competing interests (e.g. crime detection systems) –, these systems should provide a safe environment in terms of potential impacts on fundamental rights and freedoms. Just as customers do not have to check the safety of the cars they buy, in the same way the end users of AI systems should not have to check whether their rights and freedoms are safeguarded.

AI providers and AI systems users (e.g., municipalities in smart cities), and not end users (e.g., citizens), are in the best position to assess these risks to individual rights and freedoms and to develop or deploy AI systems with a rights-oriented design approach, under the supervision of competent and independent authorities. Furthermore, they are also in the best position to consider all the different interests of the various stakeholders with regard to extensive data collection and data mining.[63]

Against this background and given the data-intensive nature of the systems involved, a first line of attack might be to consider data protection law as the reference framework for AI regulation, broadening its scope. This has been done in the literature with regard to the GDPR, focusing on open clauses such as fairness of data processing[64] or promoting the data protection impact assessment (DPIA) as a general-purpose methodology.[65]

However, looking at the big picture and not just specific elements, existing data protection regulations are still focused on the traditional pillars of the so called fourth generation of data protection law:[66] the purpose specification principle, the use limitation principle and the notice and consent model (i.e. an informed, freely given and specific consent).[67]

These components of data protection regulation struggle with today's challenges, where the transformative use of data[68] often makes it impossible to know and explain all the uses of information at the time of its initial collection, or provide detailed information about AI data processing and its internal logic.[69]

---

[63] See Chap. 3.

[64] Clifford and Ausloos 2018; Kuner et al. 2018. On AI and fairness, see also Wachter et al. 2021.

[65] Kaminski and Malgieri 2021.

[66] Mayer-Schönberger 1997, pp. 219–241.

[67] Mantelero 2014c.

[68] Tene and Polonetsky 2012.

[69] Cate and Mayer-Schönberger 2013a, b, iii ("The technologies and data applications of the 21st century are rapidly combining to make data protection based on notice and choice irrelevant"); Rubinstein 2013; Rotenberg 2001, paras 29–32.

The asymmetric distribution of control over information and market concentration[70] highlighted in the previous section,[71] as well as social[72] and technological lock-ins,[73] further undermines the idea of information self-determination in AI based mainly on the user's conscious decision on the potential benefits and risks of data processing.[74]

In addition, looking at the potential impact of AI, these data-intensive systems may affect a variety of rights and freedoms[75] that is much broader than the sphere covered by data protection. This must necessarily be reflected in the assessment methodologies which should go beyond the limited perspective adopted in today's data protection impact assessment models, which are mainly centred on the processing, task allocation, data quality, and data security.[76]

Although the EU legislator recognises data processing risks such as discrimination and "any other significant economic or social disadvantage",[77] and recommends a broader assessment including analysis of the societal and ethical consequences,[78] Article 35 of the GDRP and the supervisory authorities' assessment models do not adequately consider potentially impacted rights, their diversity and complexity, or the ethical and social issues.[79]

[70] See Science and Technology Options Assessment 2014, pp. 94–99 and 116–121.

[71] See Sect. 1.2.

[72] The social lock-in effect is one of the consequences of the dominant position held by some big players and is most evident in the social media market. It is the incentive to remain on a network, given the numbers of connections and social relationships created and managed by the user of a social networking platform. This lock-in intrinsically limits the user's ability to recreate the same network elsewhere, whereas a technological lock-in is due to the technological standards and data formats adopted by the service providers. The social lock-in limits the effectiveness of legal provisions concerning data portability, due to the non-technical disadvantages inherent in migrating from one service to another offering the same features.

[73] See also Simitis 1987, p. 737 ("the value of a regulatory doctrine such as "informed consent" depends entirely on the social and economic context of the individual activity"); Schwartz 1999, p. 1607.

[74] See also Mantelero 2014b. On privacy and control over information see Westin 1970, p. 7; Miller 1971, p. 25; Solove 2008, pp. 24–29; Cohen 2019, pp. 1 and 5.

[75] See Mantelero and Esposito 2021.

[76] See Cate and Mayer-Schönberger 2013a, pp. 12–13; Esposito et al. 2018.

[77] Recital n. 75, GDPR.

[78] Article 29 Data Protection Working Party 2017; European Data Protection Supervisor – Ethics Advisory Group 2018.

[79] E.g. CNIL 2018a, b, c; Information Commissioner's Office 2018; Information Commissioner's Office. Data protection impact assessments https://ico.org.uk/for-organisations/guide-to-data-protection/guide-to-the-general-data-protection-regulation-gdpr/accountability-and-governance/data-protection-impact-assessments/. Accessed 17 August 2021; Agencia Española de Protección de Datos 2021, 2018.

Finally, the impact on society of several AI-based systems raises ethical and social issues, which have been only touched on in defining the purposes of DPIA and often poorly implemented in practice.[80]

For these reasons, a holistic approach to the problems posed by AI must look beyond the traditional data protection emphasis on transparency, information, and self-determination. In the presence of complicated and often obscure AI applications, focusing on their design is key to ensuring effective safeguarding of individual rights. Such safeguards cannot simply be left to the interaction between AI manufacturers/adopters and potentially impacted individuals, given the asymmetry and bias inherent to this interaction.

Given the active and crucial role in creating a safe environment – from a legal, social and ethical perspective – of those who design, develop, deploy and adopt AI systems, it is crucial to provide them with adequate tools to consider and properly address the potential risks of AI applications for individuals and society.

1.4 A Paradigm Shift: The Focus on Risk Assessment

Risk assessment models today play an increasing role in many technology fields, including data processing,[81] as a consequence of the transformation of modern society into a risk society[82] – or at least a society in which many activities entail exposure to risks and one that is characterised by the emergence of new risks. This has led legislators to adopt a risk-based approach in various areas of the legal governance of hazardous activities.[83]

There are different assessment models possible (technology assessment, risk/benefit assessment, rights-based assessment) in different domains (e.g., legal assessment, social assessment, ethical assessment), but the first question we need to ask when defining an assessment model is whether the model is sector-specific or general. This is an important question with respect to AI too, since AI solutions are not circumscribed by a specific domain or technology.

The adoption of a technology-specific approach, for example an IoT impact assessment, a Big Data impact assessment, a smart city impact assessment seems

[80] On the contrary, this multi-criteria approach is adopted in the present book, see below in the text. See also Article 29 Data Protection Working Party 2014b ("The risk-based approach goes beyond a narrow "harm-based-approach" that concentrates only on damage and should take into consideration every potential as well as actual adverse effect, assessed on a very wide scale ranging from an impact on the person concerned by the processing in question to a general societal impact (e.g. loss of social trust)").

[81] See Articles 25 and 26, GDPR.

[82] Beck 1992.

[83] Ambrus 2017.

misguided.[84] From a rights-oriented perspective, all these technologies and technology environments are relevant insofar as they interact with individuals and society, and have a potential impact on the decision-making process.

Regardless of the different software and hardware technologies used, the focus of a human-centred approach is necessarily on the rights and values to be safeguarded. The model proposed here is thus not a technological assessment,[85] but a rights-based and values-oriented assessment.

In the context of data-driven applications, an assessment model focused on a specific technology appears inadequate or only partially effective.[86] On the other hand, given the various application domains (healthcare, crime prevention, etc.), different sets of rights, freedoms and values are at stake. A sector-specific approach must therefore focus on the rights and values in question rather than the technology.

Sectoral models concentrate their attention, not on technologies, but on the context and the values that assume relevance in a given context.[87] This does not mean that the nature of the technology has no importance in the assessment process as a whole, but that it mainly regards the type and extent of the impact.

Adopting a value-oriented approach, the assessment should focus on the societal impact which includes the potential negative outcomes on a variety of fundamental rights and principles, no longer restricted to simple privacy-related risks,[88] and encompassing the ethical and social consequences of data processing.[89]

---

[84] AI Now Institute 2018.

[85] Skorupinski and Ott 2002.

[86] In some cases it is hard to define the borders between the different data processing fields and the granularity of the subject matter (e.g. the blurred confines between well-being devices/apps and medical devices).

[87] Specific impact assessments for Big Data analytics and for AI are not necessary, but we do need separate impact assessments for data-driven decisions in healthcare and another for smart cities, given the different values underpinning the two sectors. Whereas, for example, civic engagement and participation and equal treatment will be the driving values behind smart city technology impact assessment, in healthcare freedom of choice and the no-harm principle may play a more critical role. Differing contexts have different "architectures of values" that should be taken into account as a benchmark for the assessment models.

[88] UN Universal Declaration of Human Rights (1948), Article 2; Council of Europe's Convention for the Protection of Human Rights and Fundamental Freedoms, Article 14; EU Charter of Fundamental Rights of the European Union, Article 21. See also IEEE 2019; Sartor 2017.

[89] See also Skorupinski and Ott 2002, p. 101 ("Talking about risk […] is not possible without ethical considerations […] when it comes to a decision on whether risk is to be taken, obviously an orientation on norms and values is unavoidable"); United Nations – General Assembly 2021, para 26; Mantelero 2017.

A general AI impact assessment, centred on human rights,[90] ethical and societal issues, can address the call for a broader protection of individuals in the AI context and better deal with the rising demand for ethically and socially oriented AI from citizens and companies.[91]

The inclusion of ethical and societal issues is consistent with the studies in the realm of collective data protection[92] that point out the importance of these non-legal dimensions in the context of data-intensive applications.[93] Evidence in this regard comes from predictive policing software, credit scoring models and many other algorithmic decision-support systems that increasingly target groups and society at large rather than single persons, thus highlighting the group and societal scale of the potential adverse impacts.

Although the present absence of a holistic approach to risk in AI is partially filled by a variety of bottom-up initiatives, corporate guidance or ongoing public investigations, the main limitations of these initiatives concern the variety of values, approaches and models adopted.[94] Similarly the ongoing debate on AI regulation has not yet furnished a clear assessment model.[95]

Against this background, the following sections sketch out a uniform model – whose components are discussed in greater detail in Chaps. 2 and 3 – which provides a common ground for an AI application assessment and, at the same time, offers sufficient flexibility to give voice to differing viewpoints.

1.5 HRESIA: A Multi-layered Process

The main components of the Human Rights, Ethical, and Social Impact Assessment (HRESIA) are the analysis of relevant human rights, the definition of relevant ethical and social values and the targeted application of these frameworks to given

[90] For the purposes of this book, the notions of human rights and fundamental rights are considered equivalent. See also European Union Agency for Fundamental Rights https://fra.europa.eu/en/about-fundamental-rights/frequently-asked-questions#difference-human-fundamental-rights accessed 10 January 2021 ("The term 'fundamental rights' is used in European Union (EU) to express the concept of 'human rights' within a specific EU internal context. Traditionally, the term 'fundamental rights' is used in a constitutional setting whereas the term 'human rights' is used in international law. The two terms refer to similar substance as can be seen when comparing the content in the Charter of Fundamental Rights of the European Union with that of the European Convention on Human Rights and the European Social Charter.").

[91] Jobin et al. 2019; Hagendorff 2020.

[92] Mantelero 2016; Taylor et al. 2017; Vedder 1997; Wright and Friedewald 2013; Wright and Mordini 2012; Raab and Wright 2012.

[93] See also Stahl and Wright 2018.

[94] See Chap. 3. See also Fritsch et al. 2018.

[95] See Chap. 4.

AI cases. The HRESIA therefore combines the universal approach of human rights[96] with the local dimension of societal values.

The first layer of the model is based on the common values found in human rights and related process principles,[97] whose relevance has also been recognised by Data Protection Authority (DPA) jurisprudence and the courts.[98] The second layer concerns the social and ethical values which play an important role in addressing non-legal issues associated with the adoption of certain AI solutions and their acceptability, and the balance between the different human rights and freedoms, in different contexts and periods.[99]

The proposed model therefore combines the human rights assessment with attention to the societal and ethical consequences,[100] but without becoming a broader social impact assessment, remaining focused on human rights. In this sense, ethical and social values are viewed through the lens of human rights and serve to go beyond the limitations of legal theory or practical implementation in effectively addressing the most urgent issues concerning the societal impacts of AI.

Moreover, ethical and social values are key to interpreting human rights in the regional context, in many cases representing the unspoken aspect of the legal reasoning behind the decisions of supervisory authorities or courts when ruling on large-scale impacting use of data.[101]

One option in trying to embody this theoretical framework in an assessment tool focused on concrete cases is to follow the models already adopted in the field of data

[96] Referring to this universal approach, we are aware of the underlying tensions that characterise it, the process of contextualisation of these rights and freedoms (appropriation, colonisation, vernacularisation, etc.) and the theoretical debate on universalism and cultural relativism in human rights. See Levitt and Merry 2009; Benhabib 2008; Merry 2006. See also Goldstein 2007; Leve 2007; Risse and Ropp 1999; O'sullivan 1998. However, from a policy and regulatory perspective, the human rights framework, including its nuances, can provide a more widely applicable common framework than other context-specific proposals on the regulation of the impact of AI. Furthermore, the proposed methodology includes in its planning section the analysis of the human rights background, with a contextualisation based on local jurisprudence and laws, as well as the identification and engagement of potential stakeholders who can contribute to a more context-specific characterisation of the human rights framework.

[97] The human rights-based approach includes a number of 'process principles', namely: participation and inclusion, non-discrimination and equality, and transparency and accountability. See The Danish Institute for Human Rights 2020.

[98] Apart from the central role of privacy and data protection, a first analysis of the decisions concerning data processing reveals the crucial role played by the principles of non-discrimination, transparency and participation as well as the safeguarding of human dignity, physical integrity and identity, as well as freedom of choice, of expression, of education, and of movement. See Mantelero and Esposito 2021, section 4.

[99] See Chap. 3.

[100] See below Sect. 1.7.

[101] See below Sect. 1.7.

processing.[102] This is envisaged in the recent proposals concerning AI,[103] which follows a questionnaire-based approach including, in some cases, open questions concerning human rights and social issues, though with a limited level of granularity.

However, the HRESIA model follows a different approach, in which the focus on human rights exploits different tools to the focus on ethical and social issues: the first relies on questionnaires and risk assessment tools (Chap. 2), while the second is built on the use of experts to address societal challenges associated with the development and implementation of AI solutions (Chap. 3).

Questionnaires and checklists alone are not sufficient to cover the human rights, ethical and societal components of the impact assessment. They can be useful in the HRIA (Human Rights Impact Assessment) planning and scoping phase, as well as in the collection of relevant data, but this is only one part of the assessment procedure, which includes evaluation models, data analysis, and expert evaluation.[104]

In the case of ethical and social issues, standardised questionnaires and checklists cannot grasp the specificities of the case, whereas experts interacting with relevant stakeholders can play a crucial role in understanding and exploring important questions. Questionnaires and checklists are just two of the possible tools to be used in fieldwork, along with focus groups, interviews, etc.[105]

From a methodological standpoint, an important role is played by participation[106] which makes it possible to get a better understanding of the different competing interests and societal values.[107] Both in carrying out the assessment and

---

[102] Esposito et al. 2018.

[103] Independent High-Level Expert Group on Artificial Intelligence set up by the European Commission 2020.

[104] See Chap. 2. For an example of a human rights checklist, see the Digital Rights Check realised by the Deutsche Gesellschaft für Internationale Zusammenarbeit GmbH and The Danish Institute for Human Rights, available at https://digitalrights-check.toolkit-digitalisierung.de/. Accessed 20 March 2022.

[105] See Chap. 3.

[106] The role of participatory approaches and stakeholder engagement is specifically recognised in the context of fundamental rights. The Danish Institute for Human Rights 2020, p. 116; De Hert 2012, p. 72 ("Further case law is required to clarify the scope of the duty to study the impact of certain technologies and initiatives, also outside the context of environmental health. Regardless of the terms used, one can safely adduce that the current human rights framework requires States to organise solid decision-making procedures that involve the persons affected by technologies").

[107] Participation of the different stakeholders (e.g. engagement of civil society and the business community in defining sectoral guidelines on values) can achieve a more effective result than mere transparency, although the latter has been emphasised in the recent debate on data processing. The Danish Institute for Human Rights 2020, p. 11 ("Engagement with rights-holders and other stakeholders is essential in HRIA […] Stakeholder engagement has therefore been situated as the core cross-cutting component in the Guidance and Toolbox"); Walker 2009, p. 41 ("participation is not only an end – a right – in itself, it is also a means of empowering communities to influence the policies and projects that affect them, as well as building the capacity of decision-makers to take into account the rights of individuals and communities when formulating and implementing projects and policies"). A more limited level of engagement, focused on awareness, was suggested by the Council of Europe 2018, p. 45 ("Public awareness and discourse are crucially important. All available means should be used to inform and engage the general public so that users are

in the mitigation phase – where the results of the HRESIA may suggest the engagement of specific categories of individuals –, participation can give voice to the different groups of persons potentially affected by the use of data-intensive systems and different stakeholders[108] (e.g. NGOs, public bodies)[109] facilitating a human-centred approach to AI design.

Participation is therefore a development goal for the assessment,[110] since it reduces the risk of under-representing certain groups and may also flag up critical issues that have been underestimated or ignored.[111] However, as pointed out in risk theory,[112] participation should not become a way for decision makers to avoid their responsibilities as leaders of the entire process.[113] Decision makers, in the choice and use of AI systems, must remain committed to achieving the best results in terms of minimising the potential negative impacts of data use on individuals and society.

Finally, given the social issues that underpin the HRESIA, transparency is an essential methodological requirement of this model. Transparency is crucial for an effective participation (Chap. 3) – as demonstrated in fields where impact assessments concern the societal consequences of technology (e.g. environment impact assessments) – and is also crucial in providing potentially affected people with information to give them a better understanding of the AI risks and reduce the limitations on their self-determination.

Along the lines of risk management models, the HRESIA assessment process adopts a by-design approach from the earliest stages and is characterised by a circular approach that follows the product/service throughout its lifecycle, which is also in line with the circular product development models that focus on flexibility and interaction with users to address their needs.[114]

---

empowered to critically understand and deal with the logic and operation of algorithms. This can include but is not limited to information and media literacy campaigns. Institutions using algorithmic processes should be encouraged to provide easily accessible explanations with respect to the procedures followed by the algorithms and to how decisions are made. Industries that develop the analytical systems used in algorithmic decision-making and data collection processes have a particular responsibility to create awareness and understanding, including with respect to the possible biases that may be induced by the design and use of algorithms").

[108] Stakeholders, unlike those groups directly affected by data processing, play a more critical role in those contexts where direct consultation may put groups at risk, due to the lack of adequate legal safeguards provided by local jurisdictions to human rights. See also Kemp and Vanclay 2013, p. 92 ("For situations where direct consultation may put groups at risk, it may be necessary to engage third parties, such as NGOs or other agencies or individuals who have worked closely with particular groups. Assessment teams must be vigilant about ensuring that individuals and groups are not put at risk by virtue of the human rights assessment itself").

[109] For a different approach to participation, more oriented towards the participation of lay people in expert committees, in the context of Technology Assessment, see Skorupinski and Ott 2002, pp. 117–120.

[110] See also United Nations Office of the High Commissioner for Human Rights 2006.

[111] Wright and Mordini 2012, p. 402.

[112] Palm and Hansson 2006, pp. 550–551.

[113] See Chap. 2.

[114] See Chap. 2, Sect. 2.3.2 and Chap. 3. See also Manifesto for Agile Software Development http://agilemanifesto.org/, accessed 5 February 2018; Gürses and Van Hoboken 2017.

1.6 The Role of Experts

The combination of these different layers in the model proposed here is intended to provide a self-assessment tool enabling AI system developers, deployers, and users to identify key values guiding the design and implementation of AI products and services. However, general background values and their contextual application may be not enough to address the societal changes when designing data-intensive systems. Although balanced with respect to the context, the definition of such rights and values may remain theoretical and need to be further tailored to the specific application.

To achieve a balance in specific cases, individuals with the right skills are needed to apply this set of rights and values in the given situation. The difficulty of bridging the gap between the theory of rights and values and their concrete application, given the nature of data use and the complexity of the associated risks, means that experts can play an important role in applying general principles and guidelines to a specific case (see Chap. 3).

Experts are therefore a key component of model implementation as they assist AI developers and users in this contextualisation and in applying the HRESIA benchmark values to the given case, balancing interests that may be in conflict, assessing risks and mitigating them.

The need for an expert view in data science has already been perceived by AI companies. The increasing and granular availability of data about individuals gathered from various devices, sensors, and online services enable private companies to collect huge amounts of data from which they can extract further information about individuals and groups. Private companies are therefore now more easily able to conduct large-scale social investigations, which can be classed as research activities, traditionally carried out by research bodies. This raises new issues since private firms often do not have the same ethical[115] and scientific background as researchers in academia or research centres.[116]

To address this lack of expertise, the adoption of ethical boards has been suggested, which may act at a national level, providing general guidelines, or at a company level, supporting data controllers on specific data applications.[117] Several companies have already set up ethical boards, appointed ethical advisors or adopted ethical guidelines.[118]

However, these boards have a limited focus on ethical issues and do not act within a broader framework of rights and values. Such shortcomings highlight the self-regulatory nature of these solutions lacking a strong general framework that could provide a common baseline for a holistic approach to human-centred AI.

On the other hand, committees of experts within the HRESIA framework could build on the human rights framework outlined above, representing a sound and

[115] See also Chap. 3.

[116] E.g., Schechter and Bravo-Lillo 2014; Kramer et al. 2014; Calo 2014, pp. 1046; boyd 2016.

[117] Calo 2013; Polonetsky et al. 2015. See Chap. 4.

[118] See Chap. 3.

common set of values to guide expert decisions and complemented by the ethical and social values taken into account by the HRESIA.

These aspects will clearly have an influence on the selection of the experts involved. Legal expertise, an ethical and sociological background, as well as domain-specific knowledge (of data applications) are required. Moreover, the background and number of experts will also depend on the complexity of AI use.[119]

The main task of the experts is to consider the specific AI use and place it in the local context, providing a tailored and more granular application of the legal and societal values underpinning the HRESIA model. In this process, the experts may decide that this contextual application of general principles and values requires the engagement of the groups of individuals potentially affected by AI[120] or institutional stakeholders. In this sense, the HRESIA is not a mere desk analysis, but takes a participatory approach – as described earlier[121] – which may be enhanced by the work of the experts involved in the HRESIA implementation.

To guarantee the transparency and the independence of these experts and their deliberations, specific procedures to regulate their activity, including stakeholder engagement should be adopted. In addition, full documentation of the decisional process should be recorded and archived for a specific period of time depending on the type of data use.

1.7 Assessing the Impact of Data-Intensive AI Applications: HRESIA Versus PIA/DPIA, SIA and EtIA

When comparing the HRESIA model with the impact assessment solutions adopted in the field of data-centred systems, the main reference is the experience gained in data protection.

The focus on the risks arising from data processing has been an essential element of data protection regulation from the outset, though over the years this risk has evolved in a variety of ways.[122] The original concern about government surveillance[123] has been joined by new concerns regarding the economic exploitation of personal information (risk of unfair or unauthorised uses of personal information[124]) and, more recently, by

[119] To offset the related costs, permanent expert committees might be set up by groups of enterprises or serving all SMEs in a given area.

[120] On the nature of these groups and its potential influence on the difficulty of engaging them in the assessment, Mantelero 2016.

[121] See Sect. 1.5.

[122] See fn 18.

[123] Westin 1970.

[124] See also Acquisti et al. 2015; Brandimarte et al. 2010; Turow et al. 2007.

the increasing number of decision-making processes based on information (risk of discrimination, large scale social surveillance, bias in predictive analyses[125]).

From a theoretical perspective, this focus on the potential adverse effects of data use has not been an explicit element of data protection law. The main purpose of many of the provisions is the safeguarding of specific values, rights and freedoms (e.g. human dignity, non-discrimination, freedom of thought, freedom of expression) against potential prejudices, adopting a procedural approach that leaves in the shadows these interests, which are encapsulated in the broad and general notion of data protection.

Moreover, compared to other personality rights, such as right to image or name, data protection has a proteiform nature, as data may consist of name, numbers, behavioural information, genetic data or many other types of information. The progressive datafication of our world makes it difficult to find something that is not or cannot be transformed into data. The resulting broad notion of data protection covers different fields and has partially absorbed some elements traditionally protected by other personality rights.[126]

Against this background, the idea of control over information was used to aggregate the various forms of data protection and to find a common core.[127] The procedural approach is consistent with this idea, as it secures all stages of data processing, from data collection to communication of data to third parties. Nevertheless, control over information describes the nature of the power that the law grants to the data subject, not its theoretical foundations.

In this regard, part of the legal doctrine has emphasised the role of human dignity as the cornerstone of data protection in Europe.[128] However, the interplay with the non-discrimination principle[129] and the role of data protection in the public sphere and digital citizenship[130] suggest that a broader range of values underpin data protection.

Although, over the years, data protection regulations[131] and practices[132] have adopted a more explicit risk-based approach to address the varying challenges of data use, they still focus on the procedural aspects. Data management procedures therefore represent a form of risk management based on the regulation of the different stages of data processing (collection, analysis and communication) and the definition of the powers and tasks of the various actors involved in this process.

---

[125] See, *inter alia*, Wachter et al. 2021; Zuiderveen Borgesius 2020; Hildebrandt 2021; Selbst 2017; Hildebrandt 2016, pp. 191–195; Barocas and Selbst 2016; Mantelero 2016.

[126] See also van der Sloot 2015, pp. 25–50 ("the right to privacy has been used by the Court to provide protection to a number of matters which fall primarily under the realm of other rights and freedoms contained in the Convention").

[127] See also Solove 2008, pp. 12–38; Westin 1970, pp. 330–399.

[128] Whitman 2004.

[129] See, in this sense, the notion of special categories of data in Article 6 of Council of Europe Convention 108 and in Article 9 of the GDPR. See also The White House 2015, and 2012, Appendix A: The Consumer Privacy Bill of Rights.

[130] Rodotà 2004.

[131] See Articles 24 and 35, GDPR.

[132] Wright and De Hert 2012.

This procedural approach and the focus of risk assessment on data management have led data protection authorities to propose assessment models (Privacy Impact Assessment, PIA) primarily centred on data quality and data security, leaving aside the nature of safeguarded interests. Instead, these interests are taken into account by DPAs and courts in their decisions, but – since data protection laws provide limited explicit references to the safeguarded values, rights and freedoms – the analysis of the relevant interest is often curtailed or not adequately elaborated.[133]

Data protection authorities and courts prefer arguments grounded on the set of criteria provided by data protection regulations.[134] The lawfulness and fairness of processing, transparency, purpose limitation, data minimisation, accuracy, storage limitation, data integrity and confidentiality are general principles frequently used by data protection authorities in their argumentations.[135] However, these principles are only an indirect expression of the safeguarded interests. Most of them are general clauses that may be interpreted more or less broadly and require an implicit consideration of the interests underpinning data use.

Moreover, the indefinite nature of these clauses has frequently led to the adoption of the criterion of proportionality[136], which amounts to a synthesis of the different competing interests and rights by courts or the DPAs. In fact, this balancing of interests and the reasoning that has resulted in a precise distinction between them is often implicit in the notion of proportionality and not discussed in the decisions taken by the DPAs or only discussed in an axiomatic manner.[137]

---

[133] See, e.g., the following decisions: Garante per la protezione dei dati personali (Italian DPA), 1 February 2018, doc. web n. 8159221; Garante per la protezione dei dati personali, 8 September 2016, n. 350, doc. web 5497522; Garante per la protezione dei dati personali, 4 June 2015, n. 345, doc. web n. 4211000; Garante per la protezione dei dati personali, 8 May 2013, n. 230, doc. web n. 2433401; Agencia Española de Protección de Datos (Spanish DPA), Expediente n. 01769/2017; Agencia Española de Protección de Datos, Expediente n. 01760/2017; Agencia Española de Protección de Datos, Resolución R/01208/2014; Agencia Española de Protección de Datos, (Gabinet Juridico) Informe 0392/2011; Agencia Española de Protección de Datos, (Gabinet Juridico) Informe 368/2006; Commission de la protection de la vie privée (Belgian DPA), 15 December 2010, recommandation n. 05/2010; Commission Nationale de l'Informatique et des Libertés (French DPA), 17 July 2014, deliberation n. 2014–307; Commission Nationale de l'Informatique et des Libertés, 21 June 1994, deliberation n. 94–056.

[134] Regarding the focus of DPAs' decisions on national data protection laws and their provisions, see also the results of the empirical analysis carried out by Porcedda 2017.

[135] See above fn 133.

[136] De Hert 2012, p. 46, who describes the application of the principle of proportionality as a "political" test. With regard to the jurisprudence of the European Court of Human Rights, this author also points out how "The golden trick for Strasbourg is to see almost every privacy relevant element as one that has to do with the required legal basis".

[137] See e.g. Court of Justice of the European Union, 13 May 2014, Case C-131/12, Google Spain SL, Google Inc. v Agencia Española de Protección de Datos, Mario Costeja González, para 81 ("In the light of the potential seriousness of that interference, *it is clear that* it cannot be justified by merely the economic interest which the operator of such an engine has in that processing", emphasis added).

Against this scenario, it is difficult for data controllers to understand and acknowledge the set of legal and social values that they should take into account in developing their data-intensive devices and services, since these values and their mutual interaction remain unclear and undeclared. Nor is this difficulty solved by the use of PIAs, since these assessment models merely point out the need to consider aspects other than data quality and data security, without specifying them or providing effective tools to identify and enlist broader social values.

Equally, the recent requirements of the GDPR – according to the models proposed by the DPAs – fail to offer a more satisfactory answer. Despite specific references in the GDPR to the safeguarding of rights and freedoms in general as well as to societal issues,[138] the new assessment models do nothing to pay greater attention to the societal consequences than the existing PIAs.[139]

The HRESIA fills this gap, providing an assessment model focused on the rights and freedoms that may be affected by data use[140] offering a more appropriate contextualisation of the various rights and freedoms that are relevant to data-intensive systems. The latter are no longer limited to data protection and should therefore be considered separately rather than absorbed in a broad notion of data protection.

Moreover, the HRESIA makes explicit the relevant social and ethical values considered in the evaluation of the system, while data protection laws, as well as proposed AI regulations, use general principles (e.g. fairness or proportionality) and general clauses (e.g. necessity, legitimacy[141]) to introduce non-legal social values into the legal framework. Legal scholars have also highlighted how the application

---

[138] See Recital n. 75.

[139] For a proposed integration of PIA and EIA, see Wright and Friedewald 2013, pp. 760–762. However, these authors do not adopt a broader viewpoint focused on human rights assessment.

[140] Despite this difference, HRESIA and PIA/DPIA take a common approach in terms of architecture, since both are rights-based assessments. See also The Danish Institute for Human Rights 2020, p. 98 ("Human rights impacts cannot be subject to 'offsetting' in the same way that, for example, environmental impacts can be. For example, a carbon offset is a reduction in emissions of carbon dioxide made in order to compensate for or to offset an emission made elsewhere. With human rights impacts, on the other hand, due to the fact that human rights are indivisible and interrelated, it is not appropriate to offset one human rights impact with a 'positive contribution' elsewhere").

[141] Bygrave 2002, pp. 61–63 and 339 on processing data for legitimate purpose ("solid grounds exist for arguing that the notion of 'legitimate' denotes a criterion of social acceptability, such that personal data should only be processed for purposes that do not run counter to predominant social mores […] The bulk of data protection instruments comprehend legitimacy *prima facie* in terms of procedural norms hinging on a criterion of lawfulness […] Very few expressly operate with a broader criterion of social justification. Nevertheless, the discretionary powers given by some national laws to national data protection authorities have enabled the latter to apply a relatively wide-ranging test of social justification"). See also New South Wales Privacy Committee 1977; Kirby 1981.

of human rights is necessarily affected by social and political influences that are not explicitly formalised in court decisions.[142]

From this perspective, a HRESIA may be used to unveil the existing interplay between the legal and the societal dimensions,[143] making it explicit. It is important to reveal this cross-fertilization between law and society, without leaving it concealed between the lines of the decisions of the courts, DPAs or other bodies.

Finally, a model that considers the social and ethical dimensions also helps to democratise assessment procedures, removing them from the exclusive hands of the courts, mediated by legal formalities.

This change in the assessment analysis can have a direct positive impact on business practices. Although courts, DPAs and legal scholars are aware of the influence of societal issues on their reasoning, this is often not explicit in their decisions. Product developers are therefore unable to grasp the real sense of the existing provisions and their implementation. Stressing the societal values that should be taken into account in human rights assessment helps developers to carry out self-assessments of the potential and complex consequences of their product and services, from the early stages of product design.

Some may argue that one potential shortcoming of the proposed approach concerns the fact that it may introduce a paternalistic view to data processing. In this sense, a HRESIA model necessarily encourages system designers, developers and users to rule out certain processing operations due to their ethical or social implications, even though some end users may take a different view and consider them in line with their own values. The model may therefore be seen as a limitation of self-determination, indirectly reducing the range of available data use options.

The main pillar of this argument rests on individual self-determination, but this notion is largely undermined by today's AI-driven data use.[144] The lack of conscious understanding in making decisions on data processing, and the frequent lack of effective freedom of choice (due to social, economic and technical lock-ins), argue for a slightly paternalistic approach as a way to offset these limitations on individual self-determination.[145] Moreover, HRESIA is not a standard but a self-assessment tool. It aims to provide a better awareness of the human rights,

---

[142] De Hert 2012; Nardell 2010; Arai-Takahashi and Arai 2002; van Drooghenbroeck 2001; Evans and Evans 2006; Centre for European Policy Studies 2010; Greer 2000; Harris et al. 2014; De Hert 2005.

[143] HRIA has its roots in Social Impact Assessment (SIA) models; Walker 2009, p. 5. Nevertheless, due to the existing interplay between human rights and social and ethical values, it is hard to define this relationship as derivation, as human rights notions necessarily affected the values adopted in SIA models. For example, the International Association for Impact Assessment Principles refers to Article 1 of the UN Declaration on the Right to Development by which every human being and all peoples are entitled to participate in, contribute to, and enjoy economic, social, cultural and political development.

[144] Mantelero 2014c.

[145] Bygrave 2002, p. 86 ("Under many European data protection regimes, paternalistic forms of control have traditionally predominated over participatory forms, though implementation of the EC Directive changes this weighting somewhat in favour of the latter").

ethical and social implications of data use, including a bottom-up participatory approach and a context-based view, which give voice to different viewpoints.

Finally, the publicity surrounding the HRESIA (in line with the HRIA) may help to reinforce individual self-determination, as it makes explicit the implications of a certain data processing operation and fosters end users' informed choice. Publicity increases not only the data subject's awareness, but also the data controller's accountability in line with a human rights-oriented approach.[146]

There are cases in which full disclosure of the assessment results may be limited by the legitimate interests of the data controller, such as confidentiality of information, security, and competition. For example, the Guidelines on Big Data adopted by the Council of Europe in 2017[147] – following the opinions of legal scholars[148] – specify that the results of the assessment proposed in the guidelines "should be made publicly available, without prejudice to secrecy safeguarded by law. In the presence of such secrecy, controllers provide any confidential information in a separate annex to the assessment report. This annex shall not be public but may be accessed by the supervisory authorities".[149]

Having highlighted the difference between PIA/DPIA and HRESIA, it is worth noting how closely HRESIA stands to the SIA (Social Impact Assessment). They share a similar focus on societal issues and the collective dimension,[150] an interest in public participation, empowerment of individuals and groups through the assessment process, attention to non-discrimination and equal participation in the assessment, accountability procedures and circular architecture. Important similarities also exist with the EtIA (Ethical Impact Assessment) models[151] and the focus on the ethical dimension.

However, despite the similarities, there are significant differences that set the HRESIA apart from both the PIA/DPIA and the SIA and EtIA models. The main differences concern the rationale of these models, the extent of the assessment and the way the different interests are balanced in the assessment. The HRESIA aims to provide a universal tool that, at the same time, also takes into account the local dimension of the safeguarded interests. In this sense, it is based on a common architecture grounded on intentional instruments with normative force (charters of fundamental rights). The core of the architecture is represented by human rights,

---

146 Access to information is both a human right per se and a key process principle of HRIA.

147 See above fn. 13.

148 Mantelero 2013, p. 234; Richards and King 2013, p. 43; Wright 2011, p. 222.

149 Council of Europe 2017, Section IV, para 3.3; Selbst 2017, p. 190. See also Ruggie 2007.

150 MacNaughton and Hunt 2011; Vanclay et al. 2015; Walker 2009, pp. 39–42.

151 SATORI project 2017, p. 6, defines ethical impact as the "impact that concerns or affects human rights and responsibilities, benefits and harms, justice and fairness, well-being and the social good". Although other authors, Wright and Mordini 2012, use the acronym EIA for Ethical Impact Assessment, the different acronym EtIA is used here to avoid any confusion with the Environmental Impact Assessment, which is usually identified with the acronym EIA.

which also play a role in SIA models but are not pivotal, as the SIA takes a wider approach.[152]

In fact, the scope of the SIA model encompasses a wide range of issues,[153] broad theoretical categories and focuses on the specific context investigated.[154] The solutions proposed by the SIA are therefore heterogeneous and vary in different contexts,[155] making it difficult to place them within a single framework, which – on the contrary – is a key requirement in the context of the global policies on AI.

By contrast, a model grounded on human rights[156] is more closely defined and universally applicable. Moreover, the SIA is designed for large-scale social phenomena, such as policy solutions,[157] while the HRESIA focuses on specific data-intensive AI applications.

Finally, the HRESIA is largely a rights-based assessment, in line with the approach adopted in data protection (PIA, DPIA), while both the SIA and the EtIA (Ethical Impact Assessment) are risks/benefits models.

On the comparison between HRESIA and EtIA,[158] the same considerations made with regard to SIA can be made in relation to EtIA.[159] In the forms proposed in the context of data use, there is a clearer link in the EtIA model with the ethical

[152] E.g., Dietz 1987; Taylor et al. 1990; Becker 2001; Vanclay 2002; Becker and Vanclay 2003; Centre for Good Governance 2006; MacNaughton and Hunt 2011; Vanclay et al. 2015; Götzmann et al. 2016.

[153] Burdge and Vanclay 1996, p. 59 ("Social impacts include all social and cultural consequences to human populations of any public or private actions that alter the ways in which people live, work, play, relate to one another, organize to meet their needs, and generally cope as members of society"). See also Massarani et al. 2007.

[154] In this sense, the ethical and social impact assessment (ESIA) is described as the outermost circle to which the PIA can be extended by Raab and Wright 2012, pp. 379–382.

[155] See also Svensson 2011, p. 84.

[156] Kemp and Vanclay 2013, pp. 90–91 ("Human rights impact assessment (HRIA) differs from SIA in the sense that it proceeds from a clear starting point of the internationally recognised rights, whereas SIA proceeds following a scoping process whereby all stakeholders (including the affected communities) nominate key issues in conjunction with the expert opinion of the assessor in terms of what the key issues might be based on experience in similar cases elsewhere and a conceptual understanding").

[157] Vanclay 2006, p. 9.

[158] See also Palm and Hansson 2006; Kenneally et al. 2010.

[159] See, e.g., with regard to stakeholder engagement Wright and Mordini 2012, p. 397 ("One of the objectives of an ethical impact assessment is to engage stakeholders in order to identify, discuss and find ways of dealing with ethical issues arising from the development of new technologies, services, projects or whatever"). See also Chap. 3.

principles already recognised in law.[160] However, a purely ethical assessment does run the risk of overlap between ethical guidance and legal requirement.

1.8 The HRESIA and Collective Dimension of Data Use

Shifting the focus from the traditional sphere of data quality and security to fundamental rights and freedoms, the HRESIA can be of help in dealing with the emerging issues concerning the collective dimension of data processing.[161]

Data-intensive applications and their use in decision-making processes impact on a variety of fundamental rights and freedoms. Not only does the risk of discrimination represent one of the biggest challenges of these applications, but other rights and freedoms also assume relevance, such as the right to the integrity of the person, to education, to equality before the law, and freedom of movement, of thought, of expression, of assembly and freedom in the workplace.[162]

Against this scenario, the final question that the proposed model must address regarding its interplay with data protection concerns the compatibility of the collective dimension of data protection and the way human rights are framed by legal scholars. To answer to this question, it is necessary to highlight how the notion of collective data protection tried to go beyond the individual dimension of data protection and its focus on data quality and security, suggesting a broader range of safeguarded interests and considering individuals as a group.

An impact assessment focussing on the broader category of human rights, which also takes into account the ethical and societal issues related to data use, can provide an answer to this need. This broader perspective and the varied range of human rights makes it possible to consider the impacts of data use more fully, not only limited to the protection of personal information. Moreover, several principles, rights, and freedoms in the charters of human rights directly or indirectly address group or collective issues.

However, in the context of human rights[163] as well as data protection, legal doctrine and the regulatory framework focus primarily on the individual dimension.

---

160 Wright and Mordini 2012, p. 399 ("With specific regard to values, it draws on those stated in the EU Reform Treaty, signed by Heads of State and Government at the European Council in Lisbon on 13 December 2007, such as human dignity, freedom, democracy, human right protection, pluralism, non-discrimination, tolerance, justice, solidarity and gender equality"). See also Callies et al. 2017, p. 31. For a broader analysis of ethical issue in risk assessment, see also Asveld and Roeser 2009.

161 Taylor et al. 2017; Mantelero 2016; Vedder 1997.

162 Council of Europe, Committee of experts on internet intermediaries 2018; European Data Protection Supervisor – Ethics Advisory Group 2018. See also van der Sloot 2015.

163 On the limits of an approach focused on induvial rather than on the collective dimension, Walker 2009, p. 21 ("Combatting discrimination is not simply a matter of prohibiting acts of discrimination or discriminatory legislation, but also entails an obligation on the State to take action to reverse the underlying biases in society that have led to discrimination and, where

Furthermore, in some cases, human rights theory provides little detail on the rights and freedoms threatened by the challenges of innovative digital technology.[164]

In this regard, for example, the approach to classification adopted by modern algorithms does not merely focus on individuals and on the categories traditionally used for unfair or prejudicial treatment of different groups of people.[165] Algorithms create groups or clusters of people with common characteristics other than the traditionally protected grounds (e.g. customer habits, lifestyle, online and offline behaviour, network of personal relationships etc.). For this reason, the wide application of predictive technologies based on these new categories and their use in decision-making processes challenges the way discrimination has usually been understood.[166]

appropriate, take temporary special measures in favour of people living in disadvantaged situations so as to promote substantive equality"). See also Mitnick 2018; George 1989.

[164] For example, based on previous experience, discrimination is primarily viewed within the traditional categories (sex, religion, etc.). See for example Recital 71 of the GDPR on automated decision-making, which refers to "discriminatory effects on natural persons on the basis of racial or ethnic origin, political opinion, religion or beliefs, trade union membership, genetic or health status or sexual orientation". However, groups shaped by analytics and AI differ from the traditional notion of groups in the sociological sense of the term considered by the legislation: they have a variable geometry and individuals can shift from one group to another.

[165] These categories, used in discriminatory practice, are to a large extent the special categories referred to in the data protection regulations.

[166] This notion must encompass both the prejudicial treatment of groups of people – regardless of whether they belong to special categories –, and the consequences of unintentional bias in the design, data collection and decision-making stages of data-intensive applications. Indeed, these consequences may negatively impact on individuals and society, even though they do not concern forms of discrimination based on racial or ethnic origin, political opinions, religious or philosophical beliefs or other elements that traditionally characterise minorities or vulnerable groups. For example, Kate Crawford has described the case of the City of Boston and its StreetBump smartphone app to passively detect potholes. The application had a signal problem, due to the bias generated by the low penetration of smartphones among lower income and older residents. While the Boston administration took this bias into account and solved the problem, less enlightened public officials might underestimate such considerations and make potentially discriminatory decisions. See Crawford 2013; Lerman 2013. Another example is the Progressive case, in which an insurance company obliged drivers to install a small monitoring device in their cars in order to receive the company's best rates. The system considered as a negative factor driving late at night but did not take into account the potential bias against low-income individuals, who are more likely to work night shifts, compared with late-night party-goers, "forcing them [low-income individuals] to carry more of the cost of intoxicated and other irresponsible driving that happens disproportionately at night", Robinson et al. 2014, pp. 18–19. Finally, commercial practices may lead to price discrimination or the adoption of differential terms and conditions depending on the assignment of consumers to a specific cluster. Thus, consumers classified as "financially challenged" belong to a cluster "[i]n the prime working years of their lives [...] including many single parents, struggl[ing] with some of the lowest incomes and little accumulation of wealth". This implies the following predictive viewpoint, based on big data analytics and regarding all consumers in the cluster: "[n]ot particularly loyal to any one financial institution, [and] they feel uncomfortable borrowing money and believe they are better off having what they want today as they never know what tomorrow will bring" (Federal Trade Commission 2014, p. 20). It is not hard to imagine the potential discriminatory consequences of similar classifications with regard to individuals and groups. See also Poort and Zuiderveen Borgesius 2021.

Additionally, the nature of the groups created by data-intensive applications poses challenging issues from the procedural viewpoint, which concern the potential remedies to the need for collective representation in the context of algorithmic-created groups.[167] Indeed, people belonging to groups that are the traditional targets of discriminatory practices are aware of their membership of these groups and they know or may know the other members of the group. On the contrary, in the groups generated by algorithms, people do not know the other members of the group and, in many cases, are not aware of the consequences of their belonging to a group. Data subjects are not aware of the identity of the other members of the group, have no relationship with them and have a limited perception of their collective issues.

Hard law remedies in this field may not be easy to achieve in the short run and the existing or potential procedural rules often vary from one legal context to another.[168] In this scenario, an assessment tool may represent a valid alternative to address these challenges. For these reasons, a model based on a participatory approach and in which human rights are seen through the lens of ethical and social values can provide broader safeguards both in terms of the interests taken into account and the categories of individuals engaged in the process.

Finally, providing a framework for a collective and societal impact assessment of data-intensive applications is also in line with the ongoing debate on Responsible Research Innovation[169] and the demands of the data industry and product developers for practical self-assessment tools to help them address the social issues of data use. Tools should be more flexible, open to new emerging values, easily reshaped and applicable in different legal and cultural contexts. At the same time, it should be pointed out how the HRESIA model differs from the Responsible Research Innovation assessment, where the latter takes into account a variety of societal issues, which do not necessarily concern fundamental rights and freedoms[170] (e.g. interoperability, openness).[171]

---

[167] See also Mantelero 2017.

[168] See, e.g., the case of redress procedures for the protection of consumer rights.

[169] Stilgoe et al. 2013, pp. 1568–1580.

[170] Regarding this kind of hendiadys ("fundamental rights and freedoms"), see also De Hert and Gutwirth 2004, pp. 319–320 ("legal scholars in Europe have devoted much energy in transforming or translating liberty questions into questions of 'human rights'. One of the advantages of this 'rights approach' is purely strategic: it facilitates the bringing of cases before the European Court of Human Rights, a Court that is considered to have higher legal status […] There are however more reasons to think in terms of rights. It is rightly observed that the concept of human rights in legal practice is closely linked to the concept of subjective rights. Lawyers do like the idea of subjective rights. They think these offer better protection than 'liberty' or 'liberties'").

[171] Regarding this approach in the context of data processing, see also H2020 Virt-EU project https://virteuproject.eu/, accessed 19 December 2017.

1.9 Advantages of the Proposed Approach

The positive features of the proposed model for assessing the impact of data use can be briefly summarised as follows:

- The central role of human rights in HRESIA provides a universal set of values, making it suited to various legal and social contexts.
- The HRESIA is a principle-based model, which makes it better at dealing with the rapid change of technological development, not easily addressed by detailed sets of provisions.
- The proposed model follows in the footsteps of the data protection assessments, as a rights-based assessment in line with the PIA and DPIA approaches. However, it is broader in scope in that individual rights are properly and fully considered, coherent with their separate theoretical elaboration.
- The HRESIA emphasises the ethical and social dimensions, giving a better understanding of the human rights implications in a given context, and as spheres to be considered independently when deciding to implement data-intensive AI-based systems affecting individuals and society.
- By stressing ethical and social values, the HRESIA helps to make explicit the non-legal values that inform the courts and DPAs in their reasoning when they apply general data protection principles, interpret general clauses or balance conflicting interests in the context of data-intensive systems.
- In considering ethical and social issues, this model makes it possible to give flexibility to the legal framework in dealing with AI applications. A human rights assessment that operates through the lens of ethical and social values can therefore better address the challenges of the developing digital society.
- Finally, as an assessment tool, the HRESIA fosters the adoption of a preventive approach to product/service development from the earliest stages, favouring safeguards to rights and values, and a responsible approach to technology development.

1.10 Summary

The increasing use of AI in decision-making processes highlights the importance of examining the potential impact of AI data-intensive systems on individuals and society at large.

The consequences of data processing are no longer restricted to the well-known privacy and data protection issues but encompass prejudices against groups of individuals and a broader array of fundamental rights. Moreover, the tension between the extensive use of data-intensive systems, on the one hand, and the growing demand for ethically and socially responsible data use on the other, reveals the lack of a regulatory framework that can fully address the societal issues raised by AI technologies.

Against this background, neither traditional data protection impact assessment models (PIA and DPIA) nor the broader social or ethical impact assessment procedures (SIA and EtIA) appear to provide an adequate answer to the challenges of our algorithmic society.

While the former have a narrow focus – centred on data quality and data security – the latter cover a wide range of issues, employing broad theoretical categories and providing a variety of different solutions. A human rights-centred assessment may therefore offer a better answer to the demand for a more comprehensive assessment, including not only data protection, but also the effects of data use on other fundamental rights and freedoms (such as freedom of movement, freedom of expression, of assembly and freedom in the workplace) and related principles (such as non-discrimination).

Moreover, a human rights assessment is grounded on the charters of fundamental rights, which provide the common baseline for assessing data use in the context of global AI policies.

While the Human Rights Impact Assessment (HRIA) is not a new approach in itself[172] and has its roots in environmental impact assessment models and development studies,[173] HRIA has not yet been systematically applied in the context of AI.[174]

However, given the enormous changes to society brought by technology and datafication, when applied to the field of AI the HRIA must be enriched to consider ethical and societal issues, evolving into a more holistic model such as the proposed Human Rights, Ethical and Social Impact Assessment (HRESIA).

The HRESIA is also more closely aligned with the true intention of the EU legislator to safeguard not only the right to personal data protection, but also the fundamental rights and freedoms of natural persons.

Furthermore, ethical and social values, viewed through the lens of human rights, make it possible to overcome the limitations of the traditional human rights impact assessment and help to interpret human rights in line with the regional context. The HRESIA can in this way contribute to a universal tool that also takes the local dimension of the safeguarded interests into account.

---

[172] Gostin and Mann 1994; Ruggie 2007; Harrison and Stephenson 2010; Harrison 2011; World Bank and Nordic Trust Fund 2013; The Danish Institute for Human Rights 2020.

[173] Walker 2009, pp. 3–4; Massarani et al. 2007, pp. 143–149. See also Burdge and Vanclay 1996, pp. 62–64 and Ruggie 2007 ("However, the ESIA [Environmental and Social Impact Assessment] approach of studying the direct impacts of a business can miss human rights violations that are embedded in a society").

[174] An early suggestion in this sense was provided by the Council of Europe 2018, p. 45 ("Human rights impact assessments should be conducted before making use of algorithmic decision-making in all areas of public administration"). More recently, proposals on AI regulation under discussion at the European Union and the Council of Europe have highlighted the importance of assessing the impact of AI applications on human rights, albeit with some limitations; see Chap. 4. See also United Nations – General Assembly 2021, paras 51–52.

To achieve these goals the HRESIA model combines different components, from self-assessment questionnaires to participatory tools. They help define the general value framework and place it in a local context, providing a tailored and granular application of the underlying legal and social values.

On the basis of this architecture, such an assessment tool can raise awareness among AI manufacturers, developers, and users of the impact of AI-based products/services on individuals and society. At the same time, a participatory and transparent assessment model like the HRESIA also gives individuals an opportunity for more informed choices concerning the use of their data and increases their awareness about the consequences of AI applications.

This assessment may represent an additional burden for AI industry and adopters. However, even in contexts where it is not required by law,[175] it could well gain ground in those areas where people pay greater attention to ethical and social implications of AI (healthcare, services/products for kids, etc.) or where socially oriented entities or developers' communities are involved. Moreover, as has happened in other sectors, a greater attention to human rights and societal impacts may represent a competitive advantage for companies that deal with responsible consumers and partners.

Finally, the focus of policymakers, industry, and communities on ethical and responsible use of AI, and the lack of adequate tools to assess the impacts of AI on the fundamental rights and freedoms, as called for by the proposals under discussion in Europe,[176] also make the HRESIA a possible candidate as a mandatory assessment tool.

References

Acquisti A, Brandimarte L, Loewenstein G (2015) Privacy and human behavior in the age of information. Science 347(6221):509–514.

Acquisti A, Grossklags J (2005) Privacy and rationality in individual decision making. Security & Privacy, IEEE 3(1):26–33.

Agencia Española de Protección de Datos (2018) Guía práctica para las evaluaciones de impacto en la protección de los datos sujetas al RGPD. https://www.aepd.es/sites/default/files/2019-09/guia-evaluaciones-de-impacto-rgpd.pdf. Accessed 4 March 2018.

Agencia Española de Protección de Datos (2021) Gestión del riesgo y evaluación de impacto en tratamientos de datos personales. https://www.aepd.es/es/node/46578. Accessed 17 August 2021.

AI Now Institute (2018) Algorithmic Impact Assessments: Toward Accountable Automation in Public Agencies. https://medium.com/@AINowInstitute/algorithmic-impact-assessments-toward-accountable-automation-in-public-agencies-bd9856e6fdde. Accessed 4 March 2018.

[175] For an approach oriented toward a mandatory impact assessment for AI systems see the proposals of the European Commission and the Council of Europe on AI regulation discussed in Chap. 4.

[176] See Chap. 4.

Ambrus M (2017) The European Court of Human Rights as Governor of Risk. In: Ambrus M, Rayfuse R, Werner W (eds) Risk and the Regulation of Uncertain in International Law. Oxford University Press, Oxford, pp 99–115.

Arai-Takahashi Y, Arai Y (2002) The Margin of Appreciation Doctrine and the Principle of Proportionality in the Jurisprudence of the ECHR. Intersentia, Antwerp.

Article 29 Data Protection Working Party (2011) Opinion 15/2011 on the definition of consent. http://ec.europa.eu/justice/policies/privacy/docs/wpdocs/2011/wp187_en.pdf. Accessed 27 February 2014.

Article 29 Data Protection Working Party (2013a) Opinion 03/2013a on purpose limitation. http://ec.europa.eu/justice/data-protection/article-29/documentation/opinion-recommendation/files/2013a/wp203_en.pdf. Accessed 27 February 2014.

Article 29 Data Protection Working Party (2013b) Opinion 06/2013b on open data and public sector information ('PSI') reuse. http://ec.europa.eu/justice/data-protection/article-29/documentation/opinion-recommendation/files/2013b/wp207_en.pdf. Accessed 27 February 2014.

Article 29 Data Protection Working Party (2014a) Opinion 06/2014a on the notion of legitimate interests of the data controller under Article 7 of Directive 95/46/EC. http://ec.europa.eu/justice/data-protection/article-29/documentation/opinion-recommendation/files/2014a/wp217_en.pdf. Accessed 27 February 2014.

Article 29 Data Protection Working Party (2014b) Statement on the role of a risk-based approach in data protection legal frameworks. http://ec.europa.eu/justice/data-protection/article-29/documentation/opinion-recommendation/files/2014b/wp218_en.pdf. Accessed 27 February 2014b.

Article 29 Data Protection Working Party (2017) Guidelines on Data Protection Impact Assessment (DPIA) and determining whether processing is "likely to result in a high risk" for the purposes of Regulation 2016/679. Adopted on 4 April 2017 as last revised and adopted on 4 October 2017. http://ec.europa.eu/newsroom/article29/item-detail.cfm?item_id=611236. Accessed 13 April 2018.

Asveld L, Roeser S (eds) (2009) The Ethics of Technological Risk. Earthscan, London.

Barocas S, Selbst AD (2016) Big Data's Disparate Impact 104 (3) California Law Review 671

Beck U (1992) Risk Society: Towards a New Modernity. Sage, London.

Becker HA (2001) Social impact assessment. Eur. J. Oper. Res. 128(2):311–321.

Becker HA, Vanclay F (eds) (2003) The International Handbook of Social Impact Assessment. Conceptual and Methodological Advances. Edward Elgar, Cheltenham.

Bellagio Big DataWorkshop Participants (2014) Big data and positive social change in the developing world: A white paper for practitioners and researchers. http://www.rockefellerfoundation.org/uploads/files/c220f1f3-2e9a-4fc6-be6c-45d42849b897-big-data-and.pdf. Accessed 28 June 2015.

Benhabib S (2008) The Legitimacy of Human Rights. Daedalus 137:94–104.

Bennett CJ (1992) Regulating Privacy: Data Protection and Public Policy in Europe and the United States. Cornell University Press, Ithaca, New York.

Bennett CJ, Haggerty KD, Lyon D, Steeves V (eds) (2014) Transparent Lives Surveillance in Canada. Athabasca University Press, Edmonton.

Bloustein EJ (1977) Group Privacy: The Right to Huddle. Rut.-Cam. L. J. 8:219–283.

Bollier D (2010) The Promise and Perils of Big Data. Aspen Institute, Communications and Society Program. http://www.aspeninstitute.org/sites/default/files/content/docs/pubs/The_Promise_and_Peril_of_Big_Data.pdf. Accessed 27 February 2014.

boyd d (2012) Networked Privacy. Surv. & Soc. 10(3/4):348–350.

boyd d (2016) Untangling Research and Practice: What Facebook's "Emotional Contagion" Study Teaches Us. Research Ethics 12:4–13.

boyd d, Crawford K (2012) Critical Questions for Big Data: Provocations for a Cultural, Technological, and Scholarly Phenomenon. Inf., Comm. & Soc. 15(5):662–679.

Brandimarte L, Acquisti A, Loewenstein G (2010) Misplaced Confidences: Privacy and the Control Paradox. Ninth Annual Workshop on the Economics of Information Security. http://www.heinz.cmu.edu/~acquisti/papers/acquisti-SPPS.pdf. Accessed 27 February 2014.
Breckenridge AC (1970) The Right to Privacy. University of Nebraska Press, Lincoln.
Brenton M (1964) The Privacy Invaders. Coward-McCann, New York.
Brown I (2012) Government access to private-sector data in the United Kingdom. Int'l Data Privacy L. 2(4):230–238.
Brown I (2013) Lawful Interception Capability Requirements. https://www.scl.org/articles/2878-lawful-interception-capability-requirements. Accessed 12 June 2016.
Brownsword R (2009) Consent in Data Protection Law: Privacy, Fair Processing and Confidentiality. In: Gutwirth S, Poullet Y, De Hert P, de Terwangne C, Nouwt S (eds) Reinventing data protection? Springer, Dordrecht, pp 83–110.
Brüggemeier G, Colombi Ciacchi A, O'Callaghan P (2010) Personality Rights in European Tort Law. Cambridge University Press, New York.
Burdge RJ, Vanclay F (1996) Social Impact Assessment: A Contribution to the State of the Art Series. Impact Assessment 14(1):59–86.
Bygrave LA (2002) Data Protection Law. Approaching Its Rationale, Logic and Limits. Kluwer Law International, The Hague/London/New York.
Callies I, Jansen P, Reijers W, Douglas D, Gurzawska A, Kapeller A, Brey P, Benčin R, Warso Z (2017) Outline of an Ethics Assessment Framework. http://satoriproject.eu/media/SATORI-FRAMEWORK-2017-05-03.pdf. Accessed 27 April 2018.
Calo RM (2013) Against Notice Skepticism in Privacy (and Elsewhere). Notre Dame L. Rev. 87 (3):1027–1072.
Calo R (2014) Digital Market Manipulation. Geo. Wash. L. Rev. 82(4):995–1051.
Cannataci J (2008) Lex Personalitatis & Technology-Driven Law. SCRIPT-ed 5(1):1–6.
Cannataci JA, Zhao B, Torres Vives G, Monteleone S, Mifsud Bonnici J, Moyakine E (2016) Privacy, Free Expression and Transparency: Redefining Their New Boundaries in the Digital Age. United Nations Educational, Scientific and Cultural Organization, Paris.
Castells M (1996) The Rise of the network society. Blackwell Publishers, Cambridge, MA.
Cate FH (2006) The Failure of Fair Information Practice Principles. In Winn JK (ed.) Consumer Protection in the Age of the 'Information Economy. Ashgate, Hampshire, pp 341–378.
Cate FH, Dempsey JX, Rubinstein IS (2012) Systematic government access to private-sector data. Int'l Data Privacy L. 2(4):195–199.
Cate FH, Mayer-Schönberger V (2013a) Data Use and Impact. Global Workshop. http://cacr.iu.edu/sites/cacr.iu.edu/files/Use_Workshop_Report.pdf. Accessed 27 February 2014
Cate FH, Mayer-Schönberger V (2013b) Notice and consent in a world of Big Data. Int'l Data Privacy L. 3(2):67–73.
Centre for European Policy Studies (2010) Global Data Transfers: The Human Rights Implications. https://www.ceps.eu/publications/global-data-transfers-human-rights-implications. Accessed 13 November 2017.
Centre for Good Governance (2006) A Comprehensive Guide for Social Impact Assessment. http://unpan1.un.org/intradoc/groups/public/documents/cgg/unpan026197.pdf. Accessed 2 May 2018.
Clifford D, Ausloos J (2018) Data Protection and the Role of Fairness. Yearbook of European Law 37:130–187.
CNIL (2018a) Privacy Impact Assessment (PIA). Knowledge Bases. https://www.cnil.fr/sites/default/files/atoms/files/cnil-pia-3-en-knowledgebases-2018a-02-19_diffusable_en_pdf_valide_jli.pdf. Accessed 28 February 2018.
CNIL (2018b) Privacy Impact Assessment (PIA). Methodology. https://www.cnil.fr/sites/default/files/atoms/files/cnil-pia-1-en-methodology.pdf. Accessed 28 February 2018.
CNIL (2018c) Privacy Impact Assessment (PIA). Templates. https://www.cnil.fr/sites/default/files/atoms/files/cnil-pia-2-en-templates.pdf. Accessed 28 February 2018.
Cohen JE (2000) Examined Lives: Informational Privacy and the Subject as an Object. Stan. L. Rev. 52:1373–1438.

Cohen JE (2013) What Privacy is For. Harv. L. Rev. 126:1904–1933.
Cohen JE (2019) Between Truth and Power: The Legal Constructions of Informational Capitalism. Oxford University Press, New York.
Committee on Commerce, Science, and Transportation (2013) A Review of the Data Broker Industry: Collection, Use, and Sale of Consumer Data for Marketing Purposes. http://educationnewyork.com/files/rockefeller_databroker.pdf. Accessed 20 February 2014.
Congressional Research Service (2008) CRS Report for Congress. Data Mining and Homeland Security: An Overview. www.fas.org/sgp/crs/homesec/RL31798.pdf. Accessed 14 December 2013.
Council of Europe (2008) Guidelines for the cooperation between law enforcement and internet service providers against cybercrime. https://rm.coe.int/16802fa3ba. Accessed 27 February 2014.
Council of Europe (2017) Guidelines on the protection of individuals with regard to the processing of personal data in a world of Big Data. https://rm.coe.int/CoERMPublicCommonSearchServices/DisplayDCTMContent?documentId=09000016806ebe7a. Accessed 4 May 2017.
Council of Europe (2018) Algorithms and Human Rights. Study on the Human Rights Dimensions of Automated Data Processing Techniques and Possible Regulatory Implications. https://edoc.coe.int/en/internet/7589-algorithms-and-human-rights-study-on-the-human-rights-dimensions-of-automated-data-processing-techniques-and-possible-regulatory-implications.html. Accessed 5 May 2018.
Council of Europe, Committee of Ministers (2020) Recommendation CM/Rec(2020)1 of the Committee of Ministers to member States on the human rights impacts of algorithmic systems. https://unesdoc.unesco.org/ark:/48223/pf0000377881. Accessed 24 May 2020.
Council of Europe, Consultative Committee of the Convention for the Protection of Individuals with regard to Automatic Processing of Personal Data (Convention 108) (2019) Guidelines on Artificial Intelligence and Data Protection, T-PD(2019)01. https://unesdoc.unesco.org/ark:/48223/pf0000377881. Accessed 15 February 2019.
Council of Europe, Expert Committee on human rights dimensions of automated data processing and different forms of artificial intelligence (MSI-AUT) (2019) Responsibility and AI. A Study of the Implications of Advanced Digital Technologies (Including AI Systems) for the Concept of Responsibility within a Human Rights Framework. Rapporteur: Karen Yeung. https://rm.coe.int/responsability-and-ai-en/168097d9c5. Accessed 11 July 2021.
Crawford K (2013) The Hidden Biases in Big Data. Harv. Bus. Rev. April 1, 2013. https://hbr.org/2013/04/the-hidden-biasesin-big-data. Accessed 29 January 2015.
Crawford K, Schultz J (2014) Big Data and Due Process: Toward a Framework to Redress Predictive Privacy Harms. B.C.L. Rev. 55(1):93–128.
DARPA (2002) Total Information Awareness Program (TIA). System Description Document (SDD), Version 1.1. http://epic.org/privacy/profiling/tia/tiasystemdescription.pdf. Accessed 14 December 2013.
De Hert P (2005) Balancing security and liberty within the European human rights framework. A critical reading of the Court's case law in the light of surveillance and criminal law enforcement strategies after 9/11. Utrecht Law Review 1(1):68–96.
De Hert P (2012) A Human Rights Perspective on Privacy and Data Protection Impact Assessments. In: Wright D, De Hert P (eds) Privacy Impact Assessment. Springer, Dordrecht, pp 33–76.
De Hert P, Gutwirth S (2004) Rawls' political conception of rights and liberties. An unliberal but pragmatic approach to the problems of harmonisation and globalisation. In: Van Hoecke M (ed) Epistemology and methodology of comparative law in the light of European Integration. Hart Publishing, London, pp 317–357.
Dietz T (1987) Theory and method in social impact assessment. Sociol. Inq. 57(1):54–69.
Dwork C, Mulligan DK (2013) It's not Privacy and It's not Fair. Stan. L. Rev. Online 66:35–40.
Esposito MS, Mantelero A, Sarale A, Thobani S, Nemorin S (2018) Deliverable 4.3. Second Report: Report to the internal members of the consortium on the PESIA methodology and initial guidelines. Project no. 732027 Horizon 2020. Values and ethics in Innovation for

Responsible Technology in EUrope (VIRT-EU). https://cordis.europa.eu/project/id/732027/results/it. Accessed 16 January 2020.

European Commission, Directorate General for Communication Networks, Content and Technology (2018) A Multi-Dimensional Approach to Disinformation Report of the Independent High Level Group on Fake News and Online Disinformation. https://ec.europa.eu/digital-single-market/en/news/final-report-high-level-expert-group-fake-news-and-online-disinformation. Accessed 22 March 2018.

European Data Protection Supervisor (2014) Preliminary Opinion of the European Data Protection Supervisor. Privacy and competitiveness in the age of big data: The interplay between data protection, competition law and consumer protection in the Digital Economy. https://secure.edps.europa.eu/EDPSWEB/webdav/site/mySite/shared/Documents/Consultation/Opinions/2014/14-03-26_competitition_law_big_data_EN.pdf. Accessed 27 February 2014.

European Data Protection Supervisor, Ethics Advisory Group (2018) Towards a digital ethics. https://edps.europa.eu/sites/edp/files/publication/18-01-25_eag_report_en.pdf. Accessed 4 March 2018.

European Parliament (2013) Resolution of 4 July 2013 on the US National Security Agency surveillance programme, surveillance bodies in various Member States and their impact on EU citizens' privacy. http://www.europarl.europa.eu/sides/getDoc.do?pubRef=-//EP//TEXT+TA+P7-TA-2013-0322+0+DOC+XML+V0//EN. Accessed 27 February 2014.

European Parliament, Directorate General for Internal Policies, Policy Department C: Citizens' Rights and Constitutional Affairs, Civil Liberties, Justice and Home Affairs (2013a) National Programmes for Mass Surveillance of Personal data in EU Member States and Their Compatibility with EU Law. http://www.europarl.europa.eu/committees/it/libe/studies download.html?languageDocument=EN&file=98290. Accessed 27 February 2014.

European Parliament, Directorate General for Internal Policies, Policy Department C: Citizens' Rights and Constitutional Affairs, Civil Liberties, Justice and Home Affairs (2013b) The US National Security Agency (NSA) surveillance programmes (PRISM) and Foreign Intelligence Surveillance Act (FISA) activities and their impact on EU citizens. http://info.publicintelligence.net/EU-NSA-Surveillance.pdf. Accessed 14 December 2013.

European Parliamentary Research Service (2020) The Impact of the General Data Protection Regulation (GDPR) on Artificial Intelligence. https://www.europarl.europa.eu/thinktank/en/document.html?reference=EPRS_STU(2020)641530. Accessed 12 August 2021.

Evans C, Evans S (2006) Evaluating the Human Rights Performance of Legislatures. Human Rights Law Review 6(3):545–570.

Federal Trade Commission (2014) Data Brokers: A Call for Transparency and Accountability. https://www.ftc.gov/system/files/documents/reports/data-brokers-call-transparency-accountability-report-federal-trade-commission-may-2014/140527databrokerreport.pdf. Accessed 27 February 2016.

Felzmann H, Fosch-Villaronga E, Lutz C, Tamò-Larrieux A (2019) Transparency You Can Trust: Transparency Requirements for Artificial Intelligence between Legal Norms and Contextual Concerns. Big Data & Society 6(1), 2053951719860542. https://doi.org/10.1177/2053951719860542. Accessed 11 August 2021.

Floridi L (2014) Open Data, Data Protection, and Group Privacy. Philos. Technol. 27(1):1–3.

Fritsch E, Shklovski I, Douglas-Jones R (2018) Calling for a revolution: An analysis of IoT manifestos. Proceedings of the 2018 ACM Conference on Human Factors in Computing (Montreal, Canada, 21–26 April 2018). https://doi.org/10.1145/3180000/3173876/paper302.pdf?ip=80.180.146.48&id=3173876&acc=OPEN&key=4D4702B0C3E38B35%2E4D4702B0C3E38B35%2E4D4702B0C3E38B35%2E6D218144511F3437&__acm__=1525873755_622581693e4344f67627f0aec1be630b. Accessed 3 May 2018.

Fuster G (2014) The Emergence of Personal Data Protection as a Fundamental Right of the EU. Springer International Publishing, Cham.

George RP (1989) Individual rights, collective interests, public law, and American politics. Law and Philosophy 8:245–261.

Goldstein DM (2007) Human Rights as Culprit, Human Rights as Victim: Rights and Security in the State of Exception. In: Goodale M, Merry SE (eds) The Practice of Human Rights: Tracking Law between the Global and the Local. Cambridge University Press, Cambridge, pp 49–77.

Gostin L, Mann JM (1994) Towards the Development of a Human Rights Impact Assessment for the Formulation and Evaluation of Public Health Policies. Health and Human Rights 1(1):58–80.

Götzmann N, Vanclay F, Seier F (2016) Social and Human Rights Impact Assessments: What Can They Learn from Each Other? Impact Assessment and Project Appraisal 34(1):14–23.

Greer S (2000) The margin of appreciation: interpretation and discretion under the European Convention on Human Rights. Editions du Conseil de l'Europe, Strasbourg. https://www.echr.coe.int/LibraryDocs/DG2/HRFILES/DG2-EN-HRFILES-17(2000).pdf Accessed 18 January 2021.

Gürses S, Van Hoboken J (2017) Privacy after the Agile Turn. In Polonetsky J, Tene O, Selinger E (eds) Cambridge Handbook of Consumer Privacy. Cambridge University Press, Cambridge, pp 579–601.

Hagendorff T (2020) The Ethics of AI Ethics: An Evaluation of Guidelines. Minds and Machines 30: 99–120.

Harris D, O'Boyle M, Bates E, Buckley C (2014) Law of the European Convention on Human Rights. Oxford University Press, Oxford.

Harrison J (2011) Human rights measurement: Reflections on the current practice and future potential of human rights impact assessment. J Hum Rights Prac. 3(2): 162–187.

Harrison J, Stephenson M-A (2010) Human Rights Impact Assessment: Review of Practice and Guidance for Future Assessments. Scottish Human Rights Commission. http://fian-ch.org/content/uploads/HRIA-Review-of-Practice-and-Guidance-for-Future-Assessments.pdf. Accessed 29 November 2017.

Hartzog W, Selinger E (2013) Big Data in Small Hands. Stan. L. Rev. Online 66:81–88.

Hildebrandt M (2013) Slaves to Big Data. Or Are We? IDP: revista d'Internet, dret i política 17:27–44.

Hildebrandt M (2016) Smart Technologies and the End(s) of Law: Novel Entanglements of Law and Technology. Edward Elgar Publishing, Cheltenham.

Hildebrandt M (2021) The Issue of Bias. The Framing Powers of Machine Learning. In: Pelillo M, Scantamburlo T (eds) Machines We Trust. Perspectives on Dependable AI. MIT Press, Cambridge, MA, pp 44–59.

Hoofnagle C (2003) Big Brother's Little Helpers: How Choicepoint and Other Commercial Data Brokers Collect, Process, and Package Your Data for Law Enforcement. N.C.J. Int'l L. & Com. Reg. 29(4):595–637.

Hummel P, Braun M, Tretter M, Dabrock P (2021) Data Sovereignty: A Review. Big Data & Society 8, https://doi.org/10.1177/2053951720982012.

IEEE (2019) Ethically Aligned Design. A Vision for Prioritizing Human Well-Being with Autonomous and Intelligent Systems First Edition Overview. https://standards.ieee.org/content/dam/ieee-standards/standards/web/documents/other/ead1e.pdf?utm_medium=undefined&utm_source=undefined&utm_campaign=undefined&utm_content=undefined&utm_term=undefined. Accessed 21 February 2020.

Independent High-Level Expert Group on Artificial Intelligence set up by the European Commission, 'The Assessment List For Trustworthy Artificial Intelligence (ALTAI) for Self-Assessment' (2020). https://digital-strategy.ec.europa.eu/en/library/assessment-list-trustworthy-artificial-intelligence-altai-self-assessment. Accessed 17 July 2021.

Information Commissioner's Office (2018) DPIA Template v0.4. https://ico.org.uk/media/for-organisations/documents/2553993/dpia-template.docx. Accessed 17 August 2021.

Jobin A, Ienca M, Vayena E (2019) The Global Landscape of AI Ethics Guidelines. Nature Machine Intelligence 1:389–399.

Kaminski ME, Malgieri G (2021) Algorithmic impact assessments under the GDPR: producing multi-layered explanations. International Data Privacy Law 11(2):125–144.

Kemp D, Vanclay F (2013) Human rights and impact assessment: clarifying the connections in practice. Impact Assessment and Project Appraisal 31(2):86–96.
Kenneally E, Bailey M, Maughan D (2010) A Framework for Understanding and Applying Ethical Principles in Network and Security Research. In: Sion R et al (eds) Financial Cryptography and Data Security. Springer, Berlin, pp 240–246.
Kirby M (1981) Transborder Data Flows and the 'Basic Rules' of Data Privacy. Stanford J. of Int. Law 16:27–66.
Kramer ADI, Guillory JE, Hancock JT (2014) Experimental Evidence of Massive-Scale Emotional Contagion Through Social Networks. 24 Proc. Nat'l Acad. Sci. http://www.pnas.org/content/111/24/8788.full.pdf. Accessed 12 March 2018.
Kuner C (2012) The European Commission's Proposed Data Protection Regulation: A Copernican Revolution in European Data Protection Law. Privacy & Sec. L. Rep. 11:1–15.
Kuner C, Cate FH, Millard C, Svantesson DJB (2014) Systematic Government Access to Private-Sector Data Redux. Int'l Data Privacy L. 4(1):1–3.
Kuner C, Cate FH, Lynskey O, Millard C, Ni Loideain N, Svantesson DJB (2018) Expanding the Artificial Intelligence-Data Protection Debate. Int'l Data Privacy L. 8(4):289–292.
Lerman J (2013) Big Data and Its Exclusions. Stan. L. Rev. Online 66:55–63.
Lessig L (1999) Code and Other Laws of Cyberspace. Basic Books, New York.
Leve L (2007) "Secularism Is a Human Right!": Double-Binds of Buddhism, Democracy, and Identity in Nepal. In: Goodale M, Merry SE (eds) The Practice of Human Rights: Tracking Law between the Global and the Local. Cambridge University Press, Cambridge, pp 78–114.
Levitt P, Merry S (2009) Vernacularization on the Ground: Local Uses of Global Women's Rights in Peru, China, India and the United States. Global Networks 9:441–461.
Lynskey O (2015) The Foundations of EU Data Protection Law. Oxford University Press, Oxford
MacNaughton G, Hunt P (2011) A Human Rights-Based Approach to Social Impact Assessment. In: Vanclay F, Esteves AM (eds) New Directions in Social Impact Assessment. Edward Elgar, Cheltenham, https://doi.org/10.4337/9781781001196.00034.
Mahieu R (2021) The Right of Access to Personal Data: A Genealogy. Technology and Regulation 62–75.
Mantelero A (2013) Competitive value of data protection: the impact of data protection regulation on online behaviour. Int'l Data Privacy L. 3(4):229–238.
Mantelero A (2014a) Defining a New Paradigm for Data Protection in the World of Big Data Analytics. 2014a ASE BIGDATA/SOCIALCOM/CYBERSECURITY Conference, Stanford University, May 27-31, 2014. Academy of Science and Engineering, Los Angeles.
Mantelero A (2014b) Social Control, Transparency, and Participation in the Big Data World. Journal of Internet Law 17(10):23–29.
Mantelero A (2014c) The Future of Consumer Data Protection in the E.U. Re-Thinking the "Notice and Consent" Paradigm in the New Era of Predictive Analytics. Computer Law & Sec. Rev. 30(6): 643–660.
Mantelero A (2016) Personal data for decisional purposes in the age of analytics: from an individual to a collective dimension of data protection. Computer Law & Sec. Rev. 32(2):238–255.
Mantelero A (2017) Regulating Big Data. The guidelines of the Council of Europe in the Context of the European Data Protection Framework. Computer Law & Sec. Rev. 33(5):584–602.
Mantelero A, Esposito MS (2021) An Evidence-Based Methodology for Human Rights Impact Assessment (HRIA) in the Development of AI Data-Intensive Systems. Computer Law & Sec. Rev. 41, https://doi.org/10.1016/j.clsr.2021.105561.
Mantelero A, Vaciago G (2013) The "Dark Side" of Big Data: Private and Public Interaction in Social Surveillance, How data collections by private entities affect governmental social control and how the EU reform on data protection responds. Comp. L. Rev. Int'l 6:161–169.
Marsden C, Meyer T, Brown I (2020) Platform Values and Democratic Elections: How Can the Law Regulate Digital Disinformation? Computer Law & Sec. Rev. 36, https://doi.org/10.1016/j.clsr.2019.105373.

Massarani TF, Drakos MT, Pajkowska J (2007) Extracting Corporate Responsibility: Towards a Human Rights Impact Assessment. Cornell International Law Journal 40(1):135–169.
Mayer-Schönberger V (1997) Generational Development of Data Protection in Europe. In: Agre PE, Rotenberg M (eds) Technology and Privacy: The New Landscape. The MIT Press, Cambridge, pp 219–241.
Mayer-Schönberger V, Cukier K (2013) Big Data. A Revolution That Will Transform How We Live, Work and Think. John Murray, London.
Mayer-Schönberger V, Ramge T (2022) Access Rules. Freeing Data from Big Tech for a Better Future. University of California Press, Oakland.
McKinsey Global Institute (2011) Big data: The next frontier for innovation, competition, and productivity. http://www.mckinsey.com. Accessed 16 April 2012.
Merry SE (2006) Human rights and gender violence: translating international law into local justice. University of Chicago Press, Chicago.
Michaels JD (2008) All the President's Spies: Private-Public Intelligence Partnerships in the War on Terror. California Law Review 96(4):901–966.
Miller AR (1971) The Assault on Privacy - Computers, Data Banks, Dossiers. University of Michigan Press, Ann Arbor.
Mitnick EJ (2018) Rights, Groups, and Self-Invention: Group-Differentiated Rights in Liberal Theory. Routledge, London.
Nardell G QC (2010) Levelling Up: Data Privacy and the European Court of Human Rights. In: Gutwirth S, Poullet Y, De Hert P (eds) Data Protection in a Profiled World. Springer, Dordrecht, pp 43–52.
National Research Council (2008) Protecting Individual Privacy in the Struggle Against Terrorists: A Framework for Program Assessment. National Academies Press, Washington, D.C.
Negroponte N (1994) Being digital. A. Knopf, New York.
New South Wales Privacy Committee (1977) Guidelines for the operations of personal data systems. http://www.rogerclarke.com/DV/NSWPCGs.pdf. Accessed 13 April 2018
O'sullivan D (1998) The History of Human Rights across the Regions: Universalism vs Cultural Relativism. The International Journal of Human Rights 2:22–48.
OECD (1980) Annex to the Recommendation of the Council of 23rd September 1980: Guidelines on the Protection of Privacy and Transborder Flows of Personal Data. http://www.oecd.org/internet/ieconomy/oecdguidelinesontheprotectionofprivacyandtransborderflowsofpersonaldata.htm#preface. Accessed 27 February 2014.
OECD (2013) Exploring the Economics of Personal Data: A Survey of Methodologies for Measuring Monetary Value. https://www.oecd-ilibrary.org/science-and-technology/exploring-the-economics-of-personal-data_5k486qtxldmq-en. Accessed 17 August 2021.
OECD (2019) Recommendation of the Council on Artificial Intelligence. https://legalinstruments.oecd.org/en/instruments/OECD-LEGAL-0449. Accessed 23 May 2019.
Packard V (1964) The Naked Society. David McKay, New York.
Palm E, Hansson SO (2006) The case for ethical technology assessment (eTA). Technological Forecasting & Social Change 73(5):543–558.
Pasquale F (2015) The Black Box Society. The Secret Algorithms That Control Money and Information. Cambridge, MA-London, Harvard University Press.
Pell SK (2012) Systematic government access to private-sector data in the United States. Int'l Data Privacy L. 2(4):245–254.
Petrison LA, Blattberg RC, Wang P (1997) Database Marketing. Past, Present, and Future. J. Direct Marketing 11(4):109–125.
Polonetsky J, Tene O, Jerome J (2015) Beyond the Common Rule: Ethical Structures for Data Research in Non-Academic Settings. Colorado Technology Law Journal 13:333–367.
Poort J, Zuiderveen Borgesius F (2021) Personalised Pricing: The Demise of the Fixed Price? In: Eisler J, Kohl U (eds) Data-Driven Personalisation in Markets, Politics and Law. Cambridge University Press, Cambridge.
Porcedda MG (2017) Use of the Charter of Fundamental Rights by National Data Protection Authorities and the EDPS. Centre for Judicial Cooperation, Robert Schuman Centre for

Advanced Studies, European University Institute. https://papers.ssrn.com/sol3/papers.cfm?abstract_id=3157786. Accessed 24 April 2018

Poullet Y (2006) EU data protection policy. The Directive 95/46/EC: Ten years after. Computer Law & Sec. Rev. 22(3):206–201.

Raab C, Wright D (2012) Surveillance: Extending the Limits of Privacy Impact Assessment. In: Wright D, De Hert P (eds) Privacy Impact Assessment. Springer Netherlands, Dordrecht, pp 363–383.

Reidenberg J (2014) The Data Surveillance State in the US and Europe. Wake Forest L. Rev. 49:583–608.

Richards NM (2013) The Dangers of surveillance. Harv. L. Rev. 126:1934–1965.

Richards NM, King JH (2013) Three Paradoxes of Big Data. Stan. L. Rev. Online 66:41–46.

Risse T, Ropp SC (1999) International Human Rights Norms and Domestic Change: Conclusions. In: Sikkink K, Ropp SC, Risse T (eds) The Power of Human Rights: International Norms and Domestic Change. Cambridge University Press, Cambridge, pp 234–278.

Robinson D, Yu H, Rieke A (2014) Civil Rights, Big Data, and Our Algorithmic Future. A September 2014 report on social justice and technology. http://bigdata.fairness.io/wp-content/uploads/2014/09/Civil_Rights_Big_Data_and_Our_Algorithmic-Future_2014-09-12.pdf. Accessed 10 March 2015.

Rodotà S (2004) Privacy, Freedom, and Dignity: Conclusive Remarks at the 26th International Conference on Privacy and Personal Data Protection. https://www.garanteprivacy.it/home/docweb/-/docweb-display/docweb/1049293#eng. Accessed 16 December 2017.

Rodotà S (2009) Data Protection as a Fundamental Right. In: Gutwirth S, Poullet Y, de Hert P, de Terwangne C, Nouwt S (eds) Reinventing Data Protection? Springer Netherlands, Dordrecht, pp 77–82.

Rotenberg M (2001) Fair Information Practices and the Architecture of Privacy (What Larry Doesn't Get). Stan. Tech. L. Rev. 1.

Rouvroy A, Poullet Y (2009) The Right to Informational Self-Determination and the Value of Self-Development: Reassessing the Importance of Privacy for Democracy. In: Gutwirth S, Poullet Y, de Hert P, de Terwangne C, Nouwt S (eds) Reinventing Data Protection? Springer Netherlands, Dordrecht, pp 45–76.

Rubinstein IS (2013) Big Data: The End of Privacy or a New Beginning? Int'l Data Privacy L., 3 (2):74–87.

Rubinstein IS, Nojeim GT, Lee RD (2014) Systematic government access to personal data: a comparative analysis. Int'l Data Privacy L. 4(2):96–119.

Ruggie J (2007) Report of the Special Representative of the Secretary-General on the Issue of Human Rights and Transnational Corporations and Other Business Enterprises: Guiding Principles on Business and Human Rights: Implementing the United Nations "Protect, Respect and Remedy" Framework. United Nations, General Assembly, A/HRC/4/74. https://documents-dds-ny.un.org/doc/UNDOC/GEN/G07/106/14/PDF/G0710614.pdf?OpenElement. Accessed 9 October 2020.

Samuelson P (2000) Privacy as Intellectual Property? Stan. L. Rev. 52(5):1125–1173.

Sartor G (2017) Human Rights and Information Technologies. In: Brownsword R, Scotford E, Yeung K (eds) The Oxford Handbook of Law, Regulation, and Technology. Oxford University Press, Oxford, pp 424-450, https://doi.org/10.1093/oxfordhb/9780199680832.013.79.

SATORI project (2017) Ethics assessment for research and innovation — Part 2: Ethical impact assessment framework. http://satoriproject.eu/media/CWA-SATORI_part-2_WD4-20170510W.pdf. Accessed 24 April 2018

Schechter S, Bravo-Lillo C (2014) Using Ethical-Response Surveys to Identify Sources of Disapproval and Concern with Facebook's Emotional Contagion Experiment and Other Controversial Studies. http://research.microsoft.com/pubs/220718/CURRENT%20DRAFT%20-%20Ethical-Response%20Survey.pdf. Accessed 12 March 2018.

Schwartz PM (1999) Privacy and Democracy in Cyberspace. Vanderbilt Law Review 52:1609–1701.

Schwartz PM (2004) Property, Privacy and Personal Data. Harv. L. Rev. 117(7):2056–2128.

Schwartz PM (2011) Data Protection Law and the Ethical Use of Analytics 19-21. https://www.huntonak.com/files/webupload/CIPL_Ethical_Undperinnings_of_Analytics_Paper.pdf. Accessed 27 February 2014

Schwartz PM (2013) The E.U.-US Privacy Collision: A Turn to Institutions and Procedures. Harvard Law Review 126:1966–2009.

Science and Technology Options Assessment (2014) Potential and Impacts of Cloud Computing Services and Social Network Websites. https://www.europarl.europa.eu/stoa/en/document/IPOL-JOIN_ET(2014)513546. Accessed 27 February 2014.

Secretary's Advisory Committee on Automated Personal Data Systems (1973) Records, Computers and the Rights of Citizens. http://epic.org/privacy/hew1973report/. Accessed 27 February 2014.

Selbst AD (2017) Disparate Impact in Big Data Policing. Georgia Law Review 52(1):109–195.

Selbst AD, boyd d, Friedler SA, Venkatasubramanian S, Vertesi J (2019) Fairness and Abstraction in Sociotechnical Systems. Proceedings of the Conference on Fairness, Accountability, and Transparency (ACM 2019). https://doi.org/10.1145/3287560.3287598. Accessed 4 January 2020.

Simitis S (1987) Reviewing privacy in an information society. Pen. L. Rev. 135(3):707–746.

Simitis S (1995) From the Market to the Polis: The EU Directive on the Protection of Personal Data. Iowa L. Rev. 80:445–469.

Skorupinski B, Ott K (2002) Technology assessment and ethics. Poiesis & Praxis 1(2):95–122.

Solove DJ (2001) Privacy and Power: Computer Databases and Metaphors for Information Privacy. Stan. L. Rev. 53(6):1393–1462.

Solove DJ (2008) Understanding Privacy. Harvard University Press, Cambridge, MA/London.

Solove DJ (2013) Introduction: Privacy Self-management and The Consent Dilemma. Harv. L. Rev. 126:1880–1903.

Sparrow B, Liu J, Wegner DM (2011) Google Effects on Memory: Cognitive Consequences of Having Information at Our Fingertips. Science 333:776–778.

Stahl BC, Wright D (2018) Proactive Engagement with Ethics and Privacy in AI and Big Data - Implementing responsible research and innovation in AI-related projects. https://www.dora.dmu.ac.uk/xmlui/handle/2086/15328. Accessed 26 April 2018.

Stilgoe J, Owen R, Macnaghten P (2013) Developing a Framework for Responsible Innovation. (2013) 42(9) Research Policy, 1568–1580

Strömholm S (1967) Right of Privacy and Rights of the Personality. A Comparative Survey. Working Paper Prepared for the Nordic Conference on Privacy Organized by the International Commission of Jurists, Stockholm May 1967. https://www.icj.org/wp-content/uploads/1967/06/right-to-privacy-working-paper-publication-1967-eng.pdf. Accessed 4 May 2019.

Svensson J (2011) Social impact assessment in Finland, Norway and Sweden: a descriptive and comparative study. Thesis, KTH Royal Institute of Technology 2011. https://urn.kb.se/resolve?urn=urn:nbn:se:kth:diva-86850. Accessed 27 April 2021.

Swire P (2012) From real-time intercepts to stored records: why encryption drives the government to seek access to the cloud. Int'l Data Privacy L. 2(4):200–206.

Taylor L, Floridi L, van der Sloot B (eds) (2017) Group Privacy: New Challenges of Data Technologies. Springer International Publishing, Cham.

Taylor NC, Hobson Bryan C, Goodrich CG (1990) Social assessment: theory, process and techniques. Centre for Resource Management, Lincoln College, Lincoln.

Taylor L, Schroeder R (2015) Is Bigger Better? The Emergence of Big Data as a Tool for International Development Policy. GeoJournal 80:503–518.

Tene O, Polonetsky J (2012) Privacy in the Age of Big Data: A Time for Big Decisions. Stan. L. Rev. Online 64. https://www.stanfordlawreview.org/online/privacy-paradox-privacy-and-big-data/. Accessed 20 March 2019.

The Boston Consulting Group (2012) The value of our digital identity. http://www.libertyglobal.com/PDF/public-policy/The-Value-of-Our-Digital-Identity.pdf. Accessed 27 February 2014.

The Danish Institute for Human Rights (2020) Human rights impact assessment. Guidance and toolbox. https://www.humanrights.dk/sites/humanrights.dk/files/media/dokumenter/udgivelser/

hria_toolbox_2020/eng/dihr_hria_guidance_and_toolbox_2020_eng.pdf. Accessed 25 April 2021.

The European Commission's High-level Expert Group on Artificial Intelligence (2018) A Definition of Artificial Intelligence: Main Capabilities and Scientific Disciplines. https://ec.europa.eu/digital-single-market/en/news/definition-artificial-intelligence-main-capabilities-and-scientific-disciplines. Accessed 18 December 2018.

The White House (2012) Consumer Data Privacy in a Networked World: A Framework for Protecting Privacy and Promoting Innovation in the Global Digital Economy. https://obamawhitehouse.archives.gov/sites/default/files/privacy-final.pdf. Accessed 4 December 2017.

The White House (2015) Administration Discussion Draft: Consumer Privacy Bill of Rights Act 2015. https://obamawhitehouse.archives.gov/sites/default/files/omb/legislative/letters/cpbr-act-of-2015-discussion-draft.pdf. Accessed 25 June 2017.

The White House, Executive Office of the President (2014) Big Data: Seizing Opportunities, Preserving Values. https://obamawhitehouse.archives.gov/sites/default/files/docs/big_data_privacy_report_may_1_2014.pdf. Accessed 26 December 2014.

Turow J, Hoofnagle CJ, Mulligan DK, Good N (2007) The Federal Trade Commission and Consumer Privacy in the Coming Decade. ISJLP 3:723-749. https://lawcat.berkeley.edu/record/1121306. Accessed 27 February 2014.

Tzanou M (2013) Data protection as a fundamental right next to privacy? 'Reconstructing' a not so new right'. Int'l Data Privacy L. 3(2):88–99.

UNESCO (2021) Draft Text of the Recommendation on the Ethics of Artificial Intelligence, SHS/IGM-AIETHICS/2021/JUN/2. https://unesdoc.unesco.org/ark:/48223/pf0000377881. Accessed 2 July 2021.

United Nations - General Assembly (2021) Artificial Intelligence and Privacy, and Children's Privacy. Report of the Special Rapporteur on the Right to Privacy, Joseph A. Cannataci, A/HRC/46/37. https://undocs.org/pdf?symbol=en/A/HRC/46/37. Accessed 11 August 2021.

United Nations Office of the High Commissioner for Human Rights (2006) Frequently asked questions on a human rights-based approach to development cooperation. United Nations, New York/Geneva.

Van Alsenoy B, Kosta E, Dumortier J (2014) Privacy notices versus informational self-determination: Minding the gap. Int. Rev. Law. Comp. & Tech. 28(2):185–203.

van der Sloot B (2015) Privacy as Personality Right: Why the ECtHR's Focus on Ulterior Interests Might Prove Indispensable in the Age of "Big Data". Utrecht Journal of International and European Law 31(80):25–50.

van Drooghenbroeck S (2001) La proportionnalité dans le droit de la Convention européenne des droits de l'homme: prendre l'idée simple au sérieux. Publications Fac St Louis, Brussels.

Vanclay F (2002) Conceptualising social impacts. Environ. Impact. Assess. 22(3):183–211.

Vanclay F (2006) Principles for Social Impact Assessment: A Critical Comparison between the International and US Documents. Environmental Impact Assessment Review 26(1):3–14.

Vanclay F, Esteves AM, Aucamp I, Franks DM (2015) Social Impact Assessment: Guidance for assessing and managing the social impacts of projects. Fargo ND: International Association for Impact Assessment. http://www.iaia.org/uploads/pdf/SIA_Guidance_Document_IAIA.pdf. Accessed 26 April 2018.

Vedder AH (1997) Privatization, Information Technology and Privacy: Reconsidering the Social Responsibilities of Private Organizations. In: Moore G (ed) Business Ethics: Principles and Practice. Business Education Publishers, Sunderland, pp 215–226.

Wachter S, Mittelstadt B, Russell C (2018) Counterfactual Explanations without Opening the Black Box: Automated Decisions and the GDPR. Harvard Journal of Law & Technology 31 (2):841–887.

Wachter S, Mittelstadt B, Russell C (2021) Why Fairness Cannot Be Automated: Bridging the Gap between EU Non-Discrimination Law and AI. Computer Law & Sec. Rev. 41, https://doi.org/10.1016/j.clsr.2021.105567.

Walker S (2009) The Future of Human Rights Impact Assessments of Trade Agreements. Intersentia, Utrecht.

Westin AF (1970) Privacy and Freedom. Atheneum, New York.

Whitman JQ (2004) The Two Western Cultures of Privacy: Dignity versus Liberty. The Yale Law Journal 113:1151–1221.

World Bank and Nordic Trust Fund (2013) Human Rights Impact Assessments: A Review of the Literature, Differences with other forms of Assessments and Relevance for Development. Washington, World Bank and Nordic Trust Fund.

World Economic Forum (2013) Unlocking the Value of Personal Data: From Collection to Usage. http://www3.weforum.org/docs/WEF_IT_UnlockingValuePersonalData_CollectionUsage_Report_2013.pdf. Accessed 27 February 2014.

Wright D (2011) A framework for the ethical impact assessment of information technology. Ethics and Information Technology 13(3):199–226.

Wright D, De Hert P (eds) (2012) Privacy Impact Assessment. Springer, Dordrecht.

Wright D, Friedewald M (2013) Integrating privacy and ethical impact assessments. Science and Public Policy 40(6):755–766.

Wright D, Mordini E (2012) Privacy and Ethical Impact Assessment. In: Wright D, De Hert P (eds) Privacy Impact Assessment. Springer Netherlands, Dordrecht, pp 397–418.

Zarsky T (2016) The Trouble with Algorithmic Decisions: An Analytic Road Map to Examine Efficiency and Fairness in Automated and Opaque Decision Making. Science, Technology, & Human Values 41(1):118–132.

Zuiderveen Borgesius F (2020) Strengthening Legal Protection against Discrimination by Algorithms and Artificial Intelligence. The International Journal of Human Rights 24(10): 1572–1593.

Chapter 2
Human Rights Impact Assessment and AI

Contents

Abstract The recent turn in the debate on AI regulation from ethics to law, the wide application of AI and the new challenges it poses in a variety of fields of human activities are urging legislators to find a paradigm of reference to assess the impacts of AI and to guide its development. This cannot only be done at a general level, on the basis of guiding principles and provisions, but the paradigm must be embedded into the development and deployment of each application. To this end, this chapter suggests a model for human rights impact assessment (HRIA) as part of the broader HRESIA model. This is a response to the lack of a formal methodology to facilitate an ex-ante approach based on a human-oriented design of AI. The result is a tool that can be easily used by entities involved in AI development from the outset in the design of new AI solutions and can follow the product/service throughout its lifecycle, providing specific, measurable and comparable evidence on potential impacts, their probability, extension, and severity, and facilitating comparison between possible alternative options.

A. Mantelero, *Beyond Data*, Information Technology and Law Series 36,
https://doi.org/10.1007/978-94-6265-531-7_2

Keywords Data ethics · Democracy · Human rights by design · Human Rights Impact Assessment · Participation · Precautionary principle · Smart cities · Smart toys · Transparency

2.1 Introduction

The debate that has characterised the last few years on data and Artificial Intelligence (AI) has been marked by an emphasis on the ethical dimension of the use of data (data ethics)[1] and by a focus on potential bias and risk of discrimination.[2]

While data processing regulation has been focused for decades on the law, including the interplay between data use and human rights, this debate on data-intensive AI systems has rapidly changed its trajectory, from law to ethics.[3] This is evident not only in the literature,[4] but also in the political and institutional discourse.[5] In this regard, an important turning point was the European Data Protection Supervisor (EDPS) initiative on digital ethics[6] which led to the creation of the Ethics Advisory Group.[7]

As regards the debate on data ethics, it is interesting to consider two different and chronologically consecutive stages: the academic debate and the institutional initiatives. These contributions to the debate are different and have given voice to different underlying interests.

The academic debate on the ethics of machines is part of the broader and older reflection on ethics and technology. It is rooted in known and framed theoretical models, mainly in the philosophical domain, and has a methodological maturity. In contrast, the institutional initiatives are more recent, have a non-academic nature and aim at moving the regulatory debate forward, including ethics in the sphere of data protection. The main reason for this emphasis on ethics in recent years has been the growing concern in society about the use of data and new data-intensive applications, from Big Data[8] to AI.

---

[1] Floridi et al. 2018; Mittelstadt et al. 2016.

[2] Wachter et al. 2021; Algorithm Watch 2020; Myers West et al. 2019, p. 33; Zuiderveen Borgesius 2020; Mann and Matzner 2019.

[3] Raab 2020, para 3; Bennett and Raab 2018.

[4] E.g. Floridi and Taddeo 2016.

[5] In the context of the legal debate on computer law, at the beginning of the last decade only a few authors focused on the ethical impact of IT, e.g. Wright 2010. Although the reflection on ethics and technology is not new in itself, it has become deeper in the field of data use where new technology development in the information society has shown its impact on society. See also Verbeek 2011; Spiekermann 2016; Bohn et al. 2005, pp. 19–29.

[6] European Data Protection Supervisor 2015b.

[7] European Data Protection Supervisor 2015a.

[8] Council of Europe, Consultative Committee of the Convention for the Protection of Individuals with regard to Automatic Processing of Personal Data (Convention 108) 2017.

Although similar paths are known in other fields, the shift from the theoretical analysis to the political arena represents a major change. The political attention to these issues has necessarily reduced the level of analysis, ethics being seen as an issue to be flagged rather than developing a full-blown strategy for ethically-oriented solutions. In a nutshell, the message of regulatory bodies to the technology environment was this: law is no longer enough, you should also consider ethics.

This remarkable step forward in considering the challenges of new paradigms had the implicit limitation of a more general and basic ethical framework, compared to the academic debate. In some cases, only general references to the need to consider ethical issues has been added to AI strategy documents, leaving the task of further investigation to the recipients of these documents. At other times, as in the case of the EDPS, a more ambitious goal of providing ethical guidance was pursued.

Methodologically, the latter goal has often been achieved by delegating the definition of guidelines to committees of experts, including some forms of wider consultation. As in the tradition of expert committees, a key element of this process is the selection of experts.

These committees were not only composed of ethicists or legal scholars but had a different or broader composition defined by the appointing bodies.[9] Their heterogeneous nature made them more similar to multi-stakeholder groups.

Another important element of these groups advising policymakers concerns their internal procedures: the actual amount of time given to their members to deliberate, the internal distribution of assigned tasks (in larger groups this might involve several sub-committees with segmentation of the analysis and interaction between sub-groups), and the selection of the rapporteurs. These are all elements that have an influence in framing the discussion and its results.

All these considerations clearly show the differences between the initial academic debate on ethics and the same debate as framed in the context of institutional initiatives. Moreover, this difference concerns not only structure and procedures, but also outcomes. The documents produced by the experts appointed by policymakers are often minimalist in terms of theoretical framework and focus mainly on the policy message concerning the relevance of the ethical dimension.

The variety of the ethical approaches, the lack of clear indications on the frame of reference or the reasons for preferring a certain ethical framework make it difficult to understand the key choices on the proposed ethical guidelines.[10] Moreover, the local perspective of the authors of these documents, in line with the context-dependent nature of ethical values, undermines the ambition to provide global standards or, where certain values are claimed to have general relevance, may betray a risk of ethical colonialism.

---

[9] This is the case, for example, of the Independent High-Level Expert Group on Artificial Intelligence set up by the European Commission, which brought together 52 experts, the majority (27) from industry and the rest from academia (15, including 3 with a legal background and 3 with an ethical background), civil society (6) and governmental or EU bodies (4). See also Access Now 2019; Veale 2020.

[10] Ienca and Vayena 2020.

These shortcomings that characterise a purely ethical discourse on AI regulation – which are analysed in more detail in Chap. 3 – lead us to turn our gaze towards more well-established and commonly accepted frameworks such as that provided by human rights, the implementation of which in the field of AI is discussed in the following sections.

2.2 A Legal Approach to AI-Related Risks

In considering the impact of AI on human rights, the dominant approach in many documents is mainly centred on listing the rights and freedoms potentially impacted[11] rather than operationalising this potential impact and proposing assessment models.

However, case-specific assessment is more effective in terms of risk prevention and mitigation than using risk presumptions based on an abstract classification of high-risk sectors or high-risk uses/purposes, where sectors, uses and purposes are very broad categories which include different kind of applications – some of them continuously evolving – with a variety of potential impacts on rights and freedoms that cannot be clustered *ex ante* on the basis of risk thresholds, but require a case-by-case impact assessment.[12]

Similarly, the adoption of a centralised technology assessment carried out by national ad hoc supervisory authorities[13] can provide useful guidelines for technology development and can be used to fix red lines[14] but must necessarily be complemented by a case-specific assessment of the impact of each application developed.

For these reasons, a case specific impact assessment remains the main tool to ensure accountability and the safeguarding of individual and collective rights and freedoms. In this regard, a solution to the problem could easily be drawn from the human rights impact assessment models already adopted in several fields.

However, these models are usually designed for different contexts than those of AI applications.[15] The latter are not necessarily large-scale projects involving entire

---

[11] Raso et al. 2018; Independent High-Level Expert Group on Artificial Intelligence set up by the European Commission 2019; Council of Europe, Committee of Ministers 2020; Council of Europe 2018.

[12] Chapter 4, Sect. 4.3.2.

[13] European Parliament 2020, Article 14.2 ("the risk assessment of artificial intelligence, robotics and related technologies, including software, algorithms and data used or produced by such technologies, shall be carried out, in accordance with the objective criteria provided for in paragraph 1 of this Article and in the exhaustive and cumulative list set out in the Annex to this Regulation, by the national supervisory authorities referred to in Article 18 under the coordination of the Commission and/or any other relevant institutions, bodies, offices and agencies of the Union that may be designated for this purpose in the context of their cooperation") and Chap. 4, Sect. 4.3.2.

[14] On the debate on the adoption of specific red lines regarding the use of AI in the field of facial recognition, European Digital Rights (EDRi) 2021. See also Chap. 4.

[15] See below fn 40 and fn 137.

regions with multiple social impacts. Although there are important data-intensive projects in the field of smart cities, regional services (e.g. smart mobility) or global services (e.g. online content moderation provided by big players in social media), the AI operating context for the coming years will be more fragmented and distributed in nature, given the business environment in many countries, often dominated by SMEs, and the variety of communities interested in setting-up AI-based projects. The growing number of data scientists and the decreasing cost of hardware and software solutions, as well as their delivery as a service, will facilitate this scenario characterised by many projects with a limited scale, but involving thousands of people in data-intensive experiments.

For such projects, the traditional HRIA models are too articulated and oversized, which is why it is important to provide a more tailored model of impact assessment, at the same time avoiding mere theoretical abstractions based on generic decontextualised notions of human rights.

Against this background, it is worth briefly considering the role played by impact assessment tools with respect to the precautionary principle as an alternative way of dealing with the consequences of AI.

As in the case of potential technology-related risks, there are two different legal approaches to the challenges of AI: the precautionary approach and the risk assessment. These approaches are alternative, but not incompatible. Indeed, complex technologies with a plurality of different impacts might be better addressed though a mix of these two remedies.[16]

As risk theory states, their alternative nature is related to the notion of uncertainty.[17] Where a new application of technology might produce potential serious risks for individuals and society, which cannot be accurately calculated or quantified in advance, a precautionary approach should be taken.[18] In this case, the uncertainty associated with applications of a given technology makes it impossible

---

[16] Council of Europe, Consultative Committee of the Convention for the Protection of Individuals with regard to Automatic Processing of Personal Data (Convention 108) 2017, Section IV, paras 1 and 2, where the precautionary approach is coordinated with an impact assessment that also includes ethical and social issues.

[17] On the distinction between the precautionary approach and the precautionary principle, Peel 2004 ("One way of conceptualising what might be meant by precaution as an approach […] is to say that it authorises or permits regulators to take precautionary measures in certain circumstances, without dictating a particular response in all cases. Rather than a principle creating an obligation to act to address potential harm whenever scientific uncertainty arises, an approach could give regulators greater flexibility to respond").

[18] Commission of the European Communities 2000, pp. 8–16; Hansson 2020. Only few contributions in law literature take into account the application of the precautionary approach in the field of data protection, Costa 2012 and Gonçalves 2017; Pieters 2011, p. 455 ("generalised to information technology, it can serve as a trigger for government to at last consider the social implications of IT developments. Whereas the traditional precautionary principle targets environmental sustainability, information precaution would target social sustainability"). On the precautionary approach in data protection, Narayanan et al. 2016; Raab and Wright 2012, p. 364; Lynskey 2015, p. 83; Raab 2004, p. 15.

to conduct a concrete risk assessment, which requires specific knowledge of the extent of the negative consequences, albeit in specific classes of risks.[19]

Where the potential consequences of AI cannot be fully envisaged, as in the case of the ongoing debate on facial recognitions and its applications, a proper impact assessment is impossible, but the potentially high impact on society justifies specific precautionary measures (e.g., a ban or restriction on the use of AI-based facial recognition technologies).[20] This does not mean limiting innovation, but investigating more closely its potentially adverse consequences and guiding the innovation process and research,[21] including the mitigation measures (e.g. containment strategies, licensing, standards, labelling, liability rules, and compensation schemes).

On the other hand, where the level of uncertainty is not so high, the risk-assessment process is a valuable tool in tackling the risks stemming from technology applications. According to the general theory on the risk-based approach, the process consists of four separate stages: (1) identification of risks, (2) analysis of the potential impact of these risks, (3) selection and adoption of the measures to prevent or mitigate the risks, (4) periodic review of the effectiveness of these measures.[22] Furthermore, to enable subsequent monitoring of the effective level of compliance, duty bearers should document both the risk assessment and the measures adopted.

Since neither the precautionary principle nor the risk assessment are an empty list but rather focus on specific rights and freedoms to be safeguarded, they can be seen as two tools for developing a human rights-centred technology. While the uncertainty of some technology solutions will lead to the application of the precautionary principle, a better awareness and management of related risk will enable a proper assessment.

However, the relationship between risk assessment and the precautionary principle is rather complicated and cannot be reduced to a strict alterative. Indeed, when a precautionary approach suggests that a technology should not be used in a certain social context, this does not necessary entail halting its development. On the contrary, where there is no incompatibility with human rights[23] the technology can be developed further to reach a sufficient level of maturity that shows awareness of the related risks and the effective solutions.

This means that, in these cases, human rights can play an additional role in guiding development such that, once it reaches a level of awareness of the potential consequences that exclude uncertainty, will be subject to risk assessment.

---

[19] Tosun 2013; Aven 2011; Stirling and Gee 2002.

[20] European Parliament – Committee on Civil Liberties, Justice and Home Affairs 2020, paras 14, 15 and 20; Council of Europe, Consultative Committee of the Convention for the Protection of Individuals with regard to Automatic Processing of Personal Data (Convention 108) 2021, para 1.1. See Chap. 4.

[21] Commission of the European Communities 2000, p. 4 ("measures based on the precautionary principle should be maintained so long as scientific information is incomplete or inconclusive, and the risk is still considered too high to be imposed on society").

[22] Koivisto and Douglas 2015.

[23] Article 5, European Commission, Proposal for Regulation of the European Parliament and of the Council laying down harmonised rules on Artificial Intelligence (Artificial Intelligence Act) and amending legislative acts, COM(2021) 206 final, Brussels, 21 April 2021.

Under this reasoning, two different scenarios are possible. One in which the precautionary principle becomes an outright ban on a specific use of technology and the other in which it restricts the adoption of certain technologies but not their further development. In the latter case, a precautionary approach and a risk assessment are two different phases of the same approach rather than an alternative response.

2.3 Human Rights Impact Assessment of AI in the HRESIA Model

Having defined the importance of a human rights-oriented approach in AI design and use, and the role that impact assessment procedure can play in this respect,[24] it is worth noting that traditional Human Rights Impact Assessment (HRIA) models are often territory-based considering the impact of business activities in a given local area and community, whereas in the case of AI applications this link with a territorial context may be less significant.

There are two different scenarios: cases characterised by use of AI in territorial contexts with a high-impact on social dynamics (e.g. smart cities plans, regional smart mobility plans, predictive crime programmes) and those where AI solutions have a more limited impact as they are embedded in globally distributed products/services (e.g. AI virtual assistants, autonomous cars, recruiting AI-based software, etc.) and do not focus on a given socio-territorial community. While in the first case the context is very close to the traditional HRIA cases, where large-scale projects affect whole communities and the potential impacts cover a wide range of human rights, the second case is characterised by a more limited social impact, often focusing more on individuals rather than on society at large.[25] This difference has a direct effect on the structure and complexity of the model, as well as the tool employed.

Criteria such as the AAAQ framework,[26] for example, or issues concerning property and lands, can be used in assessing a smart city plan, but are unnecessary or disproportionate in the case of an AI-based recruitment software. Similarly, a large-scale mobility plan may require a significant monitoring of needs through interviews of rightsholders and stakeholders, while in the case of an AI-based personal IoT device this phase can be much reduced.

In both these scenarios, the two most relevant novelties introduced by the HRESIA with regard to its HRIA module concern the *ex ante* nature of the assessment carried and the greater focus on quantifiable risk thresholds.

Regarding the former, the *ex ante* approach is required by the guiding role that HRESIA aims to play in project design and development, as opposed to the *ex post*

[24] See also Chap. 1.

[25] This does not mean that the collective dimension does not plays an important role and should be adequately considered in the assessment process, Mantelero 2016.

[26] The Danish Institute for Human Rights 2014.

evaluation centred on corrective policies that often characterises traditional HRIA.[27] Moreover, here, the pervasive and varied nature of data-intensive AI systems and their components leads to a reflection on the challenges that large-scale AI poses with respect to multi-factor scenarios.[28]

Concerning the focus on risk thresholds, this is in line with the requirements emerging in the regulatory debate on AI[29] where the definition of different risk levels is crucial in acceptability of AI products/services and has a direct impact on the obligations of AI manufacturers, providers and users. A quantitative dimension of assessment, in terms of ranges of risks, is therefore needed both for AI deign guidance and legal compliance.

Notwithstanding these important differences influencing the assessment methodology, the main building blocks of the model described here – planning and scoping, data collection (including rightsholder and stakeholder consultation) and analysis – remain the same as those used in HRIA and are examined in detail in the following sub-sections.

2.3.1 *Planning and Scoping*

The first stage deals with definition of the HRIA target, identifying the main features of the product/service and the context in which it will be placed, in line with the context-dependent nature of the HRIA. Three are the main areas to consider at this stage:

- description and analysis of the type of product/service, including data flows and data processing purposes
- the human rights context (contextualisation on the basis of local jurisprudence and laws)
- identification of rightsholders and stakeholders.

The Table 2.1 provides a non-exhaustive list of potential questions for HRIA planning and scoping.[30] The extent and content of these questions will depend on the specific nature of the product/service and the scale and complexity of its development and deployment.[31] This list is therefore likely to be further supplemented with project-specific questions.[32]

[27] World Bank and Nordic Trust Fund 2013, pp. 8–9.

[28] See Sect. 2.4.2.

[29] See Chap. 4.

[30] Regarding the structure and nature of the questions, Selbst forthcoming, pp. 33–35 and 69–70, who points out how open-end questions are better than top-down questions ("With open-ended questions, you do not need to anticipate the particular problems that might come up, and the answers to them emerge naturally. With top-down questions, no matter how thoughtful they are, the picture will be coarse and general").

[31] E.g. The Danish Institute for Human Rights 2020b, g.

[32] For similar questionnaires, e.g., The Danish Institute for Human Rights 2020a, pp. 30–39.

Table 2.1 Planning and scoping.

Description and analysis of the type of product/service, including related data flows and data processing purposes	– What are the main features of the product/service? – In which countries will the product/service be offered? – Identification of rights-holders: who are the target-users of the product/service? – What types of data are collected (personal, non-personal, special categories)? – What are the main purposes of data processing? – Identification of the duty-bearers: which subjects are involved in data management and what is their role in data processing?
Human rights context (contextualisation based on local jurisprudence and laws)	– Which human rights are potentially affected by the product/service? – Which international/regional legal instruments have been implemented at an operational level? – Which are the most relevant courts or authoritative bodies dealing with human rights issues in the given context? – What are the relevant decisions and provisions in the field of human rights?
Controls in place	– What policies and procedures are in place to assess the potential impact on human rights, including rightsholder and stakeholder engagement? – Has an impact assessment been carried out, developed and implemented in relation to specific issues or some features of the product/service (e.g. use of biometrics)?
Rightsholder and stakeholder engagement	– Which are the main groups or communities potentially affected by the service/product, including its development? – What other stakeholders should be involved, in addition to affected community and groups, (e.g. civil society and international organisations, experts, industry associations, journalists)? – Are there any other duty-bearers to be involved, apart from the product/service developer and users[33] (e.g. national authorities, governmental agencies)?

(continued)

[33] On the distinction between AI system users and end users, see Chap. 1, Sect. 1.3.

Table 2.1 (continued)

	– Were business partners, including suppliers (e.g. subcontractors in AI systems and datasets) involved in the assessment process? – Has the developer conducted an assessment of its supply chain to identify whether the activities of suppliers/contractors involved in product/service development might contribute to adverse human rights impacts? Has the developer promoted human rights standards or audits to ensure respect for human rights among suppliers? – Do the product/service developers publicly communicate the potential impacts on human rights of the service/product? – Does the developer provide training on human rights standards for relevant management and procurement staff?

Source The author

2.3.2 *Data Collection and the Risk Analysis Methodology*

While the first stage is mainly desk research, the second focuses on gathering relevant empirical evidence to assess the product/service's impact on human rights and freedoms. In traditional HRIA this usually involves extensive fieldwork. But in the case of AI applications, data collection and analysis is restricted to large-scale projects such as those developed in the context of smart cities, where different services are developed and integrated. For the remaining cases, given the limited and targeted nature of each application, data collection is largely related to the product/service's features and feedback from stakeholders.

Based on the information gathered in the previous stage (description and analysis of the type of product/service, human rights context, controls in place, and stakeholder engagement), we can proceed to a contextual assessment of the impact of AI use on human rights, to understand which rights and freedoms may be affected, how this may occur, and which potential mitigation measures may be taken.

Since in most cases the assessment is not based on measurable variables, the impact on rights and freedoms is necessarily the result of expert evaluation,[34] where expert opinion relies on knowledge of case law, the literature, and the legal framework. This means that it is not possible to provide precise measurement of the expected impacts but only an assessment in terms of range of risk (i.e. low, medium, high, or very high).

[34] E.g. Scheinin and Molbæk-Steensig 2021.

The benchmark for this assessment is therefore the jurisprudence of the courts and independent bodies (e.g. data protection authorities, equality bodies) that deal with human rights in their decisions. Different rights and freedoms may be relevant depending on the specific nature of the given application.

Examination of any potentially adverse impact should begin with a general overview followed by a more granular analysis where the impact is envisaged.[35] In line with normal risk assessment procedures, three key factors must be considered: risk identification, likelihood (L), and severity (S). As regards the first, the focus on human rights and freedoms already defines the potentially affected categories and the case specific analysis identifies those concretely affected, depending on the technologies used and their purposes. Since this is a rights-based model, risk concerns the prejudice to rights and freedoms, in terms of unlawful limitations and restrictions, regardless of material damage.

The expected impact of the identified risks is assessed by considering both the likelihood and the severity of the expected consequences, using a four-step scale (low, medium, high, very high) to avoid any risk of average positioning.

Likelihood is the combination of two elements: the probability of adverse consequences and the exposure. The former concerns the probability that adverse consequences of a certain risk might occur (Table 2.2) and the latter the potential number of people at risk (Table 2.3). In considering the potential impact on human rights, it is important not only to consider the probability of the impact, but also its extension in terms of potentially affected people.

Both these variables must be assessed on a contextual basis, considering the nature and features of the product and service, the application scenario, previous similar cases and applications, and any measures taken to prevent adverse consequences. Here, the engagement of relevant shareholders can help to better understand and contextualise these aspects, alongside the expertise of those carrying out the impact assessment.

These two variables are combined in the combinatorial Table 2.4 using a cardinal scale to estimate the overall likelihood level (L). This table can be further

---

[35] For an analytical description of the main components of impact analysis, based on the experience in the field of data protection, Janssen 2020, which uses four benchmarks covering the traditional areas of risk analysis in the law (impacted rights, risks at design stages and during operation, balancing risks and interests, control and agency over data processing). As for the risk assessment, the model proposed by the author does not provide a methodology to combine the different elements of impact assessment or to estimate the overall impact. Moreover, the model is used for an ex post comparative analysis, rather than for iterative design-based product/service development, as does the model we present here. In this sense, by providing two fictitious basic cases, Janssen tests her model though a comparative analysis (one case against the other) and without a clear analysis of the different risk components, in terms of individual impact and probability, with regard to each potentially affected right or freedom (e.g. "given that the monitor sensor captures every noise in its vicinity in situation (1), it probably has a high impact on a number of privacy rights, including that of intimacy of the home, communication privacy and chilling effects on the freedom of speech of (other) dwellers in the home"), and without a clear description of the assessment of their cumulative effect and overall impact. With a focus on the GDPR, Kaminski and Malgieri 2020. See also Reisman et al. 2018.

Table 2.2 Probability

	Probability	
Low	The risk of prejudice is improbable or highly improbable	1
Medium	The risk may occur	2
High	There is a high probability that the risk occurs	3
Very high	The risk is highly likely to occur	4

Source The author

Table 2.3 Exposure

	Exposure	
Low	Few or very few of the identified population of rights-holders are potentially affected	1
Medium	Some of the identified population are potentially affected	2
High	The majority of the identified population is potentially affected	3
Very high	Almost the entire identified population is potentially affected	4

Source The author

Table 2.4 Likelihood table (L)

		Probability			
		1	2	3	4
Exposure	1	1	2	3	4
	2	2	3	5	9
	3	3	5	9	12
	4	4	7	12	15

Likelihood	
Low	1
Medium	2
High	3
Very high	4

Source The author

modified on the basis of the context-specific nature of assessed AI systems and feedback received from experts, rightsholders and stakeholders.

The severity of the expected consequences (S) is estimated by considering the nature of potential prejudice in the exercise of rights and freedoms and their consequences. This is done by taking into account the gravity of the prejudice (gravity), and the effort to overcome it and to reverse adverse effects (effort) (Tables 2.5 and 2.6).

As in the case of likelihood, these two variables are combined in a table (Table 2.7) using a cardinal scale to estimate the severity level (S).

A Table 2.8 for the overall assessment charts both variables – likelihood (L) and severity (S) of the expected consequences – against each envisaged risk to rights and freedoms (R1, R2, … Rn).

Table 2.5 Gravity of the prejudice

	Gravity of the prejudice	
Low	Affected individuals and groups may encounter only minor prejudices in the exercise of their rights and freedoms	1
Medium	Affected individuals and groups may encounter significant prejudices	2
High	Affected individuals and groups may encounter serious prejudices	3
Very high	Affected individuals and groups may encounter serious or even irreversible prejudices	4

Source The author

Table 2.6 Effort to overcome the prejudice and to reverse adverse effects

	Effort	
Low	Suffered prejudice can be overcome without any problem (e.g. time spent amending information, annoyances, irritations, etc.)	1
Medium	Suffered prejudice can be overcome despite a few difficulties (e.g. extra costs, fear, lack of understanding, stress, minor physical ailments, etc.)	2
High	Suffered prejudice can be overcome albeit with serious difficulties (e.g. economic loss, property damage, worsening of health, etc.)	3
Very high	Suffered prejudice may not be overcome (e.g. long-term psychological or physical ailments, death, etc.)	4

Source The author

Table 2.7 Severity table (S)

		Gravity			
		1	2	3	4
Effort	1	1	2	4	6
	2	2	3	5	8
	3	3	5	8	10
	4	5	8	10	12

Severity	
Low	1
Medium	2
High	3
Very high	4

Source The author

The overall impact for each examined risk, taking into consideration the L and S values, is determined using a further table (Table 2.9). The colours represent the overall impact, which is very high in the dark grey sector, high in the grey sector, medium in the lighter grey sector and is low in the light grey sector.

Table 2.8 Table of envisaged risks

	L	S	Overall impact
R1			
R2			
…			
Rn			

Source The author

Table 2.9 Overall risk impact table

		Severity [impacted right/freedom]			
		Low	Medium	High	Very high
Likelihood	Low				
	Medium				
	High				
	Very high				

Source The author

Once the potentially adverse impact has been assessed for each of the rights and freedoms considered, a radial graph is charted to represent the overall impact on them. This graph is then used to decide the priority of intervention in altering the characteristics of the product/service to reduce the expected adverse impacts. See Fig. 2.1.[36]

To reduce the envisaged impacts, factors that can exclude the risk from a legal perspective (EFs) – such as the mandatory nature of certain impacting features or the prevalence of competing interests recognised by law – and those that can reduce the risk by means of appropriate mitigation measures (MMs) should be considered.

After the first adoption of the appropriate measures to mitigate the risk, further rounds of assessment can be conducted according to the level of residual risk and its acceptability, enriching the initial table with new columns (Table 2.10).

The first two new columns show any risk excluding factors (EFs) and mitigation measures (MMs), while the following two columns show the residual likelihood (rL) and severity (rS) of the expected consequences, after accounting for excluding and mitigation factors. The last column gives the final overall impact, using rL and rS values and the overall impact table (Table 2.9); this result can also be represented in a new radial graph. Note that it is also possible to estimate the total overall impact, as an average of the impacts on all the areas analysed. But this necessarily treats all the different impacted areas (i.e. rights and freedoms) as having the same importance and is therefore a somewhat imprecise synthesis.[37]

[36] This approach is also in line with the adoption of the Agile methodology in software development.

[37] See also Chap. 4, Sect. 4.3.2.

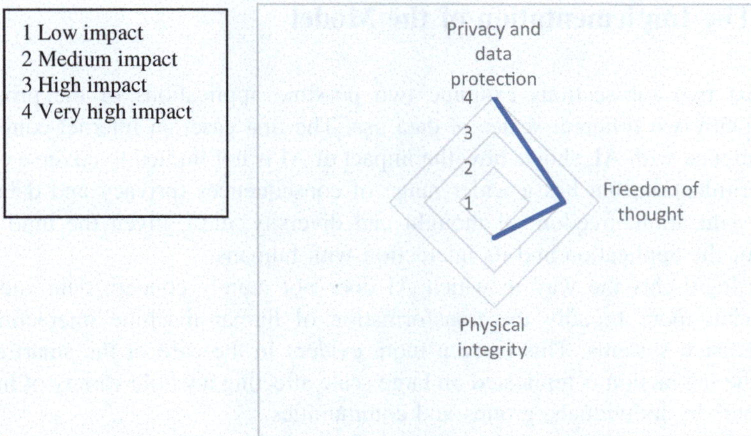

Fig. 2.1 Radial graph (impact) example. *Source* The author

Table 2.10 Comparative risk impact analysis table (before/after mitigation measures and excluding factors)

	L	S	Overall impact	EFs	MMs	rL	rS	Final Impact
R1								
R2								
…								
Rn								

Source The author

In terms of actual effects on operations, the radial graph is therefore the best tool to represent the outcome of the HRIA, showing graphically the changes after introducing mitigation measures. However, an estimation of overall impact could also be made in future since several legislative proposals on AI refer to an overall impact of each AI-based solution,[38] using a single risk scale covering all potential consequences.

[38] Data Ethics Commission 2019, p. 18. See Chap. 4.

2.4 The Implementation of the Model

The next two sub-sections examine two possible applications of the proposed model, with two different scales of data use. The first case, an Internet-connected doll equipped with AI, shows how the impact of AI is not limited to adverse effects on discrimination, but has a wider range of consequences (privacy and data protection, education, freedom of thought and diversity, etc.), given the innovative nature of the application and its interaction with humans.

This highlights the way in which AI does not merely concern data and data quality but more broadly the transformation of human-machine interaction by data-intensive systems. This is even more evident in the case of the smart cities, where the interaction is replicated on large scale affecting a whole variety of human behaviours by individuals, groups and communities.

The first case study (an AI-powered doll) shows in detail how the HRIA methodology can be applied in a real-life scenario. In the second case (a smart city project) we do not repeat the exercise for all the various data-intensive components, because a full HRIA would require extensive information collection, rightsholder and stakeholder engagement, and supply-chain analysis,[39] which go beyond the scope of this chapter.[40] But above all, the purpose of this second case study is different: to shed light on the dynamics of the HRIA in multi-factor scenarios where many different AI systems are combined.

Indeed, a smart city environment is not a single device, but encompasses a variety of technical solutions based on data and algorithms. The cumulative effect of integrating many layers results in a whole system that is greater and more complicated than the sum of its parts.

This explains why the assessment of potential risks to human rights and freedoms cannot be limited to a fragmented case-by-case analysis of each application. Rather, it requires an integrated approach that looks at the whole system and the interaction among its various components, which may have a wider impact than each component taken separately.

Scale and complexity, plus the dominant role of one or a few actors, can produce a cumulative effect which may entail multiple and increased impacts on rights and freedoms, requiring an additional integrated HRIA to give an overall assessment of the large-scale project and its impacts.

---

[39] Crawford and Joler 2018.

[40] A proper HRIA would require a multidisciplinary team working locally for a significant period of time. For example, the human rights impact assessment of the Bisha Mine in Eritrea, which started in July 2013, issued its final HRIA report in February 2014, followed by an auditing procedure in 2015. See LKL International Consulting Inc. 2014; LKL International Consulting Inc. 2015. See also Abrahams and Wyss 2010.

2.4.1 A Case Study on Consumer Devices Equipped with AI

Hello Barbie was an interactive doll produced by Mattel for the English-speaking market, equipped with speech recognition systems and AI-based learning features, operating as an IoT device. The doll was able to interact with users but did not interact with other IoT devices.[41]

The design goal was to provide a two-way conversation between the doll and the children playing with it, including capabilities that make the doll able to learn from this interaction, e.g. tailoring responses to the child's play history and remembering past conversations to suggest new games and topics.[42] The doll is no longer marketed by Mattel due to several concerns about system and device security.[43]

This section discusses the hypothetical case, imagining how the proposed assessment model[44] could have been used by manufactures and developers and the results that might have been achieved.

2.4.1.1 Planning and Scoping

Starting with the questions listed in Table 2.1 above and information on the case examined, the planning and scoping phase would summarise the key product characteristics as follows:

(a) A connected toy with four main features: (i) programmed with more than 8,000 lines of dialogue[45] hosted in the cloud, enabling the doll to talk with the user about "friends, school, dreams and fashion";[46] (ii) speech recognition technology[47] activated by a push-and-hold button on the doll's belt buckle; (iii) equipped with a microphone, speaker and two tri-colour LEOs embedded

---

[41] Mattel, 'Hello Barbie FAQ' Version 2 (2015). http://hellobarbiefaq.mattel.com/faq/. Accessed 12 November 2020.

[42] Hello Barbie FAQ (fn 41).

[43] Shasha et al. 2019 (with regard to Hello Barbie, see Appendix A, para A.3).

[44] On the safeguard of human rights and the use of HRIA in the business context, United Nations 2011 ("The State duty to protect is a standard of conduct. Therefore, States are not per se responsible for human rights abuse by private actors. However, States may breach their international human rights law obligations where such abuse can be attributed to them, or where they fail to take appropriate steps to prevent, investigate, punish and redress private actors' abuse") and more specifically Principles 13, 18 and 19.

[45] The comprehensive list of all the lines Hello Barbie says as of 17 November 2015 is available at http://hellobarbiefaq.mattel.com/wp-content/uploads/2015/11/hellobarbie-lines-v2.pdf. Accessed 28 November 2020.

[46] Hello Barbie FAQ (fn 41). Cloud service was provided by ToyTalk, see the following footnote.

[47] This technology and services were provided by ToyTalk, a Mattel partner.

in the doll's necklace, which light up when the device is active; (iv) a Wi-Fi connection to provide for two-way conversation.[48]

(b) The target-user is an English-speaking child (minor). Theoretically the product could be marketed worldwide in many countries, but the language barrier represents a limitation.

(c) The right-holders can be divided into three categories: direct users (minors), supervisory users (parents, who have partial remote control over the doll and the doll/user interaction) and third parties (e.g. friends of the direct user or re-users of the doll).

(d) Regarding data processing, the doll collects and stores voice-recording tracks based on dialogues between the doll and the user; this information may include personal data[49] and sensitive information.[50]

(e) The main purpose of the data processing and AI is to create human–robot interaction (HRI) by using machine learning (ML) to build on the dialogue between the doll and its young users. There are also additional purposes: (i) educational; (ii) parental control and surveillance[51] (parents can listen, store

[48] Hello Barbie FAQ (fn 41).

[49] Hello Barbie FAQ (fn 41) ("Q: Can Hello Barbie say a child's name? No. Hello Barbie does not ask for a child's name and is not scripted to respond with a child's name, so she will not be able to recite a child's name back to them"). But Leta Jones 2016, p. 245 who reports this reply in the dialogue with the doll: "Barbie: Sometimes I get a little nervous when I tell people my middle name. But I'm really glad I told you! What's your middle name?".

[50] Hello Barbie FAQ (fn 41) ("Although Hello Barbie was designed not to ask questions which are intended to elicit answers that might contain personal information, we cannot control whether a child volunteers such information without prompting. Parents who are concerned about this can monitor their child's use of Hello Barbie, and parents have the power to review and delete any conversation their child has with Hello Barbie, whether the conversations contain personal information or not. If we become aware of any such personal information captured in recordings, it is our policy to delete such information, and we contractually require our Service Providers to do the same. This personal information is not used for any purpose").

[51] Hello Barbie FAQ (fn 41) ("Hello Barbie only requires a parent's email address to set up an account. This is necessary so that parents can give permission to activate the speech recognition technology in the doll. Other information, such as a daughter's birthday, can be provided to help personalize the experience but are not required"). See also fn 52.

and re-use recorded conversations);[52] (iii) direct advertising to parents;[53] (iv) testing and service improvement.[54]

(f) The chief duty-bearer is the producer, but in connected toys other partners – such as ToyTalk in the Hello Barbie case – may be involved in the provision of ML, cloud and marketing services.

Another important set of data to be collected at this stage concerns the potential interplay with human rights and the reference framework, including main international/regional legal instruments, relevant courts or other authoritative bodies, and relevant decisions and provisions.

As regards the rights potentially affected, depending on the product's features and purposes, data protection and the right to privacy are the most relevant due to the possible content of the dialogue between the doll and the user, and the parental monitoring. Here the legal framework is represented by a variety of regulations at different levels. Compliance with the US COPPA[55] and the EU GDPR[56] can cover large parts of the potential market of this product and international guiding Principles[57] can facilitate the adoption of global policies and solutions.

---

[52] Hello Barbie FAQ (fn 41) ("Hello Barbie recording and storing conversations girls have with the doll? Yes. Hello Barbie has conversations with girls, and these conversations are recorded. These audio recordings are used to understand what is being said to Hello Barbie so she can respond appropriately and also to improve speech recognition for children and to make the service better. These conversations are stored securely on ToyTalk's server infrastructure and parents have the power to listen to, share, and/or delete stored recordings any time").

[53] Hello Barbie FAQ (fn 41) ("Q. Are conversations used to market to children? No. The conversations captured by Hello Barbie will not be used to contact children or advertise to them." This was confirmed by the analysis carried out by Shasha et al. 2019. Regarding the advertising directs to parents, this is the answer provided in the FAQ: "Q: Your Privacy Policy says that you will use personal information to provide consumers with news and information about events, activities, promotions, special offers, etc. That sounds like consumers could be bombarded with marketing messages. Can parents elect not to receive those communications? Yes. Opting out of receiving promotional emails will be an option during the set up process and you can opt out at any time by following the instruction in those emails. Note that marketing messages will not be conveyed via the doll itself").

[54] Hello Barbie FAQ (fn 41) ("Conversations between Hello Barbie and consumers are not monitored in real time, and no person routinely reviews those conversations. Upon occasion a human may review certain conversations, such as in order to test, improve, or change the technology used in Hello Barbie, or due to support requests from parents. If in connection with such a review we come across a conversation that raises concern about the safety of a child or others, we will cooperate with law enforcement agencies and legal processes as required to do so or as we deem appropriate on a case-by-case basis").

[55] Federal Trade Commission 2017; Haber 2019.

[56] Information Commissioner's Office 2020.

[57] E.g. Council of Europe, Convention 108+. See also Council of Europe 2018, para 36 ("With respect to connected or smart devices, including those incorporated in toys and clothes, States should take particular care to ensure that data-protection principles, rules and rights are also respected when such products are directed principally at children or are likely to be regularly used by or in physical proximity to children"); Mantelero 2021.

Moreover, in relation to data processing and individual freedom of choice, the potential effects of marketing strategies can also be considered as forms of freedom of expression[58] and freedom to conduct a business.

Given the broad interaction between the doll and the user and the behavioural, cultural and educational influence that the doll may have on young users,[59] further concerns relate to freedom of thought and diversity.[60]

In the event of cyberattack and data theft or transmission of inappropriate content to the user through the doll, safety issues also arise and may impact on the right to psychological and physical safety and health.

With the potentially global distribution of the toy, the possible impacts need to be further contextualised within each relevant legal framework, taking into consideration local case law and that of regional supranational bodies like the European Court of Human rights. In this regard, it is necessary during the scoping phase to identify the significant provisions and decisions in the countries/regions where the product is distributed.

The last aspect to be considered in planning and scoping HRIA concerns the identification and engagement of potential stakeholders. In the case of connected toys, the most important stakeholders are likely to be parents' associations, educational bodies, professional associations (e.g. psychologists and educators), child, consumer and data protection supervisory bodies, as well as trade associations. Stakeholders may also include the suppliers involved in product/service development. In the latter case, the HRIA must also assess the activities by these suppliers and may benefit from an auditing procedure[61] or the adoption of standards.

The following sections describe an iterative assessment process, starting from the basic idea of the connected AI-equipped toy with its pre-set functionality and moving on to a further assessment considering additional measures to mitigate unaddressed, or only partially addressed, concerns.

---

[58] Universal Declaration of Human Rights, Article 19, and International Covenant on Civil and Political Rights, Article 19(2). See also International Covenant on Civil and Political Rights, Human Rights Committee 2011, para 11; UNICEF 2012, principle 6 (Use marketing and advertising that respect and support children's rights).

[59] Mertala 2020 ("As Hello Barbie is able to speak, the child no longer performs the role through the doll, but in relation to the doll. This changes the nature of the performative element from dominantly transitive to dominantly performative, in which the child occupies and embodies a role in relation to the toy"). See also the following statement included in the list of all the lines Hello Barbie says as of 17 November 2015 (fn 45) "It's so cool that you want to be a mom someday".

[60] Hello Barbie FAQ (fn 41) ("The doll's conversation tree has been designed to re-direct inappropriate conversations. For example, Hello Barbie will not repeat curse words. Instead, she will respond by asking a new question"). However, besides the example given, there is no clear description of what is considered appropriate or not, and this category (appropriateness) is significantly influenced by the cultural component and potentially also by corporate ethics that may create forms of censorship or oriented behavior and thinking in the young user. Even when the FAQs refer to "school age appropriate content" ("All comments made by Hello Barbie are scripted with school age appropriate content"), they implicitly refer to a benchmark dependent the educational standards of developed economies.

[61] But see European Commission 2020, pp. 73–74.

2.4.1.2 Initial Risk Analysis and Assessment

The basic idea of the toy is an interactive doll, equipped with speech recognition and learning features, operating as an IoT device. The main component is a human-robot voice interaction feature based on AI and enabled by Internet connection and cloud services.

The rights potentially impacted are data protection and privacy, freedom of thought and diversity, and psychological and physical safety and health.[62]

Data Protection and the Right to Privacy

While these are two distinct rights, for the purpose of this case study we considered them together.[63] Given the main product features, the impact analysis is based on following questions:[64]

- Does the device collect personal information? If yes, what kind of data is collected, and what are the main features of data processing? Can the data be shared with other entities/persons?
- Can the connected toy intrude into the users' private sphere?
- Can the connected toy be used for monitoring and surveillance purposes? If yes, is this monitoring continuous or can the user stop it?
- Do users belong to vulnerable categories (e.g. minors, elderly people, parents, etc.)?
- Are third parties involved in the data processing?
- Are transborder data flows part of the processing operations?

Taking into account the product's nature, features and settings (i.e. companion toy, dialogue recording, personal information collection, potential data sharing by parents) the likelihood of prejudice can be considered very high (Table 2.4). The extent and largely unsupervised nature of the dialogue between the doll and the user, as well as the extent of data collection and retention make the probability high (Table 2.2). In addition, given its default features and settings, the exposure is very high (Table 2.3) since all the doll's users are potentially exposed to this risk.

Regarding risk severity, the gravity of the prejudice (Table 2.5) is high, given the subjects involved (young children and minors), the processing of personal data in several main areas, including sensitive information,[65] and the extent of data collection. In addition, unexpected findings may emerge in the dialogue between the

---

[62] Keymolen and Van der Hof 2019 ("Smart toys come in different forms but they have one thing in common. The development of these toys is not just a feature of ongoing technological developments; their emergence also reflects an increasing commercialisation of children's everyday lives").

[63] UN Convention on the Rights of the Child, Article 16; European Convention on Human Rights, Article 8.

[64] For a more extensive list of guiding questions, see e.g. UNICEF 2018.

[65] Pre-recorded sentences containing references to, for instance, religion and ethical groups. See the full list of all lines for Hello Barbie (fn 45) (e.g. "Sorry, I didn't catch that. Was that a yes or a no to talking about Kwanzaa?").

user and the doll, as the harmless topics prevalent in the AI-processed sentences can lead young users to provide personal and sensitive information. Furthermore, the data processing also involves third parties and transborder data flows, which add other potential risks.

The effort to overcome potential prejudice or to reverse adverse effects (Table 2.6) can be considered as medium, due to the potential parental supervision and remote control, the nature of the doll's pre-selected answers and the adoption of standard data security measures that help to overcome suffered prejudice with a few difficulties (e.g. data erasure, dialogue with the minor in case of unexpected findings). Combining high gravity and medium effort, the resulting severity (Table 2.7) is medium.

If the likelihood of prejudice can be considered very high and the severity medium, the overall impact according to Table 2.9 is high.

Freedom of Thought, Parental Guidance and the Best Interest of the Child
Based on the main features of the product, the following questions can be used for this analysis:

- Is the device able to transmit content to the user?
- Which kind of relationships is the device able to create with the user?
- Does the device share any value-oriented messages with the user?
    - If yes, what kind of values are communicated?
    - Are these values customisable by users (including parents) or on the basis of user interaction? If so, what range of alterative value sets is provided?
    - Are these values the result of work by a design team characterised by diversity?

Here the case study reveals the critical impact of AI on HRI owing to the potential content imparted through the device. This is even more critical in the context of toys where the interactive nature of AI-powered dolls changes the traditional interaction into a relational experience.[66]

In the model considered (Hello Barbie), AI creates a dialogue with the young user by selecting the most appropriate sentence from the more than 8,000 lines of dialogue available in its database. On the one hand, this enables the AI to express opinions which may also include value-laden messages, as in this sentence: "It's so cool that you want to be a mom someday".[67] On the other, some value-based considerations are needed to address educational issues concerning "inappropriate questions"[68] where the problem is not the AI reaction (Hello Barbie responds "by asking a new question"[69]), as previously, but the notion of appropriateness, which necessarily involves a value-oriented content classification by the AI system.

[66] See Mertala 2020.

[67] See fn 45. On gender stereotypes in smart toys, see Norwegian Consumer Council 2016.

[68] See fn 60.

[69] Hello Barbie FAQ (fn 41).

As these value-laden features of AI are inevitably defined during the design process, the composition of the design team, its awareness of cultural diversity and pluralism are key elements that impact on freedom of thought, in terms of default values proposed and the availability of alternative settings. In addition, the decision to provide only one option or several user-customisable options in the case of value-oriented content is another aspect of the design phase that can limit parents' freedom to ensure the moral and religious education of their children in accordance with their own beliefs.

This aspect highlights the paradigm shift brought by AI to freedom of thought and the related parental guidance in supporting the exercise by children of their rights.[70] This is even more evident when comparing AI-equipped toys with traditional educational products, such as books, serious games etc., whose contents can be examined in advance by parents.[71]

The AI-equipped doll is different. It delivers messages to young users, which may include educational content and information, but no parent will read all the 8,000 lines the doll can use or ask to have access to the logic used to match them with children's statements.

As AI-based devices interact autonomously with children and convey their own cultural values,[72] this impacts on the rights and duties of parents to provide, in a manner consistent with the evolving capacities of the child, appropriate direction and guidance in the child's freedom of thought, including aspects concerning cultural diversity.

In terms of risk assessment, the probability (Table 2.2) is medium, considering the limited number of sentences involving a value-oriented statement, and the exposure (Table 2.3) is medium, due to their alignment with values commonly accepted in many cultural contexts. The likelihood is therefore medium (Table 2.4).

Taking into account the nature of the product and its main features (i.e. some value-laden sentences used in dialogue with the young user),[73] the gravity of prejudice (Table 2.5) can be considered low in the case in question, as the value-laden sentences concern cultural questions that are not particularly controversial. The effort (Table 2.6) can also be considered low, as talking with children can mitigate potential harm. Combining these two values, the severity is therefore low (Table 2.7).

Note that this assessment would be completely altered if the dialogue content were not pre-selected but generated by AI on the basis of information resulting from

---

[70] UN Convention on the Rights of the Child, Articles 5, 14, and 18. See also See UNICEF 2018, p. 9; Murdoch 2012, p. 13.

[71] UN Convention on the Rights of the Child, Articles 17(e) and 18.

[72] E.g. Norwegian Consumer Council 2016 referring to the connected doll Cayla ("Norwegian version of the apps has banned the Norwegian words for "homosexual", "bisexual", "lesbian", "atheism", and "LGBT" […]" "Other censored words include 'menstruation', 'scientology-member', 'violence', 'abortion', 'religion', and 'incest'").

[73] Steeves 2020.

web searches,[74] where the potential risk would be much higher.[75] Similarly, the inclusion in the pre-recorded database of a greater number of value-laden sentences would directly increase the risk.

Considering the likelihood as medium and the severity of the prejudice as low, the overall impact (Table 2.9) is medium.

Right to Psychological and Physical Safety

Connected toys may raise concerns about a range of psychological and physical harms deriving from their use, including access to data and remote control of the toy.[76] Based on the main features of the product examined, the following questions can be used for this analysis:

- Can the device put psychological or physical safety at risk?
- Does the device have adequate data security and cybersecurity measures in place?
- Can third parties perpetrate malicious attacks that pose a risk to the psychological or physical safety of the user?

As regards the probability, considering the third-party origin of the prejudices and the limited interest in malicious attacks (no business interest, distributed and generic target), but also how easy it is to hack the toy, the probability (Table 2.2) of an adverse impact is medium. Exposure (Table 2.3) is low, given the prevalent use of the device in a supposedly safe environment, such as schools and home, where malicious access and control of the doll is difficult and adult monitoring is more frequent. The likelihood (Table 2.4) is therefore low.

Taking into account the nature of the product examined, the young age of the user, and the potential safety and security risks,[77] the gravity of prejudice (Table 2.5) can be considered medium. This is because malicious attacks can only be carried out by speech, and no images are collected. Nor can the toy – given its size and characteristics – directly cause physical harm to the user. The effort (Table 2.6) can be considered medium since parent-child dialogue and technical solutions can combat the potential prejudice. The severity (Table 2.7) is therefore medium.

Considering the likelihood as low and the severity of the prejudice as medium, the overall impact is medium (Table 2.9).

---

[74] In the case examined, the content provided by means of the doll was handcrafted by the writing team at Mattel and ToyTalk, not derived from open web search. Hello Barbie FAQ (fn 41).

[75] E.g., Neff and Nagy 2016.

[76] E.g. de Paula Albuquerque et al. 2020, whose authors refer to harassment, stalking, grooming, sexual abuse, exploitation, paedophilia and other types of violence blackmail, insults, confidence loss, trust loss and bullying; Shasha et al. 2019. See also Federal Bureau of Investigation 2017.

[77] See fn 41.

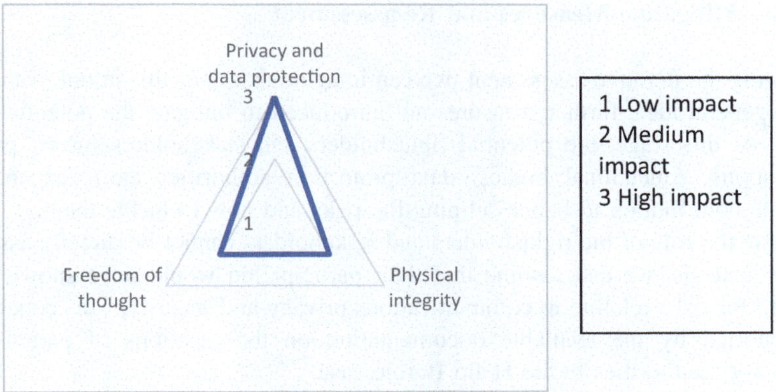

Fig. 2.2 Radial graph (impact) of the examined case. *Source* The author

2.4.1.3 Results of the Initial Assessment

The following table (Table 2.11) shows the results of the assessment carried out on the initial idea of the connected AI-equipped doll described above:

Based on this table, we can plot a radial graph representing the overall impact on all the affected rights and freedoms. The graph (Fig. 2.2) shows the priority of mitigating potentially adverse impacts on privacy and data protection, followed by risks related to physical integrity and freedom of thought.

This outcome is confirmed by the history of the actual product, where the biggest concerns of parents and the main reasons for its withdrawal related to personal data and hacking.[78]

Table 2.11 Table of envisaged risks for the examined case (L: low, M: medium; H: high; VH: very high)

Risk	L	S	Overall impact
Impact on privacy and data protection	VH	M	H
Impact on freedom of thought	M	L	M
Impact on the right to psychological and physical safety	L	M	M

Source The author

[78] Gibbs 2015.

2.4.1.4 Mitigation Measures and Re-assessment

Following the iterative assessment, we can imagine that after this initial evaluation of the general idea, further measures are introduced to mitigate the potential risks found. At this stage, the potential rightsholders and stakeholders (users, parents associations, educational bodies, data protection authorities etc.) can make a valuable contribution to better defining the risks and how to tackle them.

While the role of the rightsholders and stakeholders cannot be directly assessed in this analysis, we can assume that their participation would have shown great concern for risks relating to communications privacy and security. This conclusion is supported by the available documentation on the reactions of parents and supervisory authorities in the Hello Barbie case.[79]

After the first assessment and given the evidence on the requests of rightsholders and stakeholders, the following mitigation measures and by-design solutions could have been adopted with respect to the initial prototype.

(A) Data protection and the right to privacy

Firstly, the product must comply with the data protection regulation of the countries in which it is distributed.[80] Given the product's design, we cannot exclude the processing of personal data. The limited number of sentences provided for use by AI, as in the case of Hello Barbie, does not exclude the provision of unexpected content by the user, including personal information.[81]

Risk mitigation should therefore focus on the topics of conversation between the doll and the young user, and the safeguards in processing information collected from the user.

As regards the first aspect, an effective way to limit the potential risks would be to use a closed set of sentences, excluding phrases and questions that might induce the user to disclose personal information, and making it possible to modify these phrases and questions by the owner of the toy.[82]

---

[79] E.g. BEUC 2016; Neil 2015; McReynolds et al. 2017.

[80] In this regard Hello Barbie was certified as compliant with the US COPPA, see 'Hello Barbie FAQ' (fn 41).

[81] Hello Barbie FAQ (fn 41) ("we cannot control whether a child volunteers such information without prompting").

[82] In this case, the conditions are largely present, although there is evidence of minor issues. E.g. Hello Barbie FAQ (fn 41) ("Hello Barbie does not ask for a child's name and is not scripted to respond with a child's name, so she will not be able to recite a child's name back to them"), but see the interaction reported in Leta Jones 2016, p. 245 ("Barbie: Sometimes I get a little nervous when I tell people my middle name. But I'm really glad I told you! What's your middle name?! !"). Hello Barbie FAQ (fn 41) also points out the privacy-oriented design of the product with regard to dialogue content: "Although Hello Barbie was designed not to ask questions which are intended to elicit answers that might contain personal information".

Regarding the processing of personal data, the doll's AI-based information processing functions should be deactivated by default, giving the parents control over its activation.[83] In addition, to reduce the risk of constant monitoring, deliberate action by the child should be required to activate the doll's AI-equipped dialogue functions.[84] This would also help to make users more aware of their interaction with the system and related privacy issues.[85]

Ex post remedies can also be adopted, such as speech detection to remove personal information in recorded data.[86]

Conversations are not monitored, except to support requests from parents. To reduce the impact on the right to privacy and data protection, human review of conversations – to test, improve, or change the technology used – should be avoided, even if specific policies for unexpected findings have been adopted.[87] Individual testing phases or experiments can be carried out in a laboratory setting or on the basis of user requests (e.g. unexpected reactions and dialogues). This more restrictive approach helps to reduce the impact with respect to the initial design.

Further issues, regarding the information processing architecture and its compliance with data protection principles, concern data storage. This should be minimised and parents given the opportunity to delete stored information.[88]

With regard to the use of collected data, while access to, and sharing of, this information by parents[89] are not per se against the interest of the child, caution should be exercised in using this information for marketing purposes. Given the early age of the users and the potentially large amount of information they may

---

[83] Hello Barbie FAQ (fn 41) ("Hello Barbie only requires a parent's email address to set up an account. This is necessary so that parents can give permission to activate the speech recognition technology in the doll. Other information, such as a daughter's birthday, can be provided to help personalize the experience but are not required […] If we discover that, in violation of our terms of service, an account was created by a child, we will terminate the account and delete all data and recordings associated with it.").

[84] In the Hello Barbie case, the doll was not always on but it was activated by pressing the belt buckle.

[85] In the examined case this was also emphasized because the two tri-colour LEOs embedded in the doll's necklace lighted up to indicate she was active.

[86] Hello Barbie FAQ (fn 41) ("If we become aware of any such personal information captured in recordings, it is our policy to delete such information, and we contractually require our Service Providers to do the same. This personal information is not used for any purpose").

[87] See fn 50.

[88] Hello Barbie FAQ (fn 41) ("Parents who are concerned about this can monitor their child's use of Hello Barbie, and parents have the power to review and delete any conversation their child has with Hello Barbie, whether the conversations contain personal information or not"). Considering the young age of the user this seems not to be a disproportionate monitoring with regard to their activities and right to privacy. This does not exclude a socio-ethical relevance of this behaviour, see e.g. Leta Jones and Meurer 2016 ("the passive nature of Barbie's recording capabilities could prove perhaps more devastating to a child who may have placed an implicit trust in the doll. In order to determine the extent of the parent's involvement in their child's recordings, we extended our analysis to include the adult oversight capabilities").

[89] See above fn 52.

provide in their conversation with the doll, plus the lack of active and continuous parental control, the best solution would be not to use child-doll conversations for marketing.[90]

The complexity of data processing activities in the interaction between a child and an AI-equipped doll inevitably affects the form and content of the privacy policies and the options offered to users, as provided by many existing legislations.

A suitable notice and consent mechanism, clear and accessible and legally compliant, is therefore required,[91] but meeting this obligation is not so simple in the case in question. The nature of the connected toy and the absence of any interface limits awareness of the policies and distances them from direct interaction with the device. This accentuates the perception of the notice and consent mechanism as a mere formality to be completed to access the product.

The last crucial area concerns data security. This entails a negative impact that goes beyond personal data protection and, as such, is also analysed below under impact on the right to psychological and physical safety.

As the AI-based services are hosted by the service provider, data security issues concern both device-service communications and malicious attacks to the server and the device. Encrypted communications, secure communication solutions, and system security requirements for data hosted and processed on the server can minimise potential risks, as in the case study, which also considered access to data when the doll's user changes.[92]

None of these measures prevent the risks of hacking to the device or the local Wi-Fi connection, which are higher when the doll is used outdoors.[93] This was the chief weakness noted in the case in question and in IoT devices more generally. They are often designed with poor inherent data security and cybersecure features for cost reasons. To reduce this risk, stronger authentication and encryption solutions have been proposed in the literature.[94]

Taking into account the initial impact assessment plus all the measures described above, the exposure is reduced to low, since users are thus exposed to potential prejudices only in special circumstances, primarily malicious attack. Probability also becomes low, as the proposed measures mitigate the risks relating to dialogue

---

[90] This was the option adopted in the Hello Barbie case, see fn 53. But Steeves 2020 on the sentences used by Hello Barbie to indirectly reinforce the brand identity and encourage the child to adopt that identity for his/her own.

[91] In the case examined, one of the main weakness claimed with regard to Hello Barbie concerned the privacy policies adopted, the interplay between the different entities involved in data processing, and the design of these policies and access to them, which were considered cumbersome. Leta Jones and Meurer 2016.

[92] Hello Barbie FAQ (fn 41) ("Conversations and other information are not stored on the doll itself, but rather in the associated parent account. So, if other users are using a different Wi-Fi network and using their own account, Hello Barbie would not remember anything from the prior conversations. New users would need to set up their own account to enable conversations with Barbie").

[93] Leta Jones 2016, p. 244.

[94] See also below under (C).

between doll and user, data collection and retention. Likelihood (Table 2.4) is therefore reduced to low.

Regarding severity of prejudice, gravity can be lowered to at least medium by effect of the mitigation measures, but effort remains medium, given the potential risk of hacking. Severity is therefore lowered somewhat (from 5 to 3 in Table 2.7), though remaining medium.

If the severity and the likelihood are medium in Table 2.9, the overall impact is lowered from high to medium.

(B) Impact on freedom of thought

As described in Sect. 2.4.1.2, the impact on freedom of thought is related to the values conveyed by the doll in dialogue with the user. Here the main issue concerns the nature of the messages addressed to the user, their sources and their interplay with the rights and duties of parents to provide appropriate direction and guidance in the child's exercise of freedom of thought, including issues of cultural diversity.

A system based on Natural Language Processing allows AI various degrees of autonomy in identifying the best response or sentence in the human-machine interaction. Given the issues considered here (the nature of the values shared by the doll with its young user) the two main options are to use a closed set of possible sentences or search for potential answers in a large database, such as the Internet. A variety of solutions can also be found between these two extremes.

Since the main problem is content control, the preferable option is the first, and this was indeed the solution adopted in the Hello Barbie case.[95] Content can thus be fine-tuned to the education level of the user, given the age range of the children.[96] This reduces the risk of unexpected and inadequate content and, where full lines of dialogue are available (this was the case with Hello Barbie), parents are able to get an idea of the content offered to their children.

Some residual risks remain however, due to intentional or unintentional cultural models or values, including the difference between appropriate and inappropriate content.[97] This is due to the special relationship the toy generates[98] and the only limited mitigation provided by transparency on pre-recorded lines of dialogue.

To address these issues, concerning both freedom of thought and diversity, the AI system should embed a certain degree of flexibility (user-customizable content) and avoid stereotyping by default. To achieve this, the team working on pre-recorded sentences and dialogues should be characterised by diversity, adopting a by-design approach and bearing in mind the target user of the product.[99]

---

[95] Hello Barbie FAQ (fn 41).

[96] Hello Barbie FAQ (fn 41) ("All comments made by Hello Barbie are scripted with school age appropriate content").

[97] See fn 60.

[98] See fn 59.

[99] On the different attitude in pre-recorded sentences with regard to different religious topics, see Steeves 2020.

Moreover, taking into account the parents' point of view, mere transparency, i.e. access to the whole body of sentences used by the doll, is not enough. As is demonstrated extensively in the field of data protection, information on processing is often disregarded by the user and it is hard to imagine parents reading 8,000 lines of dialogue before buying a doll.

To increase transparency and user awareness, therefore, forms of visualisation of these values through logic and content maps could be useful to easily represent the content used. In addition, it would be important to give parents the opportunity to partially shape the AI reactions, customising the values and content, providing other options relating to the most critical areas in terms of education and freedom of thought.

With regard to the effects of these measures, they mitigate both the potentially adverse consequences of initial product design and the lack of parental supervision of content, minimising the probability of an adverse impact on freedom of thought. The probability (Table 2.2) is therefore lowered to low.

Given the wide distribution of the product, the potential variety of cultural contexts and the need for an active role of parents to minimise the risk, the exposure remains medium, although the number of affected individuals is expected to decrease (Table 2.3).

If the probability is low and the exposure is medium, the likelihood (Table 2.4) is lowered to low after the adoption of the suggested mitigation measures and design solutions.

The gravity of prejudice and the effort were originally low and the additional measures described can further reduce gravity through a more responsible management of content which might support potentially conflicting cultural models or values. Severity therefore remains low.

Considering both likelihood and severity as low, the overall impact (Table 2.9) is reduced from medium to low, compared with the original design model.

(C) Impact on the right to psychological and physical safety

The potential impact in this area is mainly related to malicious hacking activities[100] that might allow third parties to take control of the doll and use it to cause, psychological and physical harm to the user.[101] This was one of the most widely debated issues in the Hello Barbie case and one of the main reasons that led Mattel to stop producing this toy.[102] Possible mitigation measures are the exclusion of

[100] Gibbs 2015.

[101] Chang et al. 2019 ("For example, the attackers can spread content through the audio system, which is adverse for children's growth through the built-in audio in the smart toys").

[102] See also Shasha et al. 2019.

Table 2.12 Comparative risk impact analysis table (examined case)

Risk	L	S	Overall impact	MMs	rL	rS	Final impact
Impact on privacy and data protection	VH	M	H	See above sub A)	M	M	M
Impact on freedom of thought	M	L	M	See above sub B)	L	L	L
Impact on the right to psychological and physical safety	L	M	M	See above sub C)	L	M	M
Overall impact (all impacted areas)			M/H				M/L

Source The author

interaction with other IoT devices,[103] strong authentication and data encryption.[104]

As regards likelihood, considering the protection measures adopted and the low interest of third parties in this type of individual and context-specific malicious attack, the probability is low (Table 2.2). Although the suggested measures do not affect the exposure, this remains low due to the limited circumstances in which a malicious attack can be carried out (Table 2.3). The likelihood therefore remains low but is lowered (from 2 to 1 in Table 2.4).

Regarding severity, the proposed measures do not impact on the gravity of the prejudice (Table 2.5), or the effort (Table 2.6) which remain medium. Severity therefore remains medium (Table 2.7).

Since the final values of neither likelihood nor severity change, overall impact remains medium (Table 2.9), with malicious hacking being the most critical aspect of the product in terms of risk mitigation.

The Table 2.12 shows the assessment of the different impacts, comparing the results before and after the adoption of mitigation measures.

In the case in question, there is no Table 2.10 EF column since there are no factors that could exclude risk, such as certain mandatory impacting features or overriding competing interests recognised by law.

The radial graph in this Fig. 2.3 shows the concrete effect of the assessment (the blue line represents the initial impacts and the orange the impacts after adoption of the measures described above). It should be noted that the reduction of potential impact is limited as the Hello Barbie product already included several options and measures to mitigate adverse effects on rights and freedoms (pre-recorded sentences, no Internet access, data encryption, parental access to stored data, etc.). The effect would have been greater starting from a general AI-equipped doll using Natural Language Processing interacting with children, without mitigation measures.

[103] Doll's speech content was hand crafted by the writing team at Mattel and ToyTalk, not derived from open web search. See 'Hello Barbie FAQ' (fn 41).

[104] Demetzou et al. 2018; Gonçalves de Carvalho and Medeiros Eler 2018.

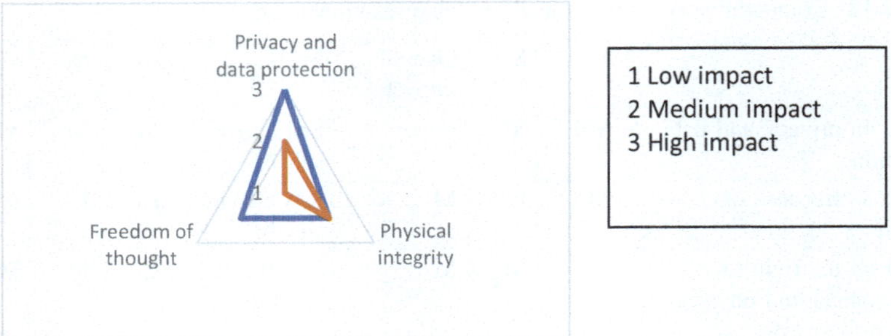

Fig. 2.3 Final radial graph of the examined case. *Source* The author. [Blue line: original impact. Orange line: final impact after adoption of mitigation measures and design solutions]

In this regard, the HRIA model proposed is in line with a human rights-by design approach, where the design team is asked to consider human rights impact from the earliest product design stages, discarding those options that have an obvious negative impact on human rights. With this approach, there is no HRIA 0 where the proposed product is completely open to the riskiest scenarios (e.g. a connected doll equipped with unsupervised AI that uses all available web sources to dialogue with young users, with unencrypted doll-user communication sent to a central datacentre where information is stored without a time limit and used for further purposes, including marketing communications direct to doll users).

In human rights-oriented design, HRIA thus becomes a tool to test, refine and improve adopted options that already entail a risk-aware approach. In this way, HRIA is a tool for testing and improving human rights-oriented design strategies.

2.4.2 A Large-Scale Case Study: Smart City Government

Large-scale projects using data-intensive AI applications are characterised by a variety of potentially impacted areas concerning individual and groups. This produces a more complex and multi-factor scenario which cannot be fully assessed by the mere aggregation of the results of HRIAs conducted for each component of these projects.

An example is provided by data-driven smart cites, where the overall effect of an integrated model including different layers affecting a variety of human activities means that the cumulative impact is greater than the sum of the impacts of each application.

In such cases, a HRIA for AI systems also needs to consider the cumulative effect of data use and the AI strategies adopted, as already happens in HRIA practice with large-scale scenario cases. This is all the more important in the field of AI where large-scale projects often feature a unique or dominant technology partner who benefits from a general overview of all the different processing activities ('platformisation'[105]).

The Sidewalk project in Toronto is an example of this 'platformisation' effect and a case study in the consequent impacts on rights and freedoms. This concluded smart city project was widely debated[106] and raised several human rights-related issues common to other data-intensive projects.

The case concerned a requalification project for the Quayside, a large urban area on Toronto's waterfront largely owned by Toronto Waterfront Revitalization Corporation. Based on an agreement between the City of Toronto and Toronto Waterfront,[107] in 2017, through a competitive Request for Proposals, Waterfront Toronto hired Sidewalk Labs (a subsidiary of Alphabet Inc.) to develop a proposal for this area.[108]

This proposal – the Master Innovation and Development Plan or MIDP[109] – outlined a vision for the Quayside site and suggested data-driven innovative solutions across the following areas: mobility and transportation; building forms and construction techniques; core infrastructure development and operations; social service delivery; environmental efficiency and carbon neutrality; climate mitigation strategies; optimisation of open space; data-driven decision making; governance and citizen participation; and regulatory and policy innovation.[110]

---

[105] Goodman and Powles 2019.

[106] Carr and Hesse 2020b; Flynn and Valverde 2019.

[107] The Waterfront Revitalization Corporation (which was renamed Waterfront Toronto) was a partnered not-for-profit corporation, created in 2003 by the City of Toronto, Province of Ontario and the Government of Canada (see also Province's Toronto Waterfront Revitalization Corporation Act) to oversee and deliver revitalization of Toronto's waterfront; further information are available at https://www.toronto.ca/city-government/accountability-operations-customer-service/city-administration/city-managers-office/agencies-corporations/corporations/waterfront-toronto/. Accessed 30 December 2020. See also Toronto Waterfront Revitalization: Memorandum of Understanding between the City of Toronto, City of Toronto Economic Development Corporation and Toronto Waterfront Revitalization Corporation. https://www.toronto.ca/legdocs/2006/agendas/council/cc060131/pof1rpt/cl027.pdf. Accessed 30 December 2020; City of Toronto, Executive Committee 2018a.

[108] Waterfront Toronto and Sidewalk Labs entered into a partnership Framework Agreement on October 16, 2017. The Framework Agreement was a confidential legal document, see City of Toronto, Executive Committee 2018a. A summary of this agreement is available in City of Toronto, Executive Committee 2018b, Comments, para 2 and Attachment 2.

[109] Sidewalk Labs was charged with providing Waterfront Toronto with a MIDP for evaluation, including public and stakeholder consultation. Following the adoption of the MIDP by the Waterfront Toronto's Board of Directors, the City of Toronto was to complete an additional assessment programme focused on feasibility and legal compliance, including public consultation. See City of Toronto, Deputy City Manager, Infrastructure and Development 2019.

[110] City of Toronto, Executive Committee 2018a.

This long list of topics shows how this data-intensive project went beyond mere urban requalification to embrace goals that are part of the traditional duties of a local administration, pursuing public interest purposes[111] with potential impacts on a variety of rights and freedoms.

The Sidewalk case[112] suggests several takeaways for the HRIA model. First, an integrated model, which combines the HRIAs of the different technologies and processes adopted within a multi-factor scenario, is essential to properly address the overall impact, including a variety of socio-technical solutions and impacted areas.

Second, the criticism surrounding civic participation in the Sidewalk project reveals how the effective engagement of relevant rightsholders and stakeholders is central from the earliest stages of proposal design. Giving voice to potentially affected groups mitigates the risk of the development of top-down and merely technology driven solutions, which have a higher risk of rejection and negative impact.

Third, the complexity and extent of large-scale integrated HRIA for multi-factor scenarios require a methodological approach that cannot be limited to an internal self-assessment but demand an independent third-party assessment by a multidisciplinary team of experts, as in traditional HRIA practice.

These elements suggest three key principles for large-scale HRIA: independence, transparency, and inclusivity. Independence requires third-party assessors with no legal or material relationship with the entities involved in the projects, including any potential stakeholders.

Transparency concerns both the assessment procedure, facilitating rightsholder and stakeholder participation, and the public availability of the assessment outcome,[113] using easily understandable language. In this sense, transparency is linked to inclusivity, which concerns the engagement of all the different rightsholders and stakeholders impacted by the activities examined (Table 2.13).

---

[111] Wylie 2020; Goodman and Powles 2019.

[112] For a more extensive discussion of this case: Scassa 2020; Morgan and Webb 2020; Artyushina 2020; Flynn and Valverde 2019; Peel and Tretter 2019; Carr and Hesse 2020a; Goodman and Powles 2019.

[113] Mantelero 2016, p. 766, fn 94 ("It is possible to provide business-sensitive information in a separate annex to the impact assessment report, which is not publicly available, or publish a short version of the report without the sensitive content").

Table 2.13 Multi-factor scenario HRIA: main stages and tasks

Main stage	Sub-section	Main tasks
I. Planning and scoping	A. Preliminary analysis	– Collection of information on the project, parties involved (including supply-chain), rightsholders, potential stakeholders, and territorial target area (country, region)[114] – Human rights reference framework: review of applicable binding and non-binding instruments, gap analysis
	B. Scoping	– Identification of main issues related to human rights to be examined – Drafting of a questionnaire for HRIA interviews and main indicators
II. Risk analysis and assessment	A. Fieldwork	– Interviews with rightsholders and internal/external project stakeholders,[115] interviews with experts, case studies on particular groups and individuals, and data collection[116] – Understanding of contextual issues (political, economic, regulatory, and social)
	B. Analysis and assessment	– Data verification and validation, comparing and combining fieldwork results and desk analysis – Further interviews and analysis, if necessary – Impact analysis for each project branch and impacted rights and freedoms – Integrated impact assessment report[117]
III. Mitigation and further implementation	A. Mitigation	– Recommendations – Prioritisation of mitigation goals
	B. Further implementation	– Post-assessment monitoring – Grievance mechanisms – Ongoing rightsholder and stakeholder engagement

Source The author

An additional important contribution of the integrated HRIA is its ability to shed light on issues that do not emerge in assessing single components of large-scale AI systems, as the cumulative effect of such projects is key. Here, the human rights layer opens up to a broader perspective which includes the impact of socio-technical solutions on democratic participation and decisions.

The Urban Data Trust created by Sidewalk and its role in the Toronto project is an example in this sense. The Urban Data Trust was tasked with establishing "a set

[114] The Danish Institute for Human Rights 2020c, pp. 13–18.

[115] Various interview techniques can be used in the assessment, such as focus groups, women-only group interviews, one-on-one interviews (key persons) and interviews with external stakeholders.

[116] Taking into account the circumstances, e.g. vulnerable groups, data could be collected anonymously through written submissions.

[117] The Danish Institute for Human Rights 2020e.

of RDU [Responsible Data Use] Guidelines that would apply to all entities seeking to collect or use urban data" and with implementing and managing "a four-step process for approving the responsible collection and use of urban data" and any entity that wishes to collect or use urban data in the district "would have to comply with UDT [Urban Data Trust] requirements, in addition to applicable Canadian privacy laws".[118]

This important oversight body was to be created by an agreement between Waterfront Toronto and Sidewalk Lab[119] and composed of a board of five members (a data governance, privacy, or intellectual property expert; a community representative; a public-sector representative; an academic representative; and a Canadian business industry representative) acting as a sort of internal review board and supported by a Chief Data Officer who, under the direction of the board, was to carry out crucial activities concerning data use.[120] In addition, the Urban Data Trust would have to enter into contracts with all entities authorised to collect or use urban data[121] in the district, and these data sharing agreements could also "potentially provide the entity with the right to enter onto property and remove sensors and other recording devices if breaches are identified".[122]

Although this model was later abandoned, due to the concerns raised by this solution,[123] it shows the intention to create an additional layer of data governance, different from both the individual dimension of information self-determination and the collective dimension of public interest managed by public bodies, within a

---

[118] Side Walk Labs 2019, vol. 2, p. 419 and vol. 3, p. 69. On the interplay the role of the Urban Data Trust in setting requirements for data processing and the legal framework into force in Canada and in Toronto, Scassa 2020.

[119] Scassa 2020, p. 55 ("in proposing the UDT, Sidewalk Labs chose a governance model developed unilaterally, and not as part of a collective process involving data stakeholders").

[120] Side Walk Labs 2019, vol. 2, p. 421 ("the Chief Data Officer would be responsible for developing the charter for the Urban Data Trust; promulgating RDU Guidelines that apply to all parties proposing to collect urban data, and that respect existing privacy laws and guidelines but also seek to apply additional guidelines for addressing the unique aspects of urban data [...]; structuring oversight and review processes; determining how the entity would be staffed, operated, and funded; developing initial agreements that would govern the use and sharing of urban data; and coordinating with privacy regulators and other key stakeholders, as necessary").

[121] The notion of urban data is a novel category proposed by Sidewalk, referring to "both personal information and information that is not connected to a particular individual [...] it is collected in a physical space in the city and may be associated with practical challenges in obtaining meaningful consent [...] Urban data would be broader than the definition of personal information and include personal, non-personal, aggregate, or de-identified data [...] collected and used in physical or community spaces where meaningful consent prior to collection and use is hard, if not impossible, to obtain", Side Walk Labs 2019, vol. 2, p. 416. But see, for critical comments on this category and its use, Scassa 2020, pp. 51–54; Goodman and Powles 2019, p. 473.

[122] Side Walk Labs 2019, vol. 2, pp. 420–422.

[123] Open Letter from Waterfront Toronto Board Chair, 31 October 2019. https://waterfrontoronto.ca/nbe/wcm/connect/waterfront/waterfront_content_library/waterfront+home/news+room/news+archive/news/2019/october/open+letter+from+waterfront+toronto+board+chair+-+october+31%2C+2019. Accessed 8 March 2021.

process of centralisation and privatisation of data governance regarding information generated within a community.[124]

In this sense, the overall impact of AI applications in urban spaces and their coordination by a dominant player providing technological infrastructure raise important questions about the cumulative effect on potentially impacted rights, and even more concerning democracy and the socio-political dimension of the urban landscape,[125] particularly in terms of the division of public and private responsibilities on matters of collective interest.

This privatisation of the democratic decision process, based on the 'platformisation' of the city, directly concerns the use of data, but is no longer just about data protection. In socio-technical contexts, data governance is about human rights in general, insofar as the use of data by different AI applications raises issues about a variety of potentially adverse effects on different rights and freedoms.[126] If data becomes a means of managing and governing society, its use necessarily has an impact on all the rights and freedoms of individuals and society. This impact is further exacerbated by the empowerment enabled by AI technologies (e.g. the use of facial recognition to replace traditional video-surveillance tools).

For these reasons, cumulative management of different data-intensive systems impacting on the social environment cannot be left to private service providers or an ad hoc associative structure, but should remain within the context of public law, centred on democratic participation in decision-making processes affecting general and public interest.[127]

Large-scale data-intensive AI projects therefore suggest using the HRIA not only to assess the overall impact of all the various AI applications used, but also to go beyond the safeguarding of human rights and freedoms. The results of this assessment therefore become a starting point for a broader analysis and planning of democratic participation in the decision-making process on the use of AI, including democratic oversight on its application.[128]

In line with the approach adopted by international human rights organisations, the human rights dimension should combine with the democratic dimension and the rule of law in guiding the development and deployment of AI projects from their earliest stages.[129]

---

[124] Artyushina 2020.

[125] Carr and Hesse 2020a; Powell 2021.

[126] E.g. Raso et al. 2018.

[127] The right to participate in public affairs (Covenant, Article 25) is based on a broad concept of public affairs, which includes public debate and dialogue between citizens and their representatives, with close links to freedom of expression, assembly and association. See UN Human Rights Committee (HRC) 1996. See also UN Committee on Economic, Social and Cultural Rights (CESCR) 1981, para 5.

[128] Mantelero 2020, pp. 82–88.

[129] See the Council of Europe's proposal discussed in Chap. 4.

The findings of the HRIA will therefore also contribute to addressing the so-called 'Question Zero' about the desirability of using AI solutions in socio-technical systems. This concerns democratic participation and the freedom of individuals, which are even more important in the case of technological solutions in an urban context, where people often have no real opportunity to opt out due to the solutions being deeply embedded in the structure of the city and its essential services.

A key issue then for the democratic use of AI concerns architecture design and its impact on rights and freedoms. The active role of technology in co-shaping human experiences[130] necessarily leads us to focus on the values underlying the technological infrastructure and how these values are transposed into society through technology.[131] The technology infrastructure cannot be viewed as neutral, but as the result of both the values, intentionally or unintentionally, embedded in the devices/services and the role of mediation played by the different technologies and their applications.[132]

These considerations on the power of designers – which are widely discussed in the debate on technology design[133] – are accentuated in the context of smart cities and in many large-scale AI systems. Here, the key role of service providers and the 'platformisation' of these environments[134] shed light on the part these providers play with respect to the overall impact of the AI systems they manage.

In this scenario, the HRIA can play an important role in assessing values and supporting a human rights-oriented design that also pays attention to participatory processes and democratic deliberation governing large-scale AI systems. This can facilitate the concrete development of a truly trustworthy AI, in which trust is based on respect for human rights, democracy and the rule of law.

---

[130] Manders-Huits and van den Hoven 2009, pp. 55–56.

[131] Ihde 1990.

[132] Latour and Venn 2002.

[133] Winner 1980; Winner 1983, p. 105 ("let us recognize that every technology of significance to us implies a set of political commitments that one can identify if one looks carefully enough. To state it more directly, what appear to be merely instrumental choices are better seen as choices about the form of the society we continually build, choices about the kinds of people we want to be"); Verbeek 2011, pp. 109, 129, and 164–165 ("Accompanying technological developments requires engagement with designers and users, identifying points of application fir moral reflection, and anticipating the social impact of technologies-in-design [...] In order to develop responsible forms of use and design, we need to equip users ad designer with frameworks and methods to anticipate, assess, ad design the mediating role of technologies in people's lives and in the ways we organize society").

[134] Council of Europe, Consultative Committee of the Convention for the Protection of Individuals with regard to Automatic Processing of Personal Data (Convention 108) 2019; Council of Europe, Committee of Ministers 2020.

2.5 Summary

The recent turn in the debate on AI regulation from ethics to law, the wide application of AI and the new challenges it poses in a variety of fields of human activities are urging legislators to find a paradigm of reference to assess the impacts of AI and to guide its development. This cannot only be done at a general level, on the basis of guiding principles and provisions, but the paradigm must be embedded into the development and deployment of each application.

With a view to providing a global approach in this field, human rights and fundamental freedoms can offer this reference paradigm for a truly human-centred AI. However, this growing interest in a human rights-focused approach needs to be turned into effective tools that can guide AI developers and key AI users, such as municipalities, governments, and private companies.

To bridge this gap with regard to the potential role of human rights in addressing and mitigating AI-related risks, this chapter has suggested a model for human rights impact assessment (HRIA) as part of the broader HRESIA model. This is a response to the lack of a formal methodology to facilitate an ex-ante approach based on a human-oriented design of product/service development.

The proposed HRIA model for AI has been developed in line with the existing practices in human rights impacts assessment, but in a way that better responds to the specific nature of AI applications, in terms of scale, impacted rights and freedoms, prior assessment of production design, and assessment of risk levels, as required by several proposals on AI regulation.[135]

The result is a tool that can be easily used by entities involved in AI development from the outset' in the design of new AI solutions, and can follow the product/service throughout its lifecycle. This assessment model provides specific, measurable and comparable evidence on potential impacts, their probability, extension, and severity, facilitating comparison between alternative design options and an iterative approach to AI design, based on risk assessment and mitigation.

In this sense, the proposed human rights module of the HRESIA is no longer just an assessment tool but a human rights management tool, providing clear evidence for a human rights-oriented development of AI products and services and their risk management.

In addition, a more transparent and easy-to-understand impact assessment model facilitates a participatory approach to AI development by rightsholders and potential stakeholders, giving them clear and structured information about possible options and the effects of changes in AI design, and contributing to the development of the ethical and social components of the HRESIA.[136]

---

135 See Chap. 4.

136 See Chap. 3.

Finally, the proposed model can also be used by supervisory authorities and auditing bodies to monitor risk management in relation to the impact of data use on individual rights and freedoms.

Based on these results, several conclusions can be drawn. The first general one is that conducting a HRIA should be seen not as a burden or a mere obligation, but as an opportunity. Given the nature of AI products/services and their features and scale, the proposed assessment model can significantly help companies and other entities to develop effective human-centric AI in challenging contexts.

The model can also contribute to a more formal and standardised assessment of AI solutions, facilitating the decision between different possible approaches. Although HRIA has already been adopted in several contexts, large-scale projects are often assessed without using a formal evaluation of risk likelihood and severity.[137] Traditional HRIA reports often describe the risks found and their potential impact, but with no quantitative assessment, providing recommendations without grading the level of impact, leaving duty bearers to define a proper action plan.

This approach to HRIA is in line with voluntary and policy-based HRIA practice in the business sector. However, once HRIA becomes a legal tool – as suggested by the European Commission and the Council of Europe[138] –, it is no longer merely a source of recommendations for better business policy. Future AI regulation will most likely bring specific legal obligations and sanctions for non-compliance in relation to risk assessment and management, as well as specific risk thresholds (e.g. high risk).

Analysis of potential impact will therefore become an element of regulatory compliance, with mandatory adoption of appropriate mitigation measures, and barriers in the event of high risk. A model that enables a graduation of risk can therefore facilitate compliance and reduce risks by preventing high-risk AI applications from being placed on the market.

With large-scale projects, such as smart cities, assessing each technological component using the proposed model and mitigating adverse effects is not sufficient. A more general overall analysis must be conducted in addition. Only an integrated assessment can consider the cumulative effect of a socio-technical system[139] by measuring its broader impacts, including the consequences in terms of democratic participation and decision-making processes.

This integrated assessment, based on broader fieldwork, citizen engagement, and a co-design process, can evaluate the overall impact of an entire AI-based environment, in a way that is closer to traditional HRIA models.

In both cases, figures such as the human rights officer and tools like a HRIA management plan, containing action plans with timelines, responsibilities and indicators, can facilitate these processes,[140] including the possibility of extending them to the supply chain and all potentially affected groups of people.

---

[137] E.g. The Danish Institute for Human Rights 2020f. But also see Salcito and Wielga 2015.

[138] See Chap. 4.

[139] Selbst et al. 2019.

[140] Abrahams and Wyss 2010.

Finally, the proposed model for the human rights component of the HRESIA model, with its more formalised assessment, can facilitate the accountability and monitoring of AI products and services during their lifecycle,[141] enabling changes in their impacts to be monitored through periodic reviews, audits, and progress reports on the implementation of the measures taken. It also makes it possible to incorporate more precise human rights indicators in internal reports and plans and make assessment results available to rightsholders and stakeholders clearly and understandably, facilitating their cooperation in a human rights-oriented approach to AI.

References

Abrahams D, Wyss Y (2010) Guide to Human Rights Impact Assessment and Management (HRIAM). International Business Leaders Forum, International Finance Corporation and UN Global Compact, Washington.

Access Now (2019) Laying down the Law on AI: Ethics Done, Now the EU Must Focus on Human Rights. https://www.accessnow.org/laying-down-the-law-on-ai-ethics-done-now-the-eu-must-focus-on-human-rights/. Accessed 7 April 2021.

Algorithm Watch (2020) Automating Society report 2020. https://automatingsociety.algorithmwatch.org/wp-content/uploads/2020/12/Automating-Society-Report-2020.pdf. Accessed 23 January 2021.

Artyushina A (2020) Is civic data governance the key to democratic smart cities? The role of the urban data trust in Sidewalk Toronto. 55 Telematics and Informatics, DOI: https://doi.org/10.1016/j.tele.2020.101456.

Aven T (2011) On Different Types of Uncertainties in the Context of the Precautionary Principle. Risk Analysis 31(10): 1515-1525.

Bennett CJ, Raab CD (2018) Revisiting the Governance of Privacy: Contemporary Policy Instruments in Global Perspective. Regulation & Governance 14(3): 447-464.

BEUC (2016) Connected Toys Do Not Meet Consumer Protection Standard. Letter to Mr Giovanni Buttarelli, European Data Protection Supervisor. https://www.beuc.eu/publications/beuc-x-2016-136_mgo_letter_to_giovanni_buttarelli_-_edps_-_connected_toys.pdf. Accessed 12 November 2020.

Bohn J, Coroamă V, Langheinrich M, Mattern F, Rohs M (2005) Social, Economic, and Ethical Implications of Ambient Intelligence and Ubiquitous Computing. In: Weber W, Rabaey JM, Aarts E (eds) Ambient Intelligence. Springer, Berlin, pp 5-29.

Carr C, Hesse M (2020a) Sidewalk Labs closed down – whither Google's smart city. Regions. https://regions.regionalstudies.org/ezine/article/sidewalk-labs-closed-down-whither-googles-smart-city/. Accessed 28 December 2020a.

Carr C, Hesse M (2020b) When Alphabet Inc. Plans Toronto's Waterfront: New Post-Political Modes of Urban Governance. Urban Planning 5:69-83.

Chang V, Li Z, Ramachandran M (2019) A Review on Ethical Issues for Smart Connected Toys in the Context of Big Data. In: Firouzi F, Estrada E, Mendez Munoz V, Chang V (eds) COMPLEXIS 2019 - Proceedings of the 4th International Conference on Complexity, Future Information Systems and Risk. SciTePress, Setúbal, pp 149–156.

[141] The Danish Institute for Human Rights 2020d, pp. 25–33.

City of Toronto, Deputy City Manager, Infrastructure and Development (2019) Report for action. EX6.1. https://www.toronto.ca/legdocs/mmis/2019/ex/bgrd/backgroundfile-133867.pdf. Accessed 30 December 2020.

City of Toronto, Executive Committee (2018a) Executive Committee consideration on January 24. 2018a.EX30. 9. http://app.toronto.ca/tmmis/viewAgendaItemHistory.do?item=2018a.EX30.9. Accessed 30 December 2020.

City of Toronto, Executive Committee (2018b) Executive Committee consideration on January 24, 2018b, 2018b.EX30. 9. Report and Attachments 1 and 2 from the Deputy City Manager, Cluster B on Sidewalk Toronto. https://www.toronto.ca/legdocs/mmis/2018b/ex/bgrd/backgroundfile-110745.pdf. Accessed 31 December 2020.

Commission of the European Communities (2000) Communication from the Commission on the precautionary principle, COM(2000) 1 final.

Costa L (2012) Privacy and the precautionary principle 28(1) Computer Law & Security Review 14–24.

Council of Europe (2018) Algorithms and Human Rights. Study on the Human Rights Dimensions of Automated Data Processing Techniques and Possible Regulatory Implications. Strasbourg.

Council of Europe, Committee of Ministers (2018) Recommendation CM/Rec(2018)7. Guidelines to Respect, Protect and Fulfil the Rights of the Child in the Digital Environment.

Council of Europe, Committee of Ministers (2020) Recommendation CM/Rec(2020)1 on the human rights impacts of algorithmic systems.

Council of Europe, Consultative Committee of the Convention for the Protection of Individuals with regard to Automatic Processing of Personal Data (Convention 108) (2017) Guidelines on the protection of individuals with regard to the processing of personal data in a world of Big Data, T-PD(2017)01.

Council of Europe, Consultative Committee of the Convention for the Protection of Individuals with regard to Automatic Processing of Personal Data (Convention 108) (2019) Guidelines on Artificial Intelligence and Data Protection, T-PD(2019)01.

Council of Europe, Consultative Committee of the Convention for the Protection of Individuals with regard to Automatic Processing of Personal Data (Convention 108) (2020) Guidelines on Facial Recognition, T-PD(2020)03rev4.

Crawford K, Joler V (2018) Anatomy of an AI System: The Amazon Echo As An Anatomical Map of Human Labor, Data and Planetary Resources. AI Now Institute and Share Lab, New York. http://www.anatomyof.ai. Accessed 27 December 2019.

Data Ethics Commission (2019) Opinion of the Data Ethics Commission. https://www.bmj.de/SharedDocs/Downloads/DE/Themen/Fokusthemen/Gutachten_DEK_EN.pdf?__blob=publicationFile&v=2. Accessed 7 June 2020.

de Paula Albuquerque O, Fantinato M, Kelner J, de Albuquerque Wheler AP (2020) Privacy in smart toys: Risks and proposed solutions. 39 Electronic Commerce Research and Applications, DOI: https://doi.org/10.1016/j.elerap.2019.100922.

Demetzou K, Böck L, Hanteer O (2018) Smart Bears don't talk to strangers: analysing privacy concerns and technical solutions in smart toys for children. In: IET Conference Proceedings. The Institution of Engineering & Technology, Stevenage, DOI: https://doi.org/10.1049/cp.2018.0005.

European Commission (2020) Study on Due Diligence Requirements through the Supply Chain: Final Report. Publications Office of the European Union.

European Commission (2021) Proposal for Regulation of the European Parliament and of the Council laying down harmonised rules on Artificial Intelligence (Artificial Intelligence Act) and amending legislative acts, COM(2021) 206 final, Brussels.

European Data Protection Supervisor (2015a) Decision of 3 December 2015a establishing an external advisory group on the ethical dimensions of data protection ('the Ethics Advisory Group') 2016/C 33/01 OJEU.

European Data Protection Supervisor (2015b) Opinion 4/2015b. Towards a new digital ethics: Data, dignity and technology.

European Digital Rights (EDRi) (2021) Civil Society Calls for AI Red Lines in the European Union's Artificial Intelligence Proposal. https://edri.org/our-work/civil-society-call-for-ai-red-lines-in-the-european-unions-artificial-intelligence-proposal/. Accessed 15 March 2021.

European Parliament (2020) Framework of ethical aspects of artificial intelligence, robotics and related Technologies European Parliament resolution of 20 October 2020 with recommendations to the Commission on a framework of ethical aspects of artificial intelligence, robotics and related technologies (2020/2012(INL)), P9_TA-PROV(2020)0275.

European Parliament - Committee on Civil Liberties, Justice and Home Affairs (2020) Opinion of the Committee on Civil Liberties, Justice and Home Affairs for the Committee on Legal Affairs on artificial intelligence: questions of interpretation and application of international law in so far as the EU is affected in the areas of civil and military uses and of state authority outside the scope of criminal justice. 2020/2013(INI).

European Union Agency for Fundamental Rights and Council of Europe (2018) Handbook on European Data Protection Law. http://fra.europa.eu/en/publication/2018/handbook-european-data-protection-law. Accessed 25 May 2018.

Federal Bureau of Investigation (2017) Consumer Notice: Internet-Connected Toys Could Present Privacy and Contact Concerns for Children' Alert Number I-071717 (Revised)-PSA. https://www.ic3.gov/Media/Y2017/PSA170717. Accessed 15 December 2020.

Federal Trade Commission (2017) Enforcement Policy Statement Regarding the Applicability of the COPPA Rule to the Collection and Use of Voice Recordings. https://www.ftc.gov/public-statements/2017/10/federal-trade-commission-enforcement-policy-statement-regarding. Accessed 28 November 2020.

Floridi L et al. (2018) AI4People – An Ethical Framework for a Good AI Society: Opportunities, Risks, Principles, and Recommendations. Minds & Machine 28:689–707.

Floridi L, Mariarosaria T (2016) What is data ethics? Phil. Trans. R. Soc. A. 374(2083), doi: https://doi.org/10.1098/rsta.2016.0360.

Flynn A, Valverde M (2019) Where The Sidewalk Ends: The Governance Of Waterfront Toronto's Sidewalk Labs Deal. Windsor Yearbook of Access to Justice 36:263–283.

Gibbs S (2015) Hackers can hijack Wi-Fi Hello Barbie to spy on your children, The Guardian, 26 November 2015. https://www.theguardian.com/technology/2015/nov/26/hackers-can-hijack-wi-fi-hello-barbie-to-spy-on-your-children. Accessed 12 November 2020.

Gonçalves ME (2017) The EU data protection reform and the challenges of big data: remaining uncertainties and ways forward. Inform. Comm. Tech. Law 26(2):90-115.

Gonçalves de Carvalho L, Medeiros Eler M (2018) Security Tests for Smart Toys. In: Proceedings of the 20th International Conference on Enterprise Information Systems 111–120. http://www.scitepress.org/DigitalLibrary/Link.aspx?doi=https://doi.org/10.5220/0006776101110120. Accessed 23 December 2020.

Goodman E, Powles J (2019) Urbanism Under Google: Lessons from Sidewalk Toronto. Fordham Law Review 88:457–498.

Haber E (2019) Toying with Privacy: Regulating the Internet of Toys. Ohio State Law Journal 80:399.

Hansson SO (2020) How Extreme Is the Precautionary Principle? NanoEthics 14:245–257.

Ienca M, Vayena E (2020) AI Ethics Guidelines: European and Global Perspectives. In: Council of Europe. Towards regulation of AI systems. Global perspectives on the development of a legal framework on Artificial Intelligence systems based on the Council of Europe's standards on human rights, democracy and the rule of law. DGI (2020)16, pp 38–60.

Ihde D (1990) Technology and the Lifeworld: from garden to earth. Indiana University Press, Bloomington.

Independent High-Level Expert Group on Artificial Intelligence set up by the European Commission (2019) Ethics Guidelines for Trustworthy AI. https://digital-strategy.ec.europa.eu/en/library/ethics-guidelines-trustworthy-ai. Accessed 15 April 2019.

Information Commissioner's Office (2020) Age appropriate design code. https://ico.org.uk/for-organisations/guide-to-data-protection/key-data-protection-themes/age-appropriate-design-a-code-of-practice-for-online-services/. Accessed 20 February 2021.

International Covenant on Civil and Political Rights, Human Rights Committee (2011) General Comment no. 34. CCPR/C/GC/34.
Janssen HL (2020) An approach for a fundamental rights impact assessment to automated decision-making. International Data Privacy Law 10(1):76–106.
Kaminski ME, Malgieri G (2021) Algorithmic Impact Assessments under the GDPR: Producing Multi-Layered Explanations. International Data Privacy Law 11(2):125–144.
Keymolen E, Van der Hof S (2019) Can I still trust you, my dear doll? A philosophical and legal exploration of smart toys and trust. Journal of Cyber Policy 4(2):143-159.
Koivisto R, Douglas D (2015) Principles and Approaches in Ethics Assessment. Ethics and Risk. Annex 1.h Ethical Assessment of Research and Innovation: A Comparative Analysis of Practices and Institutions in the EU and selected other countries. Project Stakeholders Acting Together on the Ethical Impact Assessment of Research and Innovation – SATORI. Deliverable 1.1. http://satoriproject.eu/work_packages/comparative-analysis-of-ethics-assessment-practices/. Accessed 15 February 2017.
Latour B, Venn C (2002) Morality and Technology: The End of the Means. Theory, Culture and Society 19(5-6):247-260.
Leta Jones M (2016) Your New Best Frenemy: Hello Barbie and Privacy Without Screens. Engaging Science, Technology, and Society 2:242-246.
Leta Jones M, Meurer K (2016) Can (and Should) Hello Barbie Keep a Secret? IEEE International Symposium on Ethics in Engineering, Science and Technology (ETHICS), doi: https://doi.org/10.1109/ETHICS.2016.7560047.
LKL International Consulting Inc. (2014) Human Rights Impact Assessment of the Bisha Mine in Eritrea. https://media.business-humanrights.org/media/documents/files/documents/Nevsun_HRIA_Full_Report__April_2014_.pdf. Accessed 26 October 2020.
Lynskey O (2015) The Foundations of EU Data Protection Law. Oxford University Press, Oxford.
MacNaughton G, Hunt P (2011) A Human Rights-based Approach to Social Impact Assessment. In: Vanclay F, Esteves AM (eds) New Directions in Social Impact Assessment: Conceptual and Methodological Advances. Edward Elgar, Cheltenham, doi:https://doi.org/10.4337/9781781001196.00034.
Manders-Huits N, van den Hoven J (2009) The Need for a Value-Sensitive Design of Communication Infrastructures. In: Sollie P, Düwell M (eds) Evaluating New Technologies. Methodological Problems for the Ethical Assessment of Technology Developments. Springer, Dordrecht, pp 51–60.
Mann M, Matzner T (2019) Challenging algorithmic profiling: The limits of data protection and anti-discrimination in responding to emergent discrimination. Big Data & Society 6(2), doi: https://doi.org/10.1177/2053951719895805.
Mantelero A (2016) Personal data for decisional purposes in the age of analytics: From an individual to a collective dimension of data protection. Computer Law & Security Review 32 (2):238-255.
Mantelero A (2020) Analysis of international legally binding instruments. In Council of Europe. Towards regulation of AI systems. Global perspectives on the development of a legal framework on Artificial Intelligence systems based on the Council of Europe's standards on human rights, democracy and the rule of law. DGI (2020)16, pp 61–119.
Mantelero A (2021) The future of data protection: Gold standard vs. global standard. Computer Law & Security Review 40, doi: https://doi.org/10.1016/j.clsr.2020.105500.
McReynolds E, Hubbard S, Lau T, Saraf A, Cakmak M, Roesner F (2017) Toys That Listen: A Study of Parents, Children, and Internet-Connected Toys. In: Proceedings of the 2017 CHI Conference on Human Factors in Computing Systems (ACM 2017). https://doi.org/10.1145/3025453.3025735. Accessed 12 November 2020.
Mertala P (2020) How Connectivity Affects Otherwise Traditional Toys? A Functional Analysis of Hello Barbie. Int. J. Child. Comput. Interact. 25, doi: https://doi.org/10.1016/j.ijcci.2020.100186.
Mittelstadt BD, Allo P, Taddeo M, Wachter S, Floridi L (2016) The ethics of algorithms: Mapping the debate. Big Data & Society. 3(2), doi: https://doi.org/10.1177/2053951716679679.

Morgan K, Webb B (2020) Googling the City: In Search of the Public Interest on Toronto's 'Smart' Waterfront. Urban Planning 5:84–95.

Murdoch J (2012) Protecting the Right to Freedom of Thought, Conscience and Religion under the European Convention on Human Rights. Council of Europe.

Myers West S, Whittaker M, Crawford K (2019) Discriminating Systems. https://ainowinstitute.org/discriminatingsystems.pdf. Accessed 13 June 2020.

Narayanan A, Huey J, Felten EW (2016) A Precautionary Approach to Big Data Privacy. In: Gutwirth S, Leenes R, De Hert P (eds) Data Protection on the Move. Springer, Dordrecht, pp 357-385.

Neff G, Nagy P (2016) Automation, Algorithms, and Politics| Talking to Bots: Symbiotic Agency and the Case of Tay. International Journal of Communication 10:4915–4931.

Neil M (2015) Moms Sue Mattel, Saying "Hello Barbie" Doll Violates Privacy. ABA Journal, December 9. https://www.abajournal.com/news/article/hello_barbie_violates_privacy_of_doll_owners_playmates_moms_say_in_lawsuit. Accessed 20 March 2021.

Norwegian Consumer Council (2016) #Toyfail An analysis of consumer and privacy issues in three internet-connected toys. https://fil.forbrukerradet.no/wp-content/uploads/2016/12/toyfail-report-desember2016.pdf. Accessed 14 December 2020.

Peel J (2004) Precaution - A Matter of Principle, Approach or Process? Melb. J. Int. Law 5 (2):483–501. http://www.austlii.edu.au/au/journals/MelbJlIntLaw/2004/19.html. Accessed 4 February 2017.

Peel K, Tretter E (2019) Waterfront Toronto: Privacy or Piracy? https://osf.io/xgz2s. Accessed 28 December 2020.

Pieters W (2011) Security and Privacy in the Clouds: A Bird's Eye View. In: Gutwirth S, Poullet Y, de Hert P, Leenes R (eds) Computers, Privacy and Data Protection: An Element of Choice. Springer, Dordrecht, pp 445-457.

Powell AB (2021) Undoing optimization : civic action in smart cities. Yale University Press, New Haven.

Raab C (2004) The future of privacy protection. Cyber Trust & Crime Prevention Project. https://www.piawatch.eu/node/86. Accessed 28 April 2017.

Raab C, Wright D (2012) Surveillance: Extending the Limits of Privacy Impact Assessment. In: Wright D, De Hert P (eds) Privacy Impact Assessment. Springer, Dordrecht, pp 363-383.

Raab CD (2020) Information Privacy, Impact Assessment, and the Place of Ethics. 37 Computer Law & Security Review DOI: https://doi.org/10.1016/j.clsr.2020.105404.

Raso F, Hilligoss H, Krishnamurthy V, Bavitz C, Kim L (2018) Artificial Intelligence & Human Rights Opportunities & Risks. https://cyber.harvard.edu/sites/default/files/2018-09/2018-09_AIHumanRightsSmall.pdf?subscribe=Download+the+Report. Accessed 28 September 2018.

Reisman D, Schultz J, Crawford K, Whittaker M (2018) Algorithmic Impact Assessments: A Practical Framework for Public Agency Accountability. https://ainowinstitute.org/aiareport2018.pdf. Accessed 29 June 2018.

Salcito K, Wielga M (2015) Kayelekera HRIA Monitoring Summary. http://nomogaia.org/wp-content/uploads/2015/10/KAYELEKERA-HRIA-MONITORING-SUMMARY-10-5-2015-Final.pdf. Accessed 20 February 2021.

Scassa T (2020) Designing Data Governance for Data Sharing: Lessons from Sidewalk Toronto. Technology & Regulation, Special Issue: Governing Data as a Resource, Technology and Regulation 44–56.

Scheinin M, Molbæk-Steensig H (2021) Pandemics and human rights: three perspectives on human rights assessment of strategies against COVID-19. https://cadmus.eui.eu/handle/1814/69576. Accessed 25 February 2021.

Selbst AD (forthcoming) An Institutional View Of Algorithmic Impact Assessments. 35 Harvard Journal of Law & Technology. https://papers.ssrn.com/sol3/papers.cfm?abstract_id=3867634. Accessed 7 August 2021.

Selbst AD, boyd d, Friedler SA, Venkatasubramanian S, Vertesi J (2019) Fairness and Abstraction in Sociotechnical Systems. In: Proceedings of the Conference on Fairness, Accountability, and

Transparency (ACM 2019). https://doi.org/10.1145/3287560.3287598. Accessed 4 January 2020.
Shasha S, Mahmoud M, Mannan M, Youssef A (2019) Playing With Danger: A Taxonomy and Evaluation of Threats to Smart Toys. IEEE Internet of Things Journal 6(2):2986-3002.
Side Walk Labs (2019) Toronto Tomorrow. A new approach for inclusive growth. MIDP.
Spiekermann S (2016) Ethical IT Innovation: A Value-Based System Design Approach. CRC Press, Boca Raton.
Steeves V (2020) A dialogic analysis of Hello Barbie's conversations with children. Big Data & Society, 7(1), doi: https://doi.org/10.1177/2053951720919151.
Stirling A, Gee D (2002) Science, precaution, and practice. Public Health Reports 117(6):521–533.
The Danish Institute for Human Rights (2014) The AAAQ Framework and the Right to Water: International indicators for availability, accessibility, acceptability and quality, Copenhagen. https://www.humanrights.dk/sites/humanrights.dk/files/media/migrated/aaaq_international_indicators_2014.pdf. Accessed 24 June 2019.
The Danish Institute for Human Rights (2020a) Guidance and Toolbox. https://www.humanrights.dk/sites/humanrights.dk/files/media/dokumenter/udgivelser/hria_toolbox_2020a/eng/dihr_hria_guidance_and_toolbox_2020a_eng.pdf. Accessed 20 February 2021.
The Danish Institute for Human Rights (2020b) Guidance on HRIA of Digital Activities. Phase 1: Planning and scoping. Copenhagen. https://www.humanrights.dk/sites/humanrights.dk/files/media/document/HRIA%20Toolbox_Phase%201_ENG_2020b.pdf. Accessed 20 February 2021.
The Danish Institute for Human Rights (2020c) Guidance on HRIA of Digital Activities. Phase 2: Data Collection and context analysis. https://www.humanrights.dk/sites/humanrights.dk/files/media/document/Phase%202_Data%20Collection%20and%20Context%20Analysis_ENG_accessible.pdf. Accessed 20 February 2021.
The Danish Institute for Human Rights (2020d) Guidance on HRIA of Digital Activities. Phase 4: Impact prevention, mitigation and remediation. https://www.humanrights.dk/sites/humanrights.dk/files/media/document/Phase%204_%20Impact%20prevention%20mitigation%20and%20remediation_ENG_accessible.pdf. Accessed 20 February 2021.
The Danish Institute for Human Rights (2020e) Guidance on HRIA of Digital Activities. Phase 5: Reporting and Evaluation. https://www.humanrights.dk/sites/humanrights.dk/files/media/document/HRIA%20Toolbox_Phase%205_ENG_2020e.pdf. Accessed 20 February 2021.
The Danish Institute for Human Rights (2020f) Human Rights Impact Assessment – Durex and Enfa value chains in Thailand. https://www.humanrights.dk/publications/human-rights-impact-assessment-durex-enfa-value-chains-thailand. Accessed 2 March 2021.
The Danish Institute for Human Rights (2020g) Scoping practitioner supplement. Human rights impact assessment guidance and toolbox. https://www.humanrights.dk/sites/humanrights.dk/files/media/document/HRIA%20Toolbox_Phase%201_Scoping%20Prac%20Sup_ENG_2020g_0.docx. Accessed 2 October 2021.
Tosun J (2013) How the EU Handles Uncertain Risks: Understanding the Role of the Precautionary Principle. JEPP 20(10):1517-1528.
UN Committee on Economic, Social and Cultural Rights (CESCR) (1981) General Comment No. 1: Reporting by States Parties.
UN Human Rights Committee (HRC) (1996), CCPR General Comment No. 25: The right to participate in public affairs, voting rights and the right of equal access to *public* service (Art. 25), CCPR/C/21/Rev.1/Add.7.
UNICEF (2018) Children's Online Privacy and Freedom of Expression. https://www.unicef.org/csr/files/UNICEF_Childrens_Online_Privacy_and_Freedom_of_Expression(1).pdf. Accessed 18 December 2020.
UNICEF, The Global Compact, Save the Children (2012) Children's Rights and Business Principles. https://d306pr3pise04h.cloudfront.net/docs/issues_doc%2Fhuman_rights%2FCRBP%2FChildrens_Rights_and_Business_Principles.pdf. Accessed 30 November 2020.
United Nations (2011) Guiding Principles on Business and Human Rights. https://www.ohchr.org/Documents/Publications/GuidingPrinciplesBusinessHR_EN.pdf. Accessed 8 December 2020.

Veale M (2020) A Critical Take on the Policy Recommendations of the EU High-Level Expert Group on Artificial Intelligence. European Journal of Risk Regulation, 1-10, doi:https://doi.org/10.1017/err.2019.65.

Verbeek P-P (2011) Moralizing Technology. Understanding and Designing the Morality of Things. The University of Chicago Press, Chicago.

Wachter S, Mittelstadt B, Russell C (2021) Bias Preservation in Machine Learning: The Legality of Fairness Metrics Under EU Non-Discrimination Law. West Virginia Law Review 123(3): 735-790.

Winner L (1980) Do Artifacts Have Politics? Daedalus 109(1):121–136.

Winner L (1983) Technē and Politeia: The Technical Constitution of Society. In: Durbin PT, Rapp F (eds) Philosophy and Technology. Springer, Dordrecht, pp 97-111.

World Bank, Nordic Trust Fund (2013) Human Rights Impact Assessments: A Review of the Literature, Differences with other forms of Assessments and Relevance for Development. World Bank and Nordic Trust Fund, Washington.

Wright D (2010) A framework for the ethical impact assessment of information technology. Ethics Inf. Technol. 13:199–226.

Wylie B (2020) In Toronto, Google's Attempt to Privatize Government Fails – For Now. Boston Review, 13 May.

Zuiderveen Borgesius FJ (2020) Strengthening legal protection against discrimination by algorithms and artificial intelligence. Int. J. Hum. Rights 24(10):1572-1593.

Chapter 3
The Social and Ethical Component in AI Systems Design and Management

Contents

Abstract The extensive and frequently severe impact of AI systems on society cannot be fully addressed by the human rights legal framework. Many issues involve community choices or individual autonomy requiring a contextual analysis focused on societal and ethical values. The social and ethical consequences of AI represent a complementary dimension, alongside that of human rights, that must be properly investigated in AI assessment, to capture the holistic dimension of the relationship between humans and machines. This assessment is more complicated than that of human rights, as it involves a variety of theoretical inputs on the underlying values, as well as a proliferation of guidelines. This requires a contextualised and, as far as possible, a participative analysis of the values of the community in which the AI solutions are expected to be implemented. Here the experts play a crucial role in detecting, contextualising and evaluating the AI solutions against existing ethical and social values. Ethics committees in scientific

A. Mantelero, *Beyond Data*, Information Technology and Law Series 36,
https://doi.org/10.1007/978-94-6265-531-7_3

research, bioethics and clinical trials, as well as corporate AI ethics boards, can provide inputs for future AI expert committees within the HRESIA model. Based on the experience of these committees, the assessment cannot be entrusted entirely to experts, but it should also include a participatory dimension, which is essential to effective democratic decision-making process concerning AI.

Keywords Clinical Ethics Committees · Clinical trials · Ethics committee · Data ethics · Ethical values · Ethics boards · Participation · Research Ethics Committees · Social values

3.1 Beyond Human Rights Impact Assessment

In the previous chapter, we discussed the role of human rights impact assessment (HRIA) in removing or mitigating potential adverse impacts of data-intensive systems based on AI. However, the focus on these possible consequences does not eliminate the risk of other negative social effects concerning the relation between technology and human beings.

Although legal principles, including human rights, embed ethical and societal values, not all these values assume legal relevance. Moreover, the codification of these values in legal principles necessarily embodies them in specific provisions, shaping them in a way that is different from general and abstract ethical or societal values.

There is a sphere of social and ethical issues and values that is not reflected in legal provisions but is relevant in defining a given community's approach to the use of data-intensive AI systems. If we consider, for example, smart city projects, solving all the issues concerning the impact on rights and freedoms does not exclude questions about the social acceptability of these projects.[1]

Deciding whether we want an urban environment heavily monitored by sensors, where city life is determined by the technocratic vision of the big platforms, and whether we want to give AI the responsibility for deciding student admissions to university or patient admissions to intensive care, are choices that raise big ethical societal questions.

Such questions concern the society we want to see, the way we want to shape human relationships, the role we want to leave to technology and its designers. These ethical and societal questions are very close to those we face when deciding to develop a new medical treatment impacting on individual health, entailing benefits and risks.

[1] See the Sidewalk case in Chap. 2, Sect. 2.4.2.

The latest wave of AI developments raises ethical and societal concerns about the dehumanisation of society,[2] the over-reliance on AI,[3] the value-dependent approach unintentionally or intentionally embedded in some applications, the prevalence of a socio-technical deterministic approach,[4] the dominant role of big players and their agenda in shaping the digital environment without due democratic process.

These and other similar issues are either not legal questions, or not fully addressed by the existing legal framework. It has meant interest has grown around the potential role of ethical principles, including social values in a broader notion of data ethics.

Nevertheless, from the outset, the debate on data ethics has been characterised by an improper overlap between ethics and law, in particular with regard to human rights. In this sense, it has been suggested that ethical challenges should be addressed by "fostering the development and applications of data science while ensuring the respect of human rights and of the values shaping open, pluralistic and tolerant information societies".[5] We can summarise this approach as 'ethics first': ethics plays a central role in technology regulation because it is the root of any regulatory approach, the pre-legal humus that is more important than ever where existing rules do not address or only partially address technological challenges.

Another argument in favour of the central role of ethics comes out of what that we might call the 'ethics after' approach.[6] In the concrete application of human rights we necessarily have to balance competing interests. This balance test is not based only on the rights themselves but also on the underlying ethical values, meaning that the human rights framework is largely incomplete without ethics.

Both these approaches are only partially correct. It is true that human rights have their roots in ethics. There is an extensive literature on the relationship between ethics and law, which over the years has been described by various authors as identification, separation, complementation, and interweavement.[7] Similarly, the influence of ethical values and more in general of societal issues in court decisions and balancing tests is known and has been investigated by various disciplines, including sociology, law & economics and psychology.

Here the point is not to cut off the ethical roots, but to recognise that rights and freedoms flourish on the basis of the shape given them by law provisions and case law. There is no conflict between ethical values and human rights, but the latter represent a specific crystallisation of these values that are circumscribed and contextualised by legal provisions and judicial decisions.

---

[2] Annual report of the UN High Commissioner for Human Rights and reports of the Office of the High Commissioner and the Secretary-General 2020, pp. 5–6.

[3] Jacobs et al. 2021.

[4] Holton and Boyd 2021.

[5] Floridi and Taddeo 2016, p. 374.

[6] Canca 2019.

[7] Cortina 2000.

This reflection may lead to a broader discussion of the role of ethics in the legal realm, but this study takes a more pragmatic and concrete approach by reframing the interplay between these two domains within the context of AI and focusing on the regulatory consequences of adopting an approach based on ethics rather than human rights.

The main question should be formulated as follows: what are the consequences of framing the regulatory debate around ethical issues? Four different consequences can be identified: (1) uncertainty, (2) heterogeneity, (3) context dependence, (4) risks of a 'transplant' of ethical values.

3.1.1 The Socio-ethical Framework: Uncertainty, Heterogeneity and Context Dependence

As far as uncertainty is concerned, this is due to the improper overlap between law and ethics in ethical guidelines.[8] While it is true that these two realms are intertwined in various ways, from a regulatory perspective the distinction between ethical imperatives and binding provisions is important. Taking a pragmatic approach, relying on a framework of general ethical values (such as beneficence, non-maleficence, etc.), on codes of conduct and ethical boards is not the same as adopting technological solutions on the basis of binding rules.

This difference is not only due to the different levels of enforcement, but also to the more fundamental problem of uncertainty about specific requirements. Stating that "while many legal obligations reflect ethical principles, adherence to ethical principles goes beyond formal compliance with existing laws"[9] is not enough to clarify the added value of the proposed ethical principles and their concrete additional regulatory impact.[10]

Given the different levels of binding nature and enforcement, shifting the focus from law to ethics and reformulating legal requirements as ethical duties open the doors to de-regulation and self-regulation. Rather than binding rules, business can therefore benefit from a more flexible framework based on corporate codes of ethics.[11]

---

[8] Raab 2020 ("The products in the 'turn' to ethics often look more like 'data protection-plus' than a different kind of encounter with some of the age-old issues and concepts in the study and practice of ethics, and how to embed them in practice"); van Dijk et al. 2021.

[9] Independent High-Level Expert Group on Artificial Intelligence set up by the European Commission (hereinafter AI HLEG) 2019, p. 12.

[10] Independent High-Level Expert Group on Artificial Intelligence set up by the European Commission 2019, p. 12. The principle of respect for human autonomy, for example, is detailed in self-determination, democratic process and human oversight, general categories that have an ethical origin but already have a concrete legal implementation providing a better and more detailed framework for the development of provisions relating to AI.

[11] Wagner 2018; Taylor and Dencik 2020; Ienca and Vayena 2020.

This generates uncertainty in the regulatory framework. When ethical guidelines refer to human oversight, safety, privacy, data governance, transparency, diversity, non-discrimination, fairness, and accountability as key principles, they largely refer to legal principles that already have their contextualisation in specific provisions in different fields. The added value of a new generalisation of these legal principles and their concrete applications is unclear and potentially dangerous: product safety and data governance, for instance, should not be perceived as mere ethical duties, but companies need to be aware of their binding nature and related legal consequences.

Moreover, ethical principles are characterised by an inherent heterogeneity due to the different ethical positions taken by philosophers over the centuries. Virtue ethics, deontological or consequentialist approaches[12] can lead to different conclusions on ethical issues. AI developers or manufacturers might opt for different ethical paradigms (note that those mentioned are limited to the Western tradition only), making harmonised regulation difficult.

Similarly, the context-dependence of ethical values entails their variability depending on the social context or social groups considered, as well as the different ethical traditions.

By contrast, although the universal nature of human rights necessarily entails contextualised application through national laws, which partially create context dependency and can lead to a certain degree of heterogeneity,[13] human rights seem to provide a more stable framework. The different charters, with their provisions, but also regional courts (such as the European Court of Human Rights), and a coherent legal doctrine based on international experience can all help to reduce this dependence on context.

This does not mean that human rights do not present contextual differences, but compared with ethical values, they are clearer, better defined, and stable. From a regulatory perspective, this facilitates a better harmonisation and reduces the risk of uncertainty.

3.1.2 The Risk of a 'Transplant' of Ethical Values

A largely unaddressed issue in the current debate on AI and ethics concerns the methodological approach that we might call the 'transplant' of ethical values. This is related to the risk of considering data ethics as a mere extension of ethical principles already existing and applied in other fields.

The experience of the Institutional Review Boards (IRBs) clearly shows the limitations of such an approach. As historical research has shown, the set of values

[12] Verbeek 2011, pp. 30–33 and 61–63.

[13] Levitt and Merry 2009; Benhabib 2008; Engle Merry 2006; O'sullivan 1998.

used by IRBs has, for long time, been influenced by a kind of ethical imperialism[14] in favour of the medical science, following the principles laid down after the Nazi criminal experiments involving human beings and in response to important cases of questionable studies.[15]

The important role of medical ethics in this debate has led regulators to adapt the model created for biomedical research to social science, without considering or underestimating the differences of these fields.[16] This was not the result of a deliberate intention to impose biomedical ethics on other disciplines, but the consequence of not taking in to account the variety of fields of application.

Biomedical research has a methodology based on hypotheses and testing, which means research goals defied at the outset of data collection and a specific and detailed protocol to achieve them. In addition, biomedical experiments have an impact on the physical and psychological condition of the people involved, whereas social sciences and data processing for social analysis do not necessarily produce these effects.

Finally, physicians have an ethical duty to do no harm and to benefit their patients, whereas social sciences and data analysis may be merely descriptive or, in certain circumstances, may create legitimate harm (e.g. use of data to detect crimes, with consequent harm to offenders in terms of sanction, or algorithms used to decide between alternative solutions involving potential damages, as in the case of industrial/car accidents).

Considering these differences, the 1960s debate on extending biomedical ethics to social sciences,[17] and the extensive use of AI systems for social analysis, the experience of IRBs thus provides an important warning in framing the debate on ethical assessment of AI, highlighting the consequences of a 'transplant' of ethical values.

In addition, the current ethical debate may render this transplant obscure, as many ethical guidelines and charters do not explain which ethical approach has been or should be considered, even in relation to general ethical frameworks. Deontological ethics, utilitarian ethics, virtue ethics, for example, are just some of the different possible ways of framing ethical discourse, but they imply different perspectives in setting guidelines on the moral implications of human actions.

To investigate whether these potential risks associated to the circulation of ethical models are present in the data ethics debate, an empirical analysis is required, focusing on the ethical guidelines for AI proposed and adopted by various organisations. To this end, we can benefit from several studies carried out to identify the key values of these guidelines.[18]

---

[14] Schrag 2010.

[15] Beecher 1966.

[16] Schrag 2010, pp. 84–95.

[17] Fichter and Kolb 1953; Schrag 2010, pp. 78–95.

[18] E.g. Jobin et al. 2019. The authors identified ten key ethical values within a set of 84 policy documents with the following distribution: transparency 73/84; non-maleficence 60/84; responsibility 60/84; privacy 47/84; beneficence 41/84; freedom and autonomy 34/84; trust 28/84; sustainability 14/84; dignity 13/84, and solidarity 6/84.

Although these studies suffer from certain limitations – the use of grey literature, search engines for content selection, linguistic biases, and a quantitative text-based approach that underestimates the policy perspective and contextual analysis[19] – they do provide an overview of the operational dimension of data ethics.

Based on this evidence, we can see that there is a small core of values that are present in most documents.[20] Five of them are ethical values with a strong legal implementation (transparency, responsibility, privacy, freedom and autonomy) and only two come from the ethical discourse (non-maleficence and beneficence).

Another study[21] identified several guiding values and the top nine, with a frequency of 50% or more, are: privacy protection; fairness, non-discrimination and justice; accountability; transparency and openness; safety and cybersecurity; common good, sustainability and well-being; human oversight, control and auditing; solidarity, inclusion and social cohesion; explainability and interpretability. As in the previous study, the aggregating of these principles is necessarily influenced by the categories used by the authors to reduce the variety of principles. In this case, if we exclude values with a legal implementation, the key ethical values are limited to openness, the common good, well-being and solidarity.

If we take a qualitative approach, restricting the analysis to the document adopted by the main European organisations and to those documents with a general and non-sectoral perspective,[22] we can better identify the key values that are most popular among rule makers.

Considering the four core principles[23] identified by the High-Level Expert Group on Artificial Intelligence (HLEGAI),[24] respect for human autonomy and fairness are widely developed legal principles in the field of human rights and law in general, while explicability is more a technical requirement than a principle. Regarding the seven requirements[25] identified by the HLEGAI on the basis of these principles, human agency and oversight are further specified as respect for fundamental rights, informed autonomous decisions, the right not to be subject to purely

[19] Differing sources are considered at the same level, without taking into account the difference between the guidelines adopted by governmental bodies, independent authorities, private or public ad hoc committees, big companies, NGOs, academia, intergovernmental bodies etc. The mere frequency of occurrence does not reveal the impacts of the distribution of these values among the different categories. For instance, the fact that some values are common to several intergovernmental documents may have a greater policy impact than the same frequency in a cluster of NGOs or academic documents. When the focus is on values for future regulation, albeit based on ethics, the varying relevance of the sources in terms of political impact is important.

[20] Jobin et al. 2019.

[21] Hagendorff 2020, p. 102.

[22] E.g. Council of Europe – European Commission for the Efficiency of Justice (CEPEJ) 2018.

[23] Respect for human autonomy, Prevention of harm, Fairness, Explicability.

[24] Independent High-Level Expert Group on Artificial Intelligence set up by the European Commission 2019.

[25] Human agency and oversight; Technical robustness and safety; Privacy and data governance; Transparency; Diversity, non-discrimination, and fairness; Societal and environmental wellbeing; Accountability.

automated decisions, and adoption of oversight mechanisms. These are all requirements already present in the law in various forms, especially with regard to data processing. The same applies to the remaining requirements (technical robustness and safety, privacy and data governance; transparency; diversity, non-discrimination and fairness; accountability; and environmental well-being).

Looking at the entire set of values provided by the HLEGAI, the only two elements – as framed in the document – that are partially considered by the law are the principle of harm prevention – where "harms can be individual or collective, and can include intangible harm to social, cultural and political environments" – and the broad requirement of societal wellbeing, which generally requires a social impact assessment.

Another important EU document identifies nine core ethical principles and democratic prerequisites.[26] Amongst them, four have a broader content that goes beyond the legal context (human dignity, autonomy, solidarity and sustainability). However, in the field of law and technology, human dignity and autonomy are two key values widely considered both in the human rights framework and in specific legal instruments.

Based on the results of these different analytical methodologies (quantitative, qualitative), we can identify three main groups of values that expand the legal framework. The first consists of broad principles derived from ethical and sociological theory (common good, well-being, solidarity). These principles can play a crucial role in addressing societal issues concerning the use of AI, but their broad nature might be a limitation if they are not properly investigated and contextualised.

A second group includes the principle of non-maleficence, the principle of beneficence,[27] and the related broader notion of harm prevention (harm to social, cultural, and political environments). These are not new and undefined principles, especially in the field of applied ethics and research and medical ethics. They can play an important role in AI, but we should therefore consider the potential risk of the 'transplant' of ethical values, discussed above.[28]

The last group, which includes openness, explicability and sustainability, seems already partially integrated in legal provisions although a context-specific

---

[26] European Commission – European Group on Ethics in Science and New Technologies 2018. These are the ethical principles and democratic prerequisites identified: Human dignity; Autonomy; Responsibility; Justice, equity, and solidarity; Democracy; Rule of law and accountability; Security, safety, bodily and mental integrity; Data protection and privacy; Sustainability.

[27] Although in the final version of the Independent High-Level Expert Group on Artificial Intelligence set up by the European Commission 2019, these two principles are not explicitly listed as key values, they do underpin the whole approach of the HLEGAI, as demonstrated by the draft guidelines used for the public consultation; see Independent High-Level Expert Group on Artificial Intelligence set up by the European Commission 2018 ("Ensure that AI is human-centric: AI should be developed, deployed and used with an "ethical purpose", grounded in, and reflective of, fundamental rights, societal values and the ethical principles of Beneficence (do good), Non-Maleficence (do no harm), Autonomy of humans, Justice, and Explicability. This is crucial to work towards Trustworthy AI.").

[28] See also Schrag 2010.

application of these principles in the field of AI is possible and desirable. However, these values are more closely related to a technical implementation, via specific standards or procedures to ensure their application.

This analysis of the empirical evidence on ethical values that should underpin AI-based systems shows a limited risk of 'transplant' of ethical values and, where ethical values are correctly framed, the ability to avoid improper overlap between ethical and legal realms and values.

It is therefore crucial to properly consider the social and ethical consequences of these systems as a complementary additional analysis to the human rights impact assessment, avoiding any confusion between these different layers. The ethical and societal dimensions should be included in the models and process adopted in AI design and development, to capture the holistic definition of the relationship between humans and machines.

At the same time, we should be aware that these general values, such as the common good, well-being, solidarity, are highly context based, more than human rights. This local and community dimension should therefore be considered in referring to them and properly framed.

3.1.3 Embedding Ethical and Societal Values

Assuming the existence of socio-ethical values that could or should guide us in defining the relationship between AI systems and potentially impacted individuals and groups, we need to ask whether and how these values can become part of these systems.

Looking at the evolution of the relationship between ethics and technology,[29] the original external standpoint adopted by philosophers, which viewed technology as an autonomous phenomenon with its own potentially negative impacts on society, has been progressively replaced by a greater focus on sector-specific forms of technology.

This enables us to go beyond a formal separation between ethics and technology, where the first merely concerns the social dimension without concurring in co-shaping technology itself.[30] This approach is evident, for instance, in technological mediation theory[31] which highlights the active role of technology in mediating between humans and reality as well as between individuals.

Recognising technology's active role in co-shaping human experience[32] necessarily leads us to consider how technology plays this role and to focus on the values

---

[29] Verbeek 2011, pp. 3–6 and 21–40.

[30] Latour 1999, pp. 174–215.

[31] Verbeek 2011.

[32] See also Manders-Huits and van den Hoven 2009, pp. 55–56.

underpinning technological artefacts and how they are transposed in society through technology.[33] At the same time, it is important not to describe this dynamic in terms of mere human-machine interaction, considering the machine as something given without recognising the role played by designers,[34] and their values, in defining the ethical orientation of these artefacts.

Against this background, technology cannot be considered as neutral, but as the result of both the values – intentionally or unintentionally – embedded in devices/ services and the role of mediation played by the different technologies and their applications.[35] These considerations, applied to data-intensive systems, confirm the central role of value assessment and design supporting the idea of ethical assessment and the ethical by-design approach to product/service development.

While the ethical debate focuses on the moral agency of technological artefacts[36] and the role of human-technological interaction, legal analysis focuses more closely on individual responsibility in a broader sense. Indeed, the theoretical framework of strict liability and vicarious liability encourages us to look beyond the human-technology interaction and consider a tripartite relationship between, humans (users), technology (artefacts) and those humans in a position to decide which values are embedded in the technology (designers, in general terms).

From this perspective, the issues concerning the new machine age are not circumscribed by the morality of these machines but involve the role of both the designer and the users who can shape or co-shape the ethical values embedded in the machine and transmitted through technology.

This awareness of the role of designers and users is also present in the studies on technology mediation which recommend risk assessment.[37] Moreover, AI applications and ML processes highlight how the technology has not reached a level of maturity to justify labelling AI applications as moral agents and, at the same time, how users play an active role in the applications' learning phases.[38]

For these reasons, it is important to address the general responsibility for decision-making choices in AI design, remembering that these choices contain three

---

[33] See also Latour 1992, pp. 225–58.

[34] This is also in line with the technological mediation theory; Verbeek 2011, p. 90 ("since technologies are inherently moral entities, designer have a seminal role in eventual technological mediation of moral actions and decisions").

[35] Latour 2002; Ihde 1990.

[36] Verbeek 2011, pp. 41–65.

[37] Verbeek 2011, pp. 109, 129, and 164–165 ("Accompanying technological developments requires engagement with designers and users, identifying points of application for moral reflection, and anticipating the social impact of technologies-in-design […] In order to develop responsible forms of use and design, we need to equip users ad designer with frameworks and methods to anticipate, assess, ad design the mediating role of technologies in people's lives and in the ways we organize society").

[38] In terms of practical consequences, it is unclear what benefit there is in considering AI applications as moral agents, since – as demonstrated by strict liability and vicarious liability in the field of law – it is only possible to orient the product towards specific values by having influence on designers and manufacturers.

separate components: technological feasibility, legal compliance, and socio-ethical acceptability. Thus, we avoid the simplistic conclusion that feasibility is the only driver of tech development: not everything that is feasible is also legal, and not everything that is both feasible and legal is also acceptable from an ethical and social standpoint.

As discussed above, the legislation does not cover ethical and social issues. These are either unexplored by law or irrelevant or neutral from a legal perspective (e.g., alternative policy solutions such as predictive crime prevention policing or social aid plans) and therefore outside its sphere of action. Moreover, ethical and social values are not the mere projection of individual ideas but the result of a given cultural context.

In addition, ethical values should be carefully embedded in technology, bearing in mind the known difficulties in ethically assessing unforeseen applications[39] and the potential conflict between the ethical values embedded in AI systems and freedom of choice, both at collective and individual level.[40]

In addressing these issues several approaches can be taken to recognise the importance of an ethical and societal assessment of data-intensive systems based on AI, the most frequently adopted being ethical guidelines, questionnaires, and the appointment of ethics committees.

The first two options – ethical guidelines and questionnaires – retrace the steps made in the legal realm in the socio-ethical context. Guidelines add complementary ethical provisions to the existing legal requirements, and, similarly, additional questions or sections on ethics and social issues are introduced in impact assessment models. However, both these approaches have their limitations.

As discussed in the previous section with regard to the role of ethics, guidelines can be affected by uncertainty and heterogeneity, due to an improper interplay between ethics and human rights and the variety of possible ethical approaches. In addition, ethical guidelines may reflect corporate values or approaches and, more in general, values defined outside a participatory process that reflects societal beliefs.

Regarding the use of questionnaires to embed ethical and societal values in AI system design, this option may more clearly emphasise the contextual component of the sociotechnical dimension, but again there are constraints.

First, questionnaires often contain only vague and limited questions about societal and ethical issues, in assessment models that favour other concerns, such as legal ones.

Second, criticisms of the value-oriented approaches adopted by corporations can be equally made of the way the questions are worded and the areas they investigate.

---

[39] For some examples on unforeseen and radically different applications of technology, see Verbeek 2011, pp. 57–58.

[40] Verbeek 2011, p. 112. At the collective level, a possible response to this critical issue concerning freedom of choice could be to encourage the participation of potentially affected people – see Sect. 3.4 below – and, at the individual level, to give users the opportunity to personalise the set of values embedded in AI products/services, see Chap. 2, Sect. 2.4.1.

But the biggest problem with the use of questionnaires is their mediated nature. While the human rights section of an HRIA questionnaire refers to an existing legal framework and its implementation in a given case, here this framework is absent.

Before assessing how ethical and social values are embedded in AI solutions, we need therefore to define these values, which are not specified in the provisions or in case law and vary much more widely than legal values.

As such, questions about existing ethical and social values are unable to guide the user of the questionnaire in a comparison between the As-Is and To-Be, since the second element in this equation is not defined. In the end, these questions require experts or a community able to interpret them on the basis of an understanding and familiarity with the given cultural context in which the data-intensive system will be developed and deployed.

Questionnaires on ethical and societal values underpinning AI systems are therefore important, but more a means than an end. They require panels of experts and stakeholder engagement to provide proper feedback to guide the implementation of those values in the system.

It is these expert panels and stakeholders' participation that represent the true core of the process of embedding ethical and societal values in AI systems design.

3.1.4 The Role of the Committee of Experts: Corporate Case Studies

The potential role of expert panels has been recognised by companies involved in AI development over the last few years, with the creation of committees of experts to give advice on the challenges associated with the use of data-intensive AI systems.

These panels are frequently known as ethical boards and share some common features which can help us to determine if this is the most adequate and effective way to deploy experts in AI design and development.

A well-documented case study is the Facebook Oversight Board, created by Facebook "to promote free expression by making principled, independent decisions regarding content on Facebook and Instagram and by issuing recommendations on the relevant Facebook Company Content Policy".[41] To achieve this goal the Oversight Board reviews a select number of "highly emblematic cases", determines whether decisions were made in accordance with Facebook's stated values and policies and issues binding decisions.[42]

[41] For a critical analysis of the reasons leading Facebook to this move: Klonick 2020; Douek 2019.

[42] Oversight Board Charter, Article 4 ("The board's resolution of each case will be binding and Facebook will implement it promptly, unless implementation of a resolution could violate the law") https://oversightboard.com/. Accessed 2 May 2021.

Although Facebook moderates three million posts every day[43] and in 2020 its Oversight Board reviewed only seven cases (representing a rate of 0.00023%) and 16 in 2021, it has been pointed out that even a limited but well selected sample of cases can significantly contribute to reshaping the core features of the service.[44] However, this conclusion entails two shortcomings that we should consider.

First, a supervisory body created by a company selects emblematic cases specifically to highlight weaknesses in the company's services/products. This happened in the case of the Oversight Board, where decided cases addressed the core issues of transparency of content moderation and criteria, the quantity of resources available for content moderation, harmonisation of company self-regulation standards, the role of human intervention, and the accuracy of automated content moderation systems.

Given that the main outcome of these decisions is generalised, concerning the way the company shapes its product/service, rather than on decided cases, a question arises: is an Oversight Board necessary or could the same result be achieved through an auditing process? In this case, possible issues with transparency, harmonisation, etc. could be spotted and analysed by truly independent[45] auditors[46] reviewing the content moderation decision-making process, without necessarily adopting a case-specific approach.

Second, in its analysis, the Facebook Oversight Board performs a kind of conformity assessment. By evaluating the application of Facebook's self-regulation[47] in each case – albeit within the human rights framework – the Board does not consider the overall and highly debated impact of the social network and its policies.[48] This limitation is even more significant as the Board's remit is limited to removed content and does not cover the entire service (behavioural advertising, personal data exploitation etc.).

On this basis, it is hard to see the Oversight Board as a model for a committee that can contribute to embedding societal and ethical values in the design of AI systems. The Oversight Board does not focus on the overall impact of the application, but considers it and the adopted technologies as given. The Board only assesses their functioning and how to improve some procedural aspects, without questioning the design of the AI-based social network and its broader overall impact on individuals and society.

Compared with the Facebook Oversight Board, the case of the Axon AI Ethics Board is more closely focused on product/service design. While the Oversight

---

[43] Barrett 2020, p. 4.

[44] Douek 2021.

[45] Coleman et al. 2021, who highlight the "inherent conflict that all members are on the payroll of the conglomerate. And by its very design, the FOB cannot provide truly impartial global governance and accountability, and thereby allows FB to sidestep responsibility".

[46] See also BSR 2019.

[47] See also Klonick 2018.

[48] E.g. Lewandowsky and Smillie 2020.

Board examines only a narrow part of Facebook's products/services, reviewing content moderation in contentious cases, the Axon Ethics Board's mission is "to provide expert guidance to Axon on the development of its AI products and services, paying particular attention to its impact on communities".[49]

Axon's Board was set up to give advice on specific products/services and in particular on their design while they are in the development phase.[50] More specifically, with regard to AI, the company is committed to providing the board with meaningful information about the logic involved in building its algorithms, the data on which the models are trained, and the inputs used, explaining the measures taken to mitigate adverse effects, such as bias and misuse.

This is in line with Axon's Product Evaluation Framework,[51] a risk assessment focusing on key aspects to be considered in evaluating the social benefits and costs during product development.[52] Here the main concerns, given Axon's area of operation,[53] are technology misuse, criminalisation of persons, personal data processing, potential biases and transparency, but it also includes larger categories ("violation of constitutional or other legal rights" and "potential social costs") which can broaden the analysis. The self-assessment is performed by the company during the developmental phase and then reviewed by the Ethics Board.[54]

The interaction between the company and the Board, based on the latter's recommendations[55] and the way these are addressed by the company is only partially documented in the company's reports on Ethics Board activity. While this is a limit in terms of transparency, the information presented does demonstrate a dialogue between the Board and the company on single technology applications, and a partial acceptance of the Board's recommendations by the company which has introduced changes in the products/services.[56]

A key issue in this regard concerns full access to information about products and services, as Board members are not part of the company. In this case the members of the Ethics Board signed a specific non-disclosure agreement (NDA), including

[49] https://www.axon.com/company/ai-and-policing-technology-ethics. Accessed 8 May 2021.

[50] Axon AI Ethics Board's operating principles, available at https://www.axon.com/company/ai-and-policing-technology-ethics. Accessed 8 May 2021 ("When considering a new AI application or police technology for which there may be substantial ethical risks, we will ensure that the board has an opportunity to discuss its pros and cons, and how it can be done most ethically. We will discuss new products with the board before launching a product that raises ethical concerns so that that they can provide us with guidance on new product development").

[51] Axon, Product Evaluation Framework. https://axon-2.cdn.prismic.io/axon-2/e7e5a399-30dd-47b0-98f0-55efe6f1bf28_Axon+Product+Evaluation+Framework.pdf. Accessed 8 May 2021.

[52] Axon AI Ethics Board 2020, pp. 5–6.

[53] Axon's core business covers technology and weapons for military, law enforcement and civilians, such as Taser electroshock weapons, body cameras, and cloud-based digital evidence services.

[54] Axon AI Ethics Board 2020, p. 6.

[55] Axon AI Ethics Board 2019a, b.

[56] Axon AI Ethics Board 2020, pp. 6–9.

trade secrets, proprietary information, and information about in-development products. The use of NDAs, which does not hamper the activity of the Ethics Board and facilitates dialogue with the company, raises concerns about effective interaction with potentially affected communities and stakeholders.[57]

It is worth noting that Axon has also designated two ombudspersons (a designated Axon employee who is a member of the Ethics Board and sits outside of the internal chain of command and a non-company member of the Ethics Board) who can be contacted by employees who have concerns about the implementation of the Product Evaluation Framework in specific cases, and the Board is available to hear those concerns without fear of attribution.

As with the Facebook's Oversight Board, Axon's Ethics Board does not take a participatory approach as such giving voice to potentially affected communities and groups.[58]

While the decisions of Facebook's Oversight Board are binding for the company – though limited to content moderation issues –, Axon's Ethics Board can only provide recommendations, like the Oversight Board with regard to Facebook's Content Policy. This implies that business interests can easily override any ethical concerns expressed by the Ethics Board.[59]

Despite the differences described, both Facebook and Axon created ethical boards which have had an impact on product/service design or use, and have documented this impact in their reports or decisions.

In a second group of cases, companies have set up ethical boards, but the concrete effect of their work is either unclear or, at any rate not made properly public.

This is the case of the AI Ethics Advisory Board set up in 2021 by Arena Analytics (predictive analytics and machine learning for the hiring process), bringing together experts from academia, technology, human resources, and ethics. The focus of this board is developing guidance "to help Arena manage competing ethical obligations".[60] However, the concrete outcome and impact on the business model or product/service is not documented, nor are the procedures involved in board selection and its work.

---

[57] Axon AI Ethics Board 2019a, p. 14 ("Board members have signed limited non-disclosure agreements (NDAs)").

[58] Letter to the Axon Ethics Board signed by 42 organizations in April 26, 2018. https://www.eff.org/it/document/42-organizations-letter-axons-ai-ethics-board. Accessed 8 May 2021 ("But an ethics process that does not center the voices of those who live in the most heavily policed communities will have no legitimacy. The Board must invite, consult, and ultimately center in its deliberations the voices of affected individuals and those that directly represent affected communities").

[59] Axon AI Ethics Board 2020, pp. 6–9.

[60] Area, AI Ethics Advisory Board, 13 January 2021. https://arena.io/ai-ethics-advisory-board/. Accessed 15 May 2021.

Similarly, SAP (enterprise application software) set up an AI Ethics Advisory Panel[61] of academics, policy experts and industry experts, to advise the company on the development and operationalisation of its AI guiding principles. This external body interacts with an internal AI Ethics Steering Committee which consists of company executives "from all board areas with supervision of topics that are relevant to guiding and implementing AI Ethics" and advises company teams on how specific use cases are affected by these principles.

The interesting aspect of the SAP model is the presence of an internal unit focused on ethical issues (the AI Ethics Steering Committee), which includes the figure of Chief Ethics Officer with an expanded role through the wider participation of all executives dealing with ethical issues. It is worth noting that the broader AI Ethics Steering Committee should not be considered as an alternative to the Chief Ethics Officer, since the function-based AI Ethics Steering Committee, centred on the executive position in a given area, is not necessarily related to an ethical remit. A Chief Ethics Officer could therefore be of help in internally raising and managing ethical issues. The role could be also played by an external body, such as SAP's AI Ethics Advisory Panel, but in the SAP case this panel seems not to have this function, providing the company with more general advice on the development and operationalisation of the company's guiding ethical principles, rather than case-specific advice.

A different approach is adopted by Salesforce in appointing an internal Chief Ethical and Humane Use Officer and an external Advisory Council to the Office of Ethical and Humane Use of Technology composed of "a diverse group of frontline and executive employees – as well as academics, industry experts, and society leaders from Harvard, Carnegie Mellon, Stanford, and more".[62] In this case, the positive presence of a dedicated officer with a specific background is compromised by the lack of information available on the identity of the members of external ethics body.

In all three cases, the lack of information on the workings of these bodies or documentation of their work necessarily limits our evaluation of their effectiveness in implementing ethical values in the companies' practices and products/services.

A third approach by corporations is the setting up of ethics boards without specific information on concrete objectives, compositions or procedures. This is the case of IBM's internal AI Ethics Board, which "is comprised of a cross-disciplinary team of senior IBMers, co-chaired by IBM's Chief Privacy Officer and AI Ethics Global Leader, and reports to the highest levels of the company", but the list of its members is not publicly available, nor is its concrete impact on the company's strategy.[63]

Summing up these case studies involving some of the major AI players, we can group the ethics boards into three categories. A first group of boards play an active role in the companies' business, have appointed members whose identity is known,

---

[61] https://www.sap.com/products/artificial-intelligence/ai-ethics.html. Accessed 15 May 2021.

[62] https://www.salesforce.com/company/ethical-and-humane-use/. Accessed 15 May 2021.

[63] https://www.ibm.org/responsibility/2019/case-studies/aiethicsboard ("This has created a robust governance framework that permeates IBM's culture and our decision-making – connecting principles with practice"). Accessed 15 May 2021.

put into place internal procedures, defined tasks and the firm's commitment to take into account the boards' inputs. In a second group, the boards' tasks and members are clear, but the concrete interaction and impact on company decisions is not documented. Finally, there is a third group where the identity of the board members is unknown and there is only a general description of the board's main purpose.

Such empirical evidence allows us to make some general considerations:

(i) Corporate AI ethics boards demonstrate a variety of structures, including internal and external bodies.
(ii) They also show a variety of remits, providing general advice and guidelines, product/service advice, usage policies,[64] self-assessment ethics questionnaires,[65] and in some cases more indefinite tasks.
(iii) The independence and high-profile reputation of the board members is crucial.
(iv) Greater transparency about the structure and the functioning (internal procedures) of these bodies is required, including their impact on companies' decision-making processes.
(v) Their effectiveness may be affected by decisions regarding staffing and access to information.
(vi) These bodies can be coupled with external ombudspersons/advisory councils.
(vii) Internal requests to ethical boards regarding critical issues/cases play an important role.
(viii) Accountability should be fostered with regard to company decisions on the basis of the boards' recommendations or instructions.
(ix) Only in limited cases and concerning users' interests/rights (see e.g., Facebook) are the decisions of these boards mandatory for the company.
(x) While the guiding values of these boards often refer to human rights and fundamental freedoms, companies commonly specify the principles and corporate values that drive the boards' decisions.

We can therefore conclude that there is no uniform model for corporate ethics boards in AI systems, but a wide range of solutions. Nevertheless, the various shortcomings highlighted in the case studies can help us to identify the core elements required for general AI ethical oversight: independence and reputation of the board, values-orientation, effectiveness, transparency, and accountability.

[64] Axon AI Ethics Board 2019b, p. 41.
[65] Axon AI Ethics Board 2019b, p. 46.

3.2 Existing Models in Medical Ethics and Research Committees

Medical ethics represents an interesting field for a comparative analysis with the challenges of AI, as clinical situations often face conflicts of values, where none of the proposed alternatives is entirely free of problems, even if they are not actually against the law.

For this reason, medical ethics was the first field in which the ethical review process was adopted following abuses, conflicting interests, and human rights violations.[66] In order to address the variety of medical activities (healthcare practice, research, drug production) various types of ethical committee have been set up, each with a different focus, nature and goal: (i) Clinical Ethics Committees (Healthcare/Hospital Ethics Committees); (ii) Research Ethics Committees (Institutional Review Boards or IRBs in the US); (iii) Ethics committees for clinical trials.

Some of these committees are specifically regulated by law and a legal requirement to carry out certain activities. This is the case with Ethics committees for clinical trials and Research Ethics Committees in certain fields, while the Clinical Ethics Committees, are often created on a voluntary basis, though in some cases regulated by law.

This section does not set out to investigate the regulatory framework, origin, or underpinning values of these committees, but their operational models. This is why these cases, often with a long history and consolidated structure, can help us see how to embed ethical and societal values through similar committees in the AI sector. What is more, awareness of the strengths and weakness of these models will prevent their mere transposition[67] to AI, taking the most valuable elements of the existing models to facilitate better expert committee design.

3.2.1 Clinical Ethics Committees

Given the lack of a specific regulation in many cases and their voluntary nature, Clinical Ethics Committees (CECs) might be an option to consider as a potential model for expert committees in AI, in the absence of legal requirements in this respect.

CECs, also known as Hospital Ethics Committees, are part of the larger category of clinical ethics support services[68] for healthcare professionals or patients. They

[66] Schrag 2010, Chapter 1.

[67] On the difficulty in generalising the principles established in biomedicine to other fields more recently concerned with ethical impacts, Schrag 2010; Brey et al. 2017.

[68] Doran et al. 2016, p. 26. On the historical development of the Hospital Ethics Committees in the US, where they were first emerged, McGee et al. 2002.

first appeared in the late 1970s and have spread widely across the globe with a variety of structures and functions.[69]

Their main tasks are to: (i) address ethical issues relating to medical practice (reactive role); (ii) perform an educational function with field training based on discussions during CEC meetings (proactive role); (iii) review institutional policies.[70] Meanwhile their crucial achievements are to give voice to the different actors involved in clinical practice on ethical questions (physicians, patients, patients' families), foster a multidisciplinary approach, and raise awareness on actual practices and related ethical issues.

They may be made up in different ways, an ethicist model centred on an individual ethics expert,[71] multi-disciplinary committees or small sub-groups of a larger ethics committee.[72] They may adopt a top-down or a bottom-up approach,[73] either emphasising the expert advisory role[74] or assisting healthcare personnel in handling ethical questions in day-to-day clinical practice.[75] Rights-holder and stakeholder involvement may also vary from one model to another, including a complete absence of involvement.

The main challenges they face are (i) risk of outsourcing clinicians' decisions and responsibilities to these committees, (ii) limited effective patient participation in a model that should be patient-centred,[76] and (iii) lack of adequate financial resources and organisational commitment.[77]

A possible alternative is Moral Case Deliberation[78] where all those involved in an ethical decision meet to discuss and think through the moral aspects of a particular patient case with the support of an external figure who can facilitate dialogue without having the authority to decide or suggest/recommend a certain course of action.[79] The absence of an ethical decision-maker (ethical committees or advisor) here avoids the danger of those involved putting the decision out to an ad hoc body, thereby diminishing their responsibility and engagement.[80]

The solution adopted by CECs is generally to implement a deliberative model, traditionally seen as the best way to deal with applied ethics issues. The deliberative

---

[69] For a literature review, Crico et al. 2021. See also Fournier et al. 2009; La Puma and Schiedermayer 1991.

[70] See also Slowther et al. 2001; McGee et al. 2002. For some concrete application cases, e.g. Magelssen et al. 2017.

[71] But MacRae et al. 2005, p. 257.

[72] Doran et al. 2016, suggesting a combination of them as best option. For an extensive literature review, see also Rasoal et al. 2017.

[73] Rasoal et al. 2017; Dörries et al. 2011.

[74] La Puma and Schiedermayer 1991.

[75] Hansson 2002.

[76] Ballantyne et al. 2017.

[77] See also MacRae et al. 2005.

[78] See also Janssens et al. 2015; Weidema et al. 2012; Molewijk et al. 2011.

[79] Rasoal et al. 2017, pp. 335–338; Hansson 2002.

[80] See also Molewijk et al. 2008, 2011; Weidema et al. 2012.

process fosters dialogue within the committees, giving voice to a plurality of views and stakeholders, and encourages a striving for consensus, the primary goal of these committees.

3.2.2 *Research Ethics Committees*

Compared with CECs, Research Ethics Committees (Institutional Review Boards or IRBs in the US) have a longer tradition rooted in five principal documents: the Nuremberg Code (1947), the Declaration of Helsinki (1964–2013), the Belmont Report (1978), the Oviedo Convention (1996),[81] and the Universal Declaration on Bioethics and Human Rights (2005).

They therefore have a more regulated composition and function, and give us a clearer picture of the role this model can play in the context of AI.

In addition, ethics committees, which originated in medical research, have been progressively extended to the social sciences, which is a crucial factor in assessing their value for AI. Many AI applications operate in the field of medicine, but many more concern social issues and relationships.

Social science differs from medical research as regards ethical questions, in that the latter is founded on (i) the researchers' greater knowledge of the problem than the participants (ii) a scientific method involving protocols and experiments and (iii) the duty of no-harm.[82] It is therefore impossible to simply transplant medical ethics to social science.

The existing case-history of medical ethics should therefore be examined carefully before taking this area as a model for data ethics and related practices,[83] or for the functioning of ethics boards. On the other hand, the experience of research committees, which address a variety of ethical issues not necessarily related to medical ethics, may serve to point up some valuable approaches for AI.

Research Ethics Committees (RECs) may have a local, regional or national remit, but the ethical assessment of a research project is almost always performed at a local or, in some cases, regional level.[84] Local RECs at hospitals, universities and research centres, or regional RECs can therefore be viewed as a possible model for AI expert committees.

However, the variety of approaches seen in ethical practice in non-medical sectors[85] makes it difficult to define a uniform assessment model, if not in very

[81] Andorno and Constantin 2020.

[82] In this sense Schrag 2010, p. 4.

[83] Koepsell et al. 2014.

[84] Arias Díaz et al. 2015, p. 12 ("The role of the national RECs is: (1) to supervise local and/or regional RECs, (2) to assess specific types of research ethical issues, and (3) to serve as appeal bodies. Not all of the national RECs are involved in all of these activities").

[85] Jansen et al. 2017; Koepsell et al. 2014; Brey et al. 2016.

general terms.[86] This conforms with the scope of this section to focus on the main actors (committees) and their operations, rather than on a general assessment model. It is assumed that these bodies – correctly created and working – will be in the best position to design the most suitable models for each sector-specific AI application.

The members of these committees are usually appointed by the entity they serve (university, hospital,[87] research centre) or by government bodies in the case of national and regional RECs.[88] The composition of these committees varies, but they may include different types of members based on their qualifications (ethics experts, legal experts, sector specific-experts, stakeholders' representatives) and use different selection criteria (internal experts, external experts, laypersons).

The varying mix of qualification and appointment criteria will necessarily impact on the committee's behaviour, favouring either the ethical or the technical component, internal origin or external oversight, etc. As in the case of private companies' ethics boards, the composition and selection play a crucial role in the workings and expected decisions of these bodies.

The operational approach and internal organisation of these committees also vary widely, although a number of common elements can be found: use of self-assessment questionnaires or forms to gather information from the project applicants about their proposals, regular meetings of the RECs, appointment of one or more rapporteurs for a pre-examination of the cases, adoption of deliberation methods based either on consensus or majority voting and, where necessary, interaction with applicants.

An interesting case study in the area of research committees concerns the ethics committees set up by the ERC Executive Agency (ERCEA) to assess ethical issues relating to EU-funded[89] frontier research projects in scientific excellence. The transnational composition of the ethics panels and the majority of the projects, and the wide variety of topics addressed (ERC grants cover both hard science and humanities) make this case relevant to the assessment of the impact of AI on societal issues. AI applications are developed in a variety of fields and often deployed or adopted in different countries, raising questions as to the consistency of assessment between one country and another.

The ethical issues monitored for funded research projects concern eleven areas: (i) use of human embryos/foetuses; (ii) involvement of human beings; (iii) use of

[86] Jansen et al. 2017.

[87] In medical research there is a distinction between non-interventional studies and clinical trials. The latter fall under EU Regulation 536/2014 and are discussed in Sect. 3.3.

[88] Arias Díaz et al. 2015.

[89] Regulation (EU) No 1291/2013, Article 19 and Regulation (EU) 2021/695, Article 19.

human cells/tissues; (iv) protection of personal data; (v) use of animals; (vi) non-EU countries; (vii) environment, health, and safety; (ix) dual use; (x) non-military use; (xi) misuse.[90]

Several of these areas are regulated by law at EU, international and national level, including: clinical trials;[91] human genetic material and biological samples;[92] animal experimentation;[93] data protection;[94] developing countries and politically sensitive issues;[95] environment protection and safety[96] dual use in the context of security/dissemination.[97] The presence of regulated areas in ethical screening reveals the hybrid nature of this process and the overlap between legal and ethical assessment when ethical principles are codified in law and further interpreted by the courts or other authorities (e.g. data protection authorities).

Another important aspect of ethical assessment concerns its autonomy with regard to the scientific evaluation, as the scientific quality of the projects and their conformity with ethical values is assessed by different and independent panels. Since the ethical assessment follows the scientific one, both the funding body and the applicant have an incentive to reach a compromise to avoid a promising project being rejected and the funding blocked. However, the mandatory ethical assessment and the need for a positive outcome should encourage research teams to take into account ethical issues from the earliest stages of project design to avoid this danger.

An ethical assessment may have four different outcomes. Aside from the worst-case scenario in which the project is rejected on ethical grounds, the other three possibilities are: (i) ethics clearance (the project is approved with no ethical requirements); (ii) conditional ethics clearance (the applicant must satisfy certain ethical requirements before starting the project or during project development); (iii) a further ethics assessment (the project presents major ethical issues that must be separately assessed by an ad hoc ethics committee).

Where appropriate, an ethical review may recommend a complementary ethics check/audit on specific issues at a certain point in project development (e.g., fieldwork involving human beings), which may also result in a request for a new ethical assessment.

---

[90] These are the areas that have been identified over the years in ethic assessment, but ethical issues in research also currently concern other areas, such as democracy, social justice and intellectual property, which remains unaddressed.

[91] Regulation No 536/2014 of the European Parliament; Commission Directive 2005/28/EC of 8 April 2005.

[92] Directive 2004/23/EC.

[93] Directive 2010/63/EU of the European Parliament.

[94] Regulation (EU) 2016/679.

[95] Declaration/Charter (EU Fundamental Rights; UN Rights of Child, UNESCO Universal Declaration).

[96] Directive 2001/18/EC; Directive 2009/41/EC; Regulation EC No 1946/2003; Directive 2008/56/EC; Council Directive 92/43/EEC; Council Directive 79/409/EEC and Council Regulation EC No 338/97.

[97] Council Regulation (EC) No 428/2009.

In the third case of a further ethics assessment, an ad hoc panel makes an in-depth analysis of the proposal with additional information provided by the applicant in response to the ethics screening report. The result is an assessment report which may either reach a positive conclusion (full or conditional ethics clearance) or decide the ethical issues have not been fully addressed and demand a further ethics assessment, as happens with very complex and sensitive projects. In the latter case, the further assessment may also include an interview with the applicant and, if appropriate, with competent officers of the hosting research institution (e.g., members of the REC of the hosting institution, legal advisors, data protection officer, etc.).[98]

Although the entire assessment process is centred on an ethics panel, an important role is also played by ERCEA ethics officers who carry out a pre-screening of the proposal and flag any issues not highlighted by the applicants in their mandatory ethics self-assessment. In addition, the ethics officers oversee compliance with the requirements set out in the ethics reports, including any checks and audits.

This continuous monitoring (ethics checks, audits, further assessments, oversight of compliance) is a distinctive feature of the case study, whereas RECs do not usually carry out any follow-ups to the assessments they perform before the project begins.

Another distinctive element of the ERCEA case, compared with either corporate or research committees, is the non-permanent nature of the ethics committees where a group of experts is appointed on case-by-case basis for each round of assessment. Each round of ethical screening usually involves several projects together (few or only one project in the case of an ethics assessment or further assessment of the most challenging projects), and ethics officers play an important role in selecting the panel to match the experts' profiles to the issues emerging from pre-screening.

In thinking of ERCEA ethics committees as a model for AI expert committees, there are a number of elements to be considered. The first concerns the importance of legal principles and requirements which largely transform the assessment into an evaluation of compliance, driven not by ethical values, but by their contextualisation in specific provisions.

ERCEA assessment is a hybrid, only partially grounded on ethics, highlighting the interplay between law and ethics described above as crucial in defining the different operational areas of AI assessment.

Other important factors to consider are the two aspects of the nature and activity of ERCEA ethics committees: the internal dynamics of these expert panels and the interaction between the scientific and the ethical assessment.

The first aspect, the mixed nature of the assessment – including legal compliance requirements – raises problems for interdisciplinary dialogue within the committees between those appointed for their particular expertise in regulated sectors (e.g. data

[98] When ethical issues concern the research methodology, the ethics committee includes a member of the scientific panel to consider the impact of the required changes on the scientific outcome.

protection) and those primarily involved with ethical issues. In some cases, the latter may see the legal provisions as a constraint on a broader ethical evaluation which may lead them to take positions in contrast to those of the legislator or jurisprudence.

Another important aspect of the interaction among experts concerns the risk of identification between the expert and the applicant where both operate in the same field. Peers may set softer requirements for projects deeply rooted in a shared field of work and demonstrate an unconscious bias in favour of research that pursues the same goals as their interests. This may also lead experts to overestimate the importance of the field of application or underestimate the negative impacts from different perspectives covered by the assessment.

Finally, three external elements may affect the internal dynamics of the expert panel: the workload, the role of the ethics officers and the training. When the workflow is high, this can compromise the committee's performance, reducing the time available for discussion and undervaluing criticisms in favour of race-to-the-bottom solutions. Here the ethics officers – though formally neutral – can play an important part in mediating the discussion and facilitating interaction between experts, as well as setting the agenda and deciding the time slots devoted to each proposal.

Although the ethics officers are not formally involved in the discussion and its outcome, it is evident that they can play a role in terms of moral suasion for a smoother interaction among the experts and the achievement of consensus, which is the deliberation criteria adopted by ERCEA panels. It should be noted that the consensus criterion is undoubtedly a further factor encouraging the experts to collaborate proactively in solving their differences as the evaluation cannot conclude without reaching a general agreement. On the contrary, adopting a more rapid process based on majority voting will result in a less cooperative attitude.

For these reasons, the training of the experts is an important element for a better understanding of the specific goal of the evaluation and management of the interdisciplinary nature of the committee.

Another important aspect of the nature and activity of the ERCEA ethics committees concerns the interplay between the scientific and the ethical assessment, characteristic of cases of applied ethics concerning research and innovation. As often happens with RECs,[99] the scientific assessment of the project is distinct from the ethical assessment, the latter following the project's selection for funding.

This sequence (application, scientific evaluation, project selection, ethical assessment, funding grant) is intended to provide rapid feedback to applicants on the success of their proposals, considering the high impact this has on applicants' careers and the limited number of cases with unaddressed ethical issues requiring an assessment prior to funding. However, this inevitably leads applicants to focus on the scientific side and view ethical issues as less critical and often as a 'last mile' problem. This may also partially affect the ethical assessment by the panel which is

[99] Arias Díaz et al. 2015.

responsible for blocking an innovative project on ethical grounds, in a funding model centred on scientific excellence and innovation.

Special training for researchers might raise their awareness of the ethical by-design approach to project planning, avoiding the situation of a poorly executed self-assessment due to a limited understanding of the ethical issues. It is worth noting the similarities with the dynamics seen in private sector AI development, where ethical questions are frequently considered as an add-on to the core of the application and relegated to a final-step assessment of conformity.

3.2.3 Ethics Committees for Clinical Trials

Ethics committees play a critical role in clinical trials, the main area in which ethical issues have been raised in regard to safeguarding the human dignity, human rights, safety and self-determination of research participants.

The field is therefore highly regulated at international,[100] regional and national level. In the EU, the legal framework was previously established by Directive 2001/20/EC on the implementation of good clinical practice in the conduct of clinical trials on medicinal products for human use.

Article 2.k of the Directive defined an ethics committee as "an independent body in a Member State, consisting of healthcare professionals and non-medical members". These committees were required to give their opinion, before the clinical trials began, on a wide range of issues from the scientific aspects of the trial and its design, its benefits and risks, to the rights and freedoms of trial subjects.[101] A positive opinion of the ethics committee was obligatory before the clinical trial would be allowed to go ahead.[102]

This legal framework has been recently reshaped by Regulation 536/2014 which repealed Directive 2001/20/EC introducing several changes to further harmonise and streamline clinical trial procedures. Although the role of ethics committees remains pivotal and their approval necessary for clinical trials to begin, the scope of their assessment and their composition have been modified, raising several criticisms.

Article 4 of the Regulation requires that the ethical review be performed in accordance with the law of the Member State involved, leaving its regulation up to the State itself, and stating that the review "may encompass aspects addressed in Part I of the assessment report for the authorisation of a clinical trial as referred to in Article 6 and in Part II of that assessment report as referred to in Article 7 as appropriate for each Member State concerned". Here Part I refers to the scientific

---

[100] E.g. Council of Europe, Additional Protocol to the Convention on Human Rights and Biomedicine, concerning Biomedical Research (Strasbourg, 25 January 2005).

[101] Directive 2001/20/EC, Articles 6.2 and 6.3.

[102] Directive 2001/20/EC, Article 9.

aspects of the trial (i.e. anticipated therapeutic and public health benefits, risks and inconveniences for the subject, completeness and adequateness of the investigator's brochure, and legal compliance issues), while Part II concerns the ethical issues (informed consent, reward and compensation, recruitment, data protection, suitability of the individuals conducting the trials and the trial sites, damage compensation, biological samples).

The new provisions therefore separate the scientific assessment from the ethical assessment, leaving the Member State the freedom to limit the ethics assessment to Part II alone, as some countries have done already.[103] This undermines the holistic assessment of the clinical trial[104] which comprises the scientific aspects, its design and ethical issues.[105]

Further concerns about the new Regulation regard the make-up of the ethics committees,[106] since it fails to establish rules for the composition and organisation of the committees.[107] It limits itself to the minimal requirements[108] – expertise of

---

[103] Tusino and Furfaro 2021. According to the European Federation of Pharmaceutical Industries and Associations 2021, only two Member States are not currently planning to involve Ethics Committees in Part I.

[104] Directive 2001/29/EC, Article 6. See also Roy-Toole 2016; Gefenas et al. 2017.

[105] Council for International Organizations of Medical Sciences and World Health Organization 2016, Guideline 23: Requirements for Establishing Research Ethics Committees ad for Their Review of Protocols ("Although in some instances scientific review precedes ethical review, research ethics committees must always have the opportunity to combine scientific and ethical review in order to ensure the social value of the research"); Council of Europe, Additional Protocol to the Convention on Human Rights and Biomedicine, concerning Biomedical Research (Strasbourg, 25 January 2005), Article 9. See also Scavone et al. 2019 ("Since Member States can decide whether the Part I should be included into the scope of ethics review by the EC, it is possible that some of them will skip this part. This could weaken the ethics review but also the protection of vulnerable populations since the assessment of risks and benefits will not be accessed by ECs in some member states anymore."). See also European Medicines Agency 2021, para 4.

[106] See also McHale and Hervey 2015.

[107] But Council for International Organizations of Medical Sciences and World Health Organization 2016, Guideline 23: Requirements for Establishing Research Ethics Committees ad for Their Review of Protocols ("Research ethics committees must have members capable of providing competent and thorough review of research proposals. Membership normally must include physicians, scientists and other professionals such as research coordinators, nurses, lawyers, and ethicists, as well as community members or representatives of patients' groups who can represent the cultural and moral values of study participants").

[108] Regulation 536/2014, Article 9 ("Member States shall ensure that the assessment is done jointly by a reasonable number of persons who collectively have the necessary qualifications and experience") and Recitals 18 and 19. See also Council of Europe, Additional Protocol to the Convention on Human Rights and Biomedicine, concerning Biomedical Research, Article 9.2.

the members, multidisciplinary backgrounds, participation of laypersons,[109] and the deliberative method – leaving the Member States to regulate these aspects.[110] This means that the States are free to decide both the organisational rules and the composition,[111] which are critical factors in the performance of the ethical assessment.

There is therefore significant variation among EU countries in national regulation of these committees, although their independence[112] and a degree of involvement by laypersons (in particular, patients or patients' organisations) are common requirements laid down by the Regulation.[113]

3.2.4 *Main Inputs in Addressing Ethical and Societal Issues in AI*

The above overview of ethical bodies has shown a variety of needs – in many cases not circumscribed to ethics only but to various societal issues – addressed in different ways. There are four main areas in which the experience of existing ethics committees can contribute to framing future committees of experts to assess ethical and societal issues in AI: (i) subject matter, (ii) nature of the decisions, (iii) composition, and (iv) relationship with the beneficiaries of the assessment.

Regarding the subject matter, the work of ethics committees is characterised by an interplay between ethical and legal requirements which is also present in the debate on AI regulation.[114] For the RECs this is a consequence of an historical departure from ethics to include progressively regulated fields, such as privacy, safety, dual use, etc. However, in the case of AI, ethical guidelines often show an improper overlap between law and ethics which should be avoided. Legal issues concerning human rights and fundamental freedoms are more properly addressed by the HRIA, while committees should focus on the complimentary aspects of different societal issues, not covered by human rights regulation and practice.

---

[109] See also Regulation 536/2014, Article 2.2.11. Experts have usually a clinical practice experience (physicians and nurses) or an experience in health science disciplines (e.g. epidemiology, pharmacy, biostatistics, etc.), while lay members include people with different backgrounds, such as ethicists, legal experts, psychologists, and patient representatives. See also Hernandez et al. 2009.

[110] See also Petrini 2016.

[111] E.g. the German Medicinal Products Act (Arzneimittelgesetz – AMG, last amended by Article 5 of the Act of 9 December 2020), Section 41a. https://www.gesetze-im-internet.de/englisch_amg/englisch_amg.html#p1067. Accessed 21 September 2021.

[112] Regulation 536/2014, Article 9. See also Universal Declaration on Bioethics and Human Rights, Article 19; Additional Protocol to the Convention on Human Rights and Biomedicine, concerning Biomedical Research, Article 10.

[113] Regulation 536/2014, Article 2.2.11 and rec. 18.

[114] See Chap. 4.

Another problem with the subject matter of ethical committees concerns the interplay between scientific and ethical assessment. The experience of the ECREA ethics committees and clinical trials regulation suggest that expert committees should take a holistic approach to the assessment.

In such an approach the ethical issues are confronted together with the scientific aspects from the earliest stages of project design, as also suggested by the CIOMS[115] and originally by the EU legislation on clinical trials (Directive 2004/39/EC).

This is a response not only to criticism of the two-stage model which splits the research process from the ethical assessment,[116] but also because societal values need to be embedded in AI solutions from the outset, following a by-design approach. What is more, whereas the values relating to biomedical practices are domain-centred and largely universal, the variety of AI applications and their contextual implementation mean that societal values may differ from one context to another.

As regards the nature of the decisions adopted by ethics committees, an important distinction between CECs, Research Ethics Committees and ethics committees for clinical trials is the mandatory or advisory nature of their decisions. While the function and composition of all these models can provide valuable suggestions for future AI expert committees, the pros and cons of the different nature of their decisions should be weighed in regard to AI and are further discussed in the following section. The same considerations apply to the deliberation process, based on either consensus or majority.

Another aspect of ethical assessment that must be considered with respect to AI applications is the provisional character of the evaluation, given their further development and impact, and their learning capabilities. In this regard, the continuous monitoring provided by the models implemented by the ERCEA and in clinical trials offers a better solution than the prior assessment of hospital RECs.

Regarding the panels' composition, in all the cases examined a crucial issue concerns the different levels of expertise required and the role of laypersons, including rights-holder and stakeholder participation. There is general agreement on the multidisciplinary and inclusive nature of ethics committees, but the value placed on expertise varies widely, as does the balance between internal and external experts, scientific experts and laypersons, and the engagement of rights-holders and stakeholders.

While the expert background of the committee members is crucial and impacts on the quality of the assessment, a concurrent factor is the importance of training for the components. A learn-by-doing approach is possible, but some general

---

[115] See Council for International Organizations of Medical Sciences and World Health Organization 2016.

[116] See above Sect. 3.2.3.

introductory training, even based on the most critical cases resolved, could be of help to stimulate cross-disciplinary dialogue.

Finally, with regard to the relationship with the beneficiary of the assessment, the CECs case reveals how, within the organisations setting up the committees, members who are not trained or focused on ethics may underestimate the importance of ethical issues, limiting the extent of their collaboration with ethics bodies. The presence of ethics panels may also encourage people to delegate ethical issues to them, rather than taking an ethical by-design approach to project development, as considered by the ERCEA with regard to some research projects.

3.3 Ad Hoc HRESIA Committees: Role, Nature, and Composition

As discussed in Chap. 1, the extensive and frequently severe impact of data-intensive AI systems on society cannot be fully addressed by the human rights legal framework. Many societal issues, often labelled ethical issues, concern non-legal aspects and involve community choices or individual autonomy requiring a contextual analysis focused on societal and ethical values.

In addition, human rights represent universal values accepted at international level by a large number of countries, but they are necessarily implemented in a range of contexts, and this implies a certain flexibility in the manner in which they are applied.

In the modular HRESIA model therefore, an important component in addressing these issues is the case-specific and contextualised examination which, by its nature, must inevitably be entrusted to expert assessment.

Expert committees can thus play an important role in contextualising the human rights part of the HRESIA and, at the same time, may complete the model regarding the ethical and social values most critical to the given community as well as concerns not covered by the legal framework.

A questionnaire-based approach[117] cannot fully address the complexity of AI systems and their related social and ethical issues. The case-specific nature of the problems requires a contextualised analysis with a direct involvement of experts, rights-holders and stakeholders. The longstanding focus on ethics in other fields, such as ethical committees in scientific research and medical practice, can offer input for thinking about an active role of dedicated bodies or functions within the development environment where data-intensive AI systems are created and used.

The previous sections explained how ethical assessment, which was originally applied to scientific research, has been recently endorsed by companies focusing on AI, a paradigm shift from research to industry which must be highlighted.

[117] Wright and Mordini 2012, pp. 403–404. See also The Danish Institute for Human Rights 2016.

The reason for this shift is not only the greater role that industry, with its privileged access to data and computational power, can play in AI research and development.[118] The main reason is that AI-based systems are not static, but dynamically updated and also able to learn from the environment in which they operate, a factor which complicates the distinction between the research and industrial phases.

AI products are the fruit of living continual research and experimentation (see for example, the controversial Cambridge Analytica case). The uncertain side-effects of AI products/services raise ethical questions about the outcome of research and innovation in a field where many AI products can be viewed as a sort of living social experiment.

This change in perspective justifies the interest in ethics in AI development and highlights the chance to extend to industry the safeguards and models established with regard to ethics committees in scientific research.

The experience of ethics committees in other fields suggests that AI expert committees should adopt a holistic approach, looking at both the technical/scientific aspects and the societal issues of AI projects. This would foster a by-design approach to the societal consequences from the start of product development.

Other features are also suggested by this experience: (i) independence; (ii) multidisciplinary and inclusive nature; (iii) the role of training and education, both for committee members and for those dealing with social issues inside the entities developing and using AI solutions; (iv) procedural organisation and transparency of decision-making processes; (v) access to information on the products/services being assessed; (vi) provisional nature of the assessment and lifecycle monitoring of AI applications, including further assessments.[119]

Despite the fact that these common features are shared by corporate AI ethics boards and provide a solid starting point for building future AI expert committees, the ethics committees and the corporate ethics boards discussed above vary widely in structure, including both internal and external bodies. This demonstrates that issues remain to be addressed and that various solutions are possible.

As in other fields, policy guidance on the non-legal aspects of AI can hardly be black and white and is necessarily context-based. This explains why, especially considering the nature of societal and ethical questions, the possible solutions can be combined and shaped in different ways depending on the specific AI application, its societal impact and the nature of the actors, rights-holders and stakeholders involved in its development and deployment.

---

[118] See Chap. 1.

[119] See also Council of Europe, Consultative Committee of the Convention for the Protection of Individuals with regard to Automatic Processing of Personal Data (Convention 108) 2019, para 2.10 ("AI developers, manufacturers, and service providers should adopt forms of algorithm vigilance that promote the accountability of all relevant stakeholders throughout the entire life cycle of these applications, to ensure compliance with data protection and human rights law and principles").

In defining the key aspects of AI expert committees, several contextual elements must be taken into account, which also distinguish this field from biomedicine: (i) AI applications are much more diffuse and easy-to-develop than medicines; (ii) many AI applications involve forms of automation that have no or low societal consequences; (iii) human rights issues are addressed through the HRIA; (iv) various societal issues are primarily related to large-scale projects (e.g. AI-based automated student evaluation systems).

On the other hand, biomedical and research committees, while discussing ethical questions, also have to examine human rights and legal compliance issues as do the corporate AI ethics boards. Similarly, in the HRESIA model, experts play a significant role in both the human rights and the ethical/social assessment. The difference between the two components, however, is much more marked in the HRESIA and this is reflected in the importance of the experts in the assessment.

The human rights impact assessment does not rely chiefly on experts' understanding of the legal framework, which is largely given. In the evidence-based risk assessment described in Chap. 2, experts contribute to planning and scoping the evaluation and to defining the level of risk depending on the model.

In the ethical and social component of the HRESIA, the experts' role is much more significant in recognising the community's values, which are context specific and often require active interaction with rights-holders and stakeholders to understand them fully. Here, experts operate in a less formalised context, compared with the human rights framework, and their assessment does not benefit from a quantifiable risk analysis, such as described in Chap. 2, but is closer to the deliberative processes of ethics committees discussed above.

As regards the social issues considered in the HRESIA of AI, these essentially concern the acceptability and substitution rate of the proposed AI solutions, rather than the traditional labour-related issues addressed by corporate social due diligence.

Acceptability refers to the conformity of an AI application with the societal and, in cases of customised products, individual values. For example, predictive policing systems, while authorised by law and including specific safeguards, may be seen as unacceptable by some communities.

Obviously, in the case of a conflict with human rights the problem of social acceptability does not arise. A social acceptability assessment therefore implies that the HRIA has already found the impact on human rights non-detrimental.

The same considerations apply to the substitution rate, which refers to the ability to offer feasible alternatives to AI applications,[120] where the latter entail possible, present or future, impacts on individuals and society. Substitution does not only concern technical solutions – AI-based versus non-AI embedded systems – but a

[120] See also Council of Europe, Consultative Committee of the Convention for the Protection of Individuals with regard to Automatic Processing of Personal Data (Convention 108) 2019, para 2.9 ("In order to enhance users' trust, AI developers, manufacturers and service providers are encouraged to design their products and services in a manner that safeguards users' freedom of choice over the use of AI, by providing feasible alternatives to AI applications").

wider approach to the problems AI is designed to solve. For example, a societal assessment of AI-based video-surveillance crime prevention systems should ask whether resources are best invested in these systems or in social aid measures for crime prevention.

This distinction in the scope of the impact assessment requires committee members with different backgrounds. While the HRIA involves human rights advisors and a human rights officer,[121] societal issues must be examined by figures with expertise in social science and ethics.

Given the less numerous cases in which AI applications raise ethical and social concerns, compared with the ethics committees in research and clinical trials, it is hard to imagine the institutionalisation of ethics committees as in those sectors. In this early stage of the AI era, the closest example is probably represented by the CECs, which serve to orient decision making, focus on raising awareness, and rights-holder and stakeholder engagement.

A number of contextual differences must also be considered. For example, where AI solutions are adopted by public bodies in the exercise of their powers (e.g. predictive policing, healthcare assistance, smart mobility, educational ratings, etc.) citizens often have no opt-out option and the AI systems are imposed by government on the basis of political or administrative choices.

In these cases, including those where public bodies exercise their powers in partnership with private companies, the appointment of an ad hoc expert committee, as in the ERCEA model,[122] could be a mandatory requirement. However, the increasing use of AI applications in a specific sector by a given administration might make the creation of permanent committees for clusters of similar AI applications advisable.[123]

On the other hand, where the private sector provides products and services, AI expert committees might be created on a voluntary basis to better align AI development and deployment with the societal needs and context.

In both cases the independence of the committees is key and this will impact on the member selection criteria. This concerns not only consolidated practice on conflicts of interests, but also the balance between internal or external experts where a predominance of internal members may, directly or indirectly, result in the appointing body's internal values and interests being overvalued at the expense of competing societal interests and values.[124]

---

[121] See Chap. 2.

[122] Ad hoc appointments also facilitate the assembly of case-specific expertise and reduces the risk of path-dependency or political influence.

[123] Permanent committees can benefit from better cooperation among their members, and the accumulation of practical expertise and precedent.

[124] It is worth noting that private companies, especially in the early stages of AI solution development, may be concerned about trade secrets and competition. However, this is best handled with non-disclosure agreements rather than committees composed of internal members alone.

On the other hand, as in the case of CECs,[125] AI developers may be less inclined to seek the advice of experts who have no recognised authority within the institution and who are more likely to be out of touch with them. What is more, an integrated committee within the organisation can better monitor effective implementation of its advice and interact actively with developers.

It might be more helpful therefore to envisage an internal member of the expert committee or an internal advisor on societal issues as *trait d'union* between the committee and the AI developers. In certain cases, depending on the nature of the public or private body's activity, where societal issues with AI are core and a frequent concern, a binary model could be adopted, with an expert acting as advisor on societal issues plus a committee of experts.

The advisor becomes a permanent contact for day-to-day project development, submitting the most critical issues to the committee, where the plurality of multidisciplinary views gives a greater assurance than the necessarily limited view of a single advisor. Finally, as in the model adopted by some CECs, participatory deliberation processes[126] could be implemented to facilitate a deeper understanding by developers and AI designers of the ethical and societal issues their work raises.[127]

The advisor's background here will clearly impact the entire process. For this reason and given the spectrum of issues associated with AI, rather than a background in ethics alone, the advisor should have a varied social science profile including the skills to recognise the overall impact of the proposals on society in general.

Looking at other specialist figures (e.g., the DPO in data protection law), the advisors may be either internal or external[128] but in order to have effective impact on critical issues, decisions and practices, they must be truly independent, including with regard to financial resources, and report directly to top management.

Regarding the deliberation methods and the mandatory or consultative nature of the AI committee's decisions, it is hard to drawn red lines. Consensus-based deliberations undoubtedly make for more inclusive decision-making in multidisciplinary panels, but may require more time and resources. Equally, mandatory decisions will impact AI manufacturers and developers more acutely, but involve a danger of their weaker engagement and accountability in the AI development and

[125] Dörries et al. 2011.

[126] This is, for example, the case of the Moral Case Deliberation used in healthcare, see Tan et al. 2018.

[127] See also Sendak et al. 2020.

[128] See also Polonetsky et al. 2015, pp. 353–356, who point out that the internal and external nature of committees also depends on the availability of in-house skills and the costs of setting up an internal committee. They also discuss (341) the consequences of this choice for transparency and accountability ("On the other hand, advocates would not be satisfied with a process that is governed internally and opaque. The feasibility of CSRBs thus hinges on the development of a model that can ensure rapid response and business confidentiality while at the same time guaranteeing transparency and accountability").

deployment process.[129] There is no one-size-fits-all solution, then, but different contexts probably require different approaches.

AI committees – such as RECs[130] – should play a supportive, collaborative and educational role. Alongside their main task of assessing societal impacts, they should contribute to education and policy formation within the appointing bodies.[131]

Finally, a crucial aspect concerns the role of the AI expert committee in civic participation and stakeholder engagement.[132] Participatory issues can be addressed either inside or outside the committees, by including laypersons among their members – representing rights-holders, civil society and stakeholders – or by furthering interaction between the experts, rights-holders, civil society and stakeholders through interviews, focus groups or other participation tools.[133]

The experience of the ethics committees highlights the value of giving laypersons and stakeholders – and in certain cases rights-holders – a voice directly within the committees. Nevertheless, the broader HRESIA model suggests a different approach combining in the committee human rights experts (for the HRIA) and social science experts (for the ethical and societal assessment), while adding specific tools for rightsholder and shareholder participation. It is worth remembering that participation can be valuable in assessing impacts on both human rights and societal impacts.

Meanwhile, the modular scheme keeping the three areas distinct, makes it possible to combine them according to the needs of the specific context. HRIA remains an obligatory step in the development and use of AI, but not all AI applications necessarily entail ethical and societal issues. The level of participation can also vary significantly depending on type of impact and the categories or population involved.

In addition, AI applications may impact a variety of interests and rightsholders/stakeholders, which in many cases are dispersed and not organised in civil society organisations.[134] In these cases, the HRESIA serves to identify these interests and potentially affected clusters of people who can only be involved following an initial assessment and not part of the expert committee from the outset.

Of course, this does not mean that where homogeneous impacted categories are evident from the earliest stages of an AI proposal (e.g. students and AI-based university admission tools) they cannot be given a voice or included in the assessment teams. Even here, however, given the complexity and variety of

---

[129] See Hansson 2013, p. 110 ("There is also a tendency to move risk issues from the political arena to expert committees whose members lack the mandate and the experience necessary to deal with policy issues that require negotiated solution").

[130] Tusino and Furfaro 2021.

[131] This is in line with the experience of the CECs, where the three typical functions of the ethics support services are education, policy formation and case review.

[132] See also Agich and Youngner 1991.

[133] See also Taylor et al. 1990, pp. 197–218.

[134] See Chap. 1.

interests impacted by AI, participatory tools remain an important component of HRESIA implementation in identifying additional stakeholders and ensuring a wider rights-holder engagement. Direct participation differs from the engagement of spokespersons of selected stakeholders, who often fail to represent the majority of the categories or groups of people involved.

Participation tools are therefore vital to an effective democratic decision-making process on AI,[135] an inclusive approach that ensures choice is given to minorities, underrepresented and vulnerable categories.

Finally, in the human rights, ethical and societal assessment, experts should work actively towards a degree of disclosure about the process and its outcome to facilitate this participation. At the same time, interaction with rights-holders and stakeholders should be properly documented to guarantee accountability around their effective engagement.

3.4 Rights-Holder Participation and Stakeholder Engagement

As explained above, rights-holder participation and stakeholder engagement are crucial to HRIA and societal and ethical assessments. Regarding human rights, participation can provide a better understanding of potentially affected rights, including by disaggregating HRIA to focus on specific impacted categories,[136] and a way of taking into account the vernaculisation of human rights.[137] Moreover, where AI systems are used in decision-making processes, participation can also be seen as a significant human right in itself, namely the right to participate in public affairs.[138]

As for societal and ethical assessments, given the contextual nature of the values in question, participation plays a crucial role in understanding the impact of AI systems, as a complement to the knowledge of the HRESIA experts. Here, participation is also important with regard to the specific issue of the substitution of AI-based solutions with alternative responses to the problems AI purports to address (substitution rate).[139]

---

[135] See also Ada Lovelace Institute et al. 2021, p. 49.

[136] Harrison and Stephenson 2010, p. 18.

[137] Levitt and Merry 2009; Benhabib 2008; Engle Merry 2006; O'sullivan 1998.

[138] UN Human Rights Committee (HRC), CCPR General Comment No. 25: The right to participate in public affairs, voting rights and the right of equal access to public service (Article 25), CCPR/C/21/Rev.1/Add.7, 12 July 1996; UN Committee on Economic, Social and Cultural Rights (CESCR), General Comment No. 1: Reporting by States Parties, 27 July 1981, para 5; Jacobsen 2013. See also Maisley 2017.

[139] See above Sect. 3.3.

In the AI solution design process, participation can make contributions either at the initial stage of product/service design (discovery stage[140]), during project development, or in its concrete implementation, including further post-market changes.

During the first stage, which defines only the overall goal of the product/service, rights-holders and stakeholders should be engaged in discussing the general problem and the potential substitution rate, if any.[141] Social science has suggested different forms of participation to achieve this goal[142] for implementation in the different contexts according to needs.

While it is outside the scope of this legal analysis to describe and discuss these methodologies and various results achievable,[143] it is evident that a comprehensive future regulation of AI should consider rights-holder and stakeholder engagement as crucial. This leads to two main regulatory consequences. First, the participation phase must be present in the assessment of AI projects, at least in high impact cases. Second, as participation methods require specific expertise, the HRIA and societal assessment experts should be supported by social scientists in designing participation.

Though crucial from the start of the projects, voluntary participation in detecting the key factors of the potential impacts of AI systems[144] necessarily requires a preliminary desk analysis by human rights and social science experts to identify possible impacted interests and better target any participatory initiatives. Here, underestimation or overestimation of a specific interest may affect the outcome of the entire AI project, as in the case of Toronto's Sidewalk.[145]

Having defined the targets, potential participants must be properly informed about the goals and structure of the project. Many data-intensive AI projects involve detailed technical knowledge and it is important to facilitate understanding of these aspects by providing easily accessible, general and neutral information about the technologies and their workings.

---

[140] Spiekermann 2016, p. 171.

[141] This is the case, for example, with a proposal concerning the adoption of an e-voting system. Citizens should be engaged on the decision to move towards e-voting instead of maintaining the existing on-paper model. If a general consensus is reached on the adoption of this technology, the developers will work up a concrete proposal (or a set of proposals) to achieve the final goal. On the basis of these concrete proposals, stakeholders will be further engaged in product design to provide their feedback on the development of the proposed solutions, following a sort of circular iterative approach based on feedback implementations and design adjustments. Spiekermann 2016, p. 164 ("unexpectedly, some values may turn out to be more important than initially thought, and other values may be questioned. Even if a system is developed with ethical values in mind and has been subject to rigorous ethical risk analysis, the system might turn out to be not that perfect"), pp. 172–173.

[142] See also Data Justice Lab 2021.

[143] Sloane et al. 2020.

[144] Lee et al. 2019.

[145] See Chap. 2, Sect. 2.4.2.

As disclosure about project design and content, especially in large-scale projects, may entail competition issues or, more generally, competing third party interests, limited disclosure or confidentiality agreements should be considered.

Meanwhile, participants may disclose personal or relational information at interviews or participation. In these cases, those performing the HRESIA should be subject to confidentiality obligations.

Finally, as far as is consistent with the nature and purpose of participation, participants should receive feedback about their impact on product/service design. This is particularly important where there are clearly identified and homogeneous categories of potentially affected individuals (e.g. consumers, students, etc.).

Following these guidelines, an effective and properly designed participation strategy can achieve two main results: reducing assessment bias and increasing trust in AI services and products, which are often obscure and consist in closed top-down solutions.

In terms of bias reduction, participation helps experts to think outside the box, considering new issues or examining those already identified from a different angle not necessarily reflecting their interpretation of societal values and constructs.[146] On the other hand, where the experts' views are confirmed by participatory evidence, the groundwork may offer a better understanding of the problems and the societal dimension of AI applications.

Trust, a key issue in the adoption of AI systems by individuals and communities,[147] is a complex and longstanding notion in technology development regarding the relationship between human artefacts, those who builds them, and users,[148] and comprises the capability of a given technology, often influenced by emotional and other non-rational factors.[149]

The HRESIA assessment model can give users reasons to trust in AI, conscious that the potential negative consequences have been properly considered and addressed. The active engagement of stakeholders, rights-holders and users in the design process and in the assessment can have a positive effect on the relational dimension of trust.

Participation can also evolve into a more complex relationship between AI developers and end-users, opening up to co-design approaches. Given the importance of technology in actively shaping society,[150] the public should not play a

[146] On the limits of an approach based solely on the assessment provided by experts, *inter alia*, Ferretti 2007; Sollie and Düwell 2009, pp. 96–97. See also Grunwald 2004; Karafyllis 2009, pp. 102 and 112; Swierstra et al. 2009.

[147] E.g. Independent High-Level Expert Group on Artificial Intelligence set up by the European Commission 2019.

[148] Keymolen and Voorwinden 2020.

[149] Glikson and Woolley 2020.

[150] Verbeek 2005.

passive role delegating all the design decisions to manufacturers/service providers, even where value-oriented methods are guaranteed.[151]

On the other hand, the added value of participation should not tempt us to underestimate the risks in this process. In the first place, it is crucial to combat misuse of the solution by "participation washing", guiding the target population towards expected outcomes.[152] Independent human rights and social experts should serve as a barrier to manipulation, as well as the fact that the committees themselves, and not the AI manufacturers, are responsible for the assessments.

Another critical issue concerns the voluntary nature of participation. Potential biases in the social composition of participants in favour of wealthy and educated people, polarisation due to the greater presence of highly motivated people representing minority clusters, the risk of exclusion due to the use of technology-based tools (e.g. online participation platforms), as well as cases of participants covertly acting on behalf of certain stakeholders to reinforce their position while presenting it as widely held, are challenges common to all volunteer-based approaches.

The issues with AI systems do not alter either these risks or the solutions, such as deliberative pooling and participant selection, affirmative actions and incentives for low-status and low-income citizens, and other strategies already commonly used in participation practice.

Similarly, past experience in participation may suggest limiting citizen engagement in AI design to the strictly necessary avoiding too many meetings that tend to reduce interest and the level of participation.[153] We must also remember that an enlargement of participation entails additional costs for those who build and use AI systems, so that a balance between potential risks and effort required must be reached.

The modular structure of the HRESIA can help in this regard as the level of participation required can vary significantly depending on the type of AI application and the categories or population impacted. Participatory tools can be simplified in some cases by reducing them, for instance, to rights-holder and stakeholder interviews or open consultations.

3.5 Summary

AI systems pose questions that go beyond their impact on human rights and freedoms and regard their social acceptability and coherence with the values of the community in which they are to be used. Nevertheless, this broader consideration of

---

[151] In this regard, recently proposed AI regulations in Europe underestimate both the role and the value of participation in the design of AI. See Chap. 4.

[152] See the Sidewalk case in Chap. 2, Sect. 2.4.2.

[153] See also Breuer and Pierson 2021.

the consequences of AI should not create an improper overlap between legal and ethical/social values.

The social and ethical consequences of AI represent a complementary dimension alongside that of human rights that must be properly investigated to mitigate adverse effects for individuals and society. The HRESIA therefore includes a module focused on the ethical and social impact assessment, to capture the holistic dimension of the relationship between humans and machines.

This complementarity also concerns the interests examined, with the HRIA preceding the ethical and social assessment as a preliminary step, given the binding nature of human rights. Only after the proposed solution has been found to be compliant with the human rights principles are the ethical and social consequences investigated.

The societal assessment is more complicated than that of human rights. Whereas the latter refers to a well-defined benchmark – even considering contextual implementation and vernaculisation –, the ethical and social framework involves a variety of theoretical inputs on the underlying values, as well as a proliferation of guidelines, in some cases partially affected by 'ethics washing' or reflecting corporate values.

This requires a contextualised and, as far as possible, a participative analysis of the values of the community in which the AI solutions are expected to be implemented. Here the experts play a crucial role in detecting, contextualising and evaluating the AI solutions against existing ethical and social values.

Much more than in the human rights assessment, experts are therefore decisive in grasping the relevant community values, given their context specific nature and, in many cases, the need for active interaction with rights-holders and stakeholders to better understand them.

Experts can be involved in AI assessment in a variety of ways, as demonstrated recently by the ethics boards in digital economy companies. The structure, composition and internal organisation of the expert committees are not neutral elements, but can influence the outcome of the assessment in terms of quality and reliability of the results, and the independent nature of the evaluation.

This explains how ethics committees in scientific research, bioethics and clinical trials can provide inputs for future AI expert committees within the HRESIA model. While certain key elements can be identified (e.g. independence, multidisciplinary, and inclusiveness of the committee; transparency of internal procedures and decisional processes; provisional character of their decisions), the committees present a variety of structures and types of organisation in terms of member qualifications, rights-holder, stakeholder, and layperson participation, and internal or external experts.[154] This demonstrates not only the presence of open issues that remain to be addressed, but also that there is no a one-size-fits-all solution: the differing nature and contextual importance of ethical and societal interests may require different approaches to the role of experts.

[154] See also Ruggie 2007.

One solution in organisations focused on AI and its use could be the figure of an internal advisor on societal issues as a permanent contact for day-to-day project development and a *trait d'union* with the HRESIA experts. This would also help to foster internal participatory deliberation through interaction with the AI developers.

Finally, experts tasked with performing an ethical and social impact assessment operate in a less formalised context than the human rights framework. They cannot benefit from the quantifiable risk analysis described in Chap. 2, but mainly rely on an exchange of opinions within a deliberative process similar to that discussed for ethics committees.

Just as with the HRIA, ethical and societal assessments also have an influence on the design of AI solutions, especially with regard to acceptability and the substitution rate of the proposed AI solution. They not only examine the AI product/service itself, but look at a broader range of alternative possibilities to address the needs identified, not necessarily AI-based.

Based on the experience of the ethics committees, the AI assessment cannot be entrusted entirely to experts and their interaction with stakeholders. It should also include a participatory dimension, which is essential to effective democratic decision-making process concerning AI. An inclusive approach can also contribute to a better understanding of the societal and ethical issues, as well as the context-specific human rights concerns. Furthermore, the modular HRESIA structure makes it possible to vary the level and focus of participation depending on the area under assessment.

References

Ada Lovelace Institute, AI Now Institute, Open Government Partnership (2021) Algorithmic Accountability for the Public Sector. https://www.opengovpartnership.org/documents/algorithmic-accountability-public-sector/. Accessed 15 October 2021.

Agich GJ, Youngner SJ (1991) For experts only? Access to hospital ethics committees. 21(5) Hastings Cent. Rep. 17.

Andorno R, Constantin A (2020) Human Subjects in Globalized Health Research. In: Gostin LO, Meier BM (eds) Foundations of Global Health & Human Rights. Oxford University Press, New York, https://doi.org/10.1093/oso/9780197528297.003.0019.

Arias Díaz J, Martín-Arribas MC, Herrero Olivera L, de Sola Perea L, Romare J (2015) Ethics Assessment and Guidance in Different Types of Organisations. https://satoriproject.eu/media/3.a-Research-ethics-committees.pdf. Accessed 25 June 2020.

Axon AI Ethics Board (2019a) First Report of the Axon AI & Policing Technology Ethics Board. https://static1.squarespace.com/static/58a33e881b631bc60d4f8b31/t/5d13d7e1990c4f00014c0aeb/1561581540954/Axon_Ethics_Board_First_Report.pdf. Accessed 7 May 2021.

Axon AI Ethics Board (2019b) Second Report of the Axon AI & Policing Technology Ethics Board: Automated License Plate Readers. https://static1.squarespace.com/static/58a33e881b631bc60d4f8b31/t/5dadec937f5c1a2b9d698ba9/1571679380452/Axon_Ethics_Report_2_v2.pdf. Accessed 7 May 2021.

Axon AI Ethics Board (2020) 2020 End of Year Report. https://static1.squarespace.com/static/58a33e881b631bc60d4f8b31/t/603d65a9d4ef6e4f9632b342/1614636462250/Axon+AI+Ethics+Board+2020+EOY+Report.pdf. Accessed 7 May 2021.

Ballantyne AJ, Dai E, Gray B (2017) Patient Participation in Clinical Ethics Support Services – Patient-Centered Care, Justice and Cultural Competence. 12 Clinical Ethics 11.

Barrett PM (2020) Who Moderates the Social Media Giants? A Call to End Outsourcing. New York University Stern Center for Business and Human Rights 2020. https://issuu.com/nyusterncenterforbusinessandhumanri/docs/nyu_content_moderation_report_final_version/1. Accessed 6 May 2021.

Beecher HK (1966) Ethics and Clinical Research. 274 New England Journal of Medicine 1354.

Benhabib S (2008) The Legitimacy of Human Rights. 137 Daedalus 94.

Breuer J, Pierson J (2021) The Right to the City and Data Protection for Developing Citizen-Centric Digital Cities. 24 Information, Communication & Society 797.

Brey P, Douglas D, Kapeller A, Benčin R, Ovadia D, Wolfslehner D (2016) Models for Ethics Assessment and Guidance in Higher Education. https://satoriproject.eu/media/D4.1_Annex_5_Universities.pdf. Accessed 25 June 2020.

Brey P, Shelley-Egan C, Rodrigues R, Jansen P (2017) The Ethical Assessment of Research and Innovation – A Reflection on the State of the Art (Based on Findings of the SATORI Project). In: Iphofen R (ed) Advances in Research Ethics and Integrity, vol 1. Emerald Publishing Limited, Bingley, pp 185–198. https://www.emerald.com/insight/content/doi/10.1108/S2398-601820170000001015/full/html. Accessed 5 June 2021.

BSR (2019) Human Rights Review, Facebook Oversight Board. https://www.bsr.org/reports/BSR_Facebook_Oversight_Board.pdf. Accessed 6 May 2021.

Canca C (2019) AI & Global Governance: Human Rights and AI Ethics – Why Ethics Cannot Be Replaced by the UDHR – United Nations University Centre for Policy Research. https://cpr.unu.edu/ai-global-governance-human-rights-and-ai-ethics-why-ethics-cannot-be-replaced-by-the-udhr.html. Accessed 30 April 2020.

Coleman F, Nonnecke B, Renieris EM (2021) The Promise and Pitfalls of the Facebook Oversight Board A Human Rights Perspective. Carr Center for Human Rights Policy Harvard Kennedy School, Harvard University. https://carrcenter.hks.harvard.edu/publications/promise-and-pitfalls-facebook-oversight-board-%E2%80%93-human-rights-perspective. Accessed 21 July 2021.

Cortina A (2000) Legislation, Law and Ethics. 3 Ethical Theory and Moral Practice 3.

Council for International Organizations of Medical Sciences and World Health Organization (2016) International Ethical Guidelines for Health-Related Research Involving Humans.

Council of Europe – European Commission for the Efficiency of Justice (CEPEJ) (2018) European Ethical Charter on the Use of Artificial Intelligence in Judicial Systems and their environment. https://rm.coe.int/ethical-charter-en-for-publication-4-december-2018/16808f699c. Accessed 4 December 2018.

Council of Europe, Consultative Committee of the Convention for the Protection of Individuals with regard to Automatic Processing of Personal Data (Convention 108) (2019) Guidelines on Artificial Intelligence and Data Protection', Strasbourg, T-PD(2019)01. https://rm.coe.int/guidelines-on-artificial-intelligence-and-data-protection/168091f9d8. Accessed 4 February 2019.

Crico C, Sanchini V, Casali PG, Pravettoni G (2021) Evaluating the Effectiveness of Clinical Ethics Committees: A Systematic Review. 24 Medicine, Health Care and Philosophy 135.

Data Justice Lab (2021) Advancing Civic Participation in Algorithmic Decision-Making: A Guidebook for the Public Sector. https://datajusticelab.org/wp-content/uploads/2021/06/PublicSectorToolkit_english.pdf. Accessed 14 June 2021.

Doran E, Kerridge I, Jordens C, Newson AJ (2016) Clinical Ethics Support in Contemporary Health Care: Origins, Practices, and Evaluation. In: Ferlie E, Montgomery K, Pedersen AR (eds) The Oxford Handbook of Health Care Management. Oxford University Press, Oxford, https://doi.org/10.1093/oxfordhb/9780198705109.013.13.

Dörries A, Boitte P, Borovecki A, Cobbaut J-P, Reiter-Theil S, Slowther A-M (2011) Institutional Challenges for Clinical Ethics Committees. 23 HEC Forum 193.
Douek E (2019) Facebook's "Oversight Board:" Move Fast with Stable Infrastructure and Humility. 21 N.C. J.L. & TECH. 1.
Douek E (2021) The Facebook Oversight Board's First Decisions: Ambitious, and Perhaps Impractical. Lawfare. https://www.lawfareblog.com/facebook-oversight-boards-first-decisions-ambitious-and-perhaps-impractical. Accessed 6 May 2021.
Engle Merry S (2006) Human rights and gender violence: translating international law into local justice. University of Chicago Press, Chicago.
European Commission – European Group on Ethics in Science and New Technologies (2018) Statement on Artificial Intelligence, Robotics and "Autonomous" Systems. https://op.europa.eu/en/publication-detail/-/publication/dfebe62e-4ce9-11e8-be1d-01aa75ed71a1/language-en/format-PDF/source-78120382. Accessed 11 March 2018.
European Federation of Pharmaceutical Industries and Associations (2021) CTi Monitor Survey 2020. https://www.efpia.eu/media/602602/cti-monitor-survey_-q4_2020.pdf. Accessed 26 July 2021.
European Medicines Agency (2021) ICH Guideline E6 on good clinical practice Draft ICH E6 principles. https://www.ema.europa.eu/en/ich-e6-r2-good-clinical-practice. Accessed 15 July 2021.
Ferretti MP (2007) Why public participation in risk regulation? The case of authorizing GMO products in the European Union. 16(4) Science as culture 377.
Fichter JH, Kolb WL (1953) Ethical Limitations on Sociological Reporting. 18 American Sociological Review 544.
Floridi L, Taddeo M (2016) What Is Data Ethics? 374 Philosophical Transactions of the Royal Society A: Mathematical, Physical and Engineering Sciences 20160360.
Fournier V, Rari E, Førde R, Neitzke G, Pegoraro R, Newson AJ (2009) Clinical Ethics Consultation in Europe: A Comparative and Ethical Review of the Role of Patients. 4 Clinical Ethics 131.
Gefenas E, Cekanauskaite A, Lekstutiene J, Lukaseviciene V (2017) Application Challenges of the New EU Clinical Trials Regulation. 73 European Journal of Clinical Pharmacology 795.
Glikson E, Woolley AW (2020) Human Trust in Artificial Intelligence: Review of Empirical Research. 14 Academy of Management Annals 627.
Grunwald A (2004) Vision assessment as a new element of the technology futures analysis tool-box. In Proceedings of the EU-US Scientific seminar: new technology for sight, forecasting & assessment methods. Seville 13–14 May 2004. www.jrc.es/projects/fta/index.htm. Accessed 25 March 2020.
Hagendorff T (2020) The Ethics of AI Ethics: An Evaluation of Guidelines. 30 Minds and Machines 99.
Hansson MG (2002) Imaginative Ethics – Bringing Ethical Praxis into Sharper Relief. 5 Medicine, Health Care and Philosophy 33.
Hansson SO (2013) The Ethics of Risk. Palgrave Macmillan, New York.
Harrison J, Stephenson M-A (2010) Human Rights Impact Assessment: Review of Practice and Guidance for Future Assessments. Scottish Human Rights Commission 2010.
Hernandez R et al. (2009) Harmonisation of Ethics Committees' Practice in 10 European Countries. 35 Journal of Medical Ethics 696.
Holton R, Boyd R (2021) "Where Are the People? What Are They Doing? Why Are They Doing It?" (Mindell) Situating Artificial Intelligence within a Socio-Technical Framework. 57 Journal of Sociology 179.
Ienca M, Vayena E (2020) AI Ethics Guidelines: European and Global Perspectives. In: Council of Europe. Towards regulation of AI systems. Global perspectives on the development of a legal framework on Artificial Intelligence systems based on the Council of Europe's standards on human rights, democracy and the rule of law. Council of Europe, Strasbourg, pp 38–60.
Ihde D (1990) Technology and the Lifeworld. Indiana University Press, Bloomington.

Independent High-Level Expert Group on Artificial Intelligence set up by the European Commission (2018) Draft Ethics Guidelines for Trustworthy AI. https://ec.europa.eu/digital-single-market/en/news/draft-ethics-guidelines-trustworthy-ai. Accessed 18 December 2018.

Independent High-Level Expert Group on Artificial Intelligence set up by the European Commission (2019) Ethics Guidelines for Trustworthy AI. https://digital-strategy.ec.europa.eu/en/library/ethics-guidelines-trustworthy-ai. Accessed 26 May 2020.

Jacobs M, Pradier MF, McCoy Jr TH, Perlis RH, Doshi-Velez F, Gajos KZ (2021) How Machine-Learning Recommendations Influence Clinician Treatment Selections: The Example of Antidepressant Selection. 11 Translational Psychiatry 1.

Jacobsen AF (2013) The Right to Public Participation. A Human Rights Law Update. Issue Paper. https://www.humanrights.dk/publications/right-public-participation-human-rights-law-update. Accessed 20 June 2019.

Jansen P, Sattarov F, Douglas D, Reijers W, Gurzawska A, Kapeller A, Brey P, Callies I, Benčin R, Warso Z (2017) Outline of an Ethics Assessment Framework Main Results of the SATORI Project. https://satoriproject.eu/media/D4.2_Outline_of_an_Ethics_Assessment_Framework.pdf. Accessed 4 July 2021.

Janssens RMJPA, van Zadelhoff E, van Loo G, Widdershoven GAM, Molewijk BAC (2015) Evaluation and Perceived Results of Moral Case Deliberation: A Mixed Methods Study. 22 Nursing Ethics 870.

Jobin A, Ienca M, Vayena E (2019) The Global Landscape of AI Ethics Guidelines. 1 Nature Machine Intelligence 389.

Karafyllis NC (2009) Facts or Fiction? A Critique on Vision Assessment as a Tool for Technology Assessment. In: Sollie P, Düwell M (eds) Evaluating New Technologies. Methodological Problems for the Ethical Assessment of Technology Developments. Springer, Dordrecht, pp 93–117.

Keymolen E, Voorwinden E (2020) Can We Negotiate? Trust and the Rule of Law in the Smart City Paradigm. 34 International Review of Law, Computers & Technology 233.

Klonick K (2018) The New Governors: The People, Rules, and Processes Governing Online Speech. 131 HARV. L. REV. 1598.

Klonick K (2020) The Facebook Oversight Board: Creating an Independent Institution to Adjudicate Online Free Expression. 129 Yale Law Journal 2418.

Koepsell D, Brinkman W-P, Pont S (2014) Human Research Ethics Committees in Technical Universities. 9 Journal of Empirical Research on Human Research Ethics 67.

La Puma J, Schiedermayer DL (1991) Ethics Consultation: Skills, Roles, and Training. 114 Annals of Internal Medicine 155.

Latour B (1992) Where Are the Missing Masses? The Sociology of a Few Mundane Artifacts. In: Bijker WE, Law J (eds) Shaping Technology/Building Society: Studies in Sociotechnical Change. MIT Press, Cambridge, MA, pp 225–258.

Latour B (1999) Pandora's Hope: Essays on the Reality of Science Studies. Harvard University Press, Cambridge, MA.

Latour B (2002) Morality and Technology: The End of the Means. 19 (5–6) Theory, Culture and Society 247.

Lee MK, Kysbit D, Kahng A, Tae Kim J, Yuan X, Chan A, See D, Noothigattu R, Lee S, Psomas A, Procaccia AD (2019) WeBuildAI: Participatory Framework for Algorithmic Governance. 3 Proceedings of the ACM on Human-Computer Interaction 1.

Levitt P, Merry S (2009) Vernacularization on the Ground: Local Uses of Global Women's Rights in Peru, China, India and the United States. 9 Global Networks 441.

Lewandowsky S, Smillie L (2020) Technology and Democracy: Understanding the influence of online technologies on political behaviour and decision-making. Publications Office of the European Union, Luxembourg.

MacRae S, Chidwick P, Berry S, Secker B, Hébert P, Zlotnik Shaul R, Faith K, Singer PA (2005) Clinical Bioethics Integration, Sustainability, and Accountability: The Hub and Spokes Strategy. 31 Journal of Medical Ethics 256.

Magelssen M, Miljeteig I, Pedersen R, Førde R (2017) Roles and Responsibilities of Clinical Ethics Committees in Priority Setting. 18 BMC Medical Ethics 68.
Maisley N (2017) The International Right of Rights? Article 25(a) of the ICCPR as a Human Right to Take Part in International Law-Making. 28 Eur. J. Int. Law 89.
Manders-Huits N, van den Hoven J (2009) The Need for a Value-Sensitive Design of Communication Infrastructures. In: Sollie P, Düwell M (eds) Evaluating New Technologies. Methodological Problems for the Ethical Assessment of Technology Developments. Springer, Dordrecht, pp 51–60.
McGee G, Spanogle JP, Caplan AL, Penny D, Asch DA (2002) Successes and Failures of Hospital Ethics Committees: A National Survey of Ethics Committee Chairs. 11 Cambridge Quarterly of Healthcare Ethics 87.
McHale JV, Hervey TK (eds) (2015) Risk: Clinical Trials', European Union Health Law: Themes and Implications. Cambridge University Press, Cambridge.
Molewijk AC, Abma T, Stolper M, Widdershoven G (2008) Teaching Ethics in the Clinic. The Theory and Practice of Moral Case Deliberation. 34 Journal of Medical Ethics 120.
Molewijk B, Kleinlugtenbelt D, Pugh SM, Widdershoven G (2011) Emotions and Clinical Ethics Support. A Moral Inquiry into Emotions in Moral Case Deliberation. 23 HEC Forum 257.
O'sullivan D (1998) The History of Human Rights across the Regions: Universalism vs Cultural Relativism. 2 The International Journal of Human Rights 22.
Petrini C (2016) What Is the Role of Ethics Committees after Regulation (EU) 536/2014? 42 Journal of Medical Ethics 186.
Polonetsky J, Tene O, Jerome J (2015) Beyond the Common Rule: Ethical Structures for Data Research in Non-Academic Settings. 13 Colorado Technology Law Journal 333.
Raab CD (2020) Information Privacy, Impact Assessment, and the Place of Ethics. 37 Computer Law & Security Review 105404.
Rasoal D, Skovdahl K, Gifford M, Kihlgren A (2017) Clinical Ethics Support for Healthcare Personnel: An Integrative Literature Review. 29 HEC Forum 313.
Roy-Toole C (2016) Fossil Relics: Ethics Committees under the European Clinical Trials Regulation. 4 Journal of Medical Law and Ethics 113.
Ruggie J (2007) Report of the Special Representative of the Secretary-General on the Issue of Human Rights and Transnational Corporations and Other Business Enterprises: Guiding Principles on Business and Human Rights: Implementing the United Nations "Protect, Respect and Remedy" Framework. United Nations, General Assembly, A/HRC/4/74. https://digitallibrary.un.org/record/593080#record-files-collapse-header. Accessed 9 October 2020.
Scavone C et al. (2019) The European Clinical Trials Regulation (No 536/2014): Changes and Challenges. 12 Expert Review of Clinical Pharmacology 1027.
Schrag ZM (2010) Ethical Imperialism. Institutional Review Boards and the Social Sciences 1965–2009. Johns Hopkins University Press, Baltimore.
Sendak M, Elish MC, Gao M, Futoma J, Ratliff W, Nichols M, Bedoya A, Balu S, O'Brien C (2020) "The Human Body is a Black Box": Supporting Clinical Decision-Making with Deep Learning. In FAT* '20: Proceedings of the 2020 Conference on Fairness, Accountability, and Transparency, 99. https://doi.org/10.1145/3351095.3372827.
Sloane M, Moss E, Awomolo O, Forlano L (2020) Participation Is Not a Design Fix for Machine Learning. In: Proceedings of the 37th International Conference on Machine Learning, Vienna, Austria, PMLR, 119.
Slowther A, Bunch C, Woolnough B, Hope T (2001) Clinical Ethics Support Services in the UK: An Investigation of the Current Provision of Ethics Support to Health Professionals in the UK. 27(suppl 1) Journal of Medical Ethics i2.
Sollie P, Düwell M (eds) (2009) Evaluating New Technologies. Methodological Problems for the Ethical Assessment of Technology Developments. Springer, Dordrecht.
Spiekermann S (2016) Ethical IT Innovation. A Value-Based System Design Approach. CRC Press, Boca Raton.
Swierstra T, Stemerding D, Boenink M (2009) Exploring Techno-Moral Change: The Case of ObesityPill. In: Sollie P, Düwell M (eds) Evaluating New Technologies. Methodological

Problems for the Ethical Assessment of Technology Developments. Springer, Dordrecht, pp 119–138.

Tan DYB, ter Meulen BC, Molewijk A, Widdershoven G (2018) Moral Case Deliberation. 18 Practical Neurology 181.

Taylor L, Dencik L (2020) Constructing Commercial Data Ethics. Technology and Regulation 1. https://techreg.org/article/view/10988. Accessed 18 May 2020.

Taylor CN, Hobson Bryan C, Goodrich CG (1990) Social Assessment: Theory, Process and Techniques. Centre for Resource Management, Lincoln University, New Zealand.

The Danish Institute for Human Rights. (2016). Human rights impact assessment guidance and toolbox. Copenhagen: The Danish Institute for Human Rights.

Tusino S, Furfaro M (2021) Rethinking the Role of Research Ethics Committees in the Light of Regulation (EU) No 536/2014 on Clinical Trials and the COVID-19 Pandemic. British Journal of Clinical Pharmacology. https://bpspubs.onlinelibrary.wiley.com/doi/abs/10.1111/bcp.14871. Accessed 4 June 2021.

UN Committee on Economic, Social and Cultural Rights (CESCR) (1981) General Comment No. 1: Reporting by States Parties.

UN High Commissioner for Human Rights and reports of the Office of the High Commissioner and the Secretary-General (2020) Promotion and protection of all human rights, civil political, economic, social and cultural rights, including the right to development. Question of the realization of economic, social and cultural rights in all countries: the role of new technologies for the realization of economic, social and cultural rights. A/HRC/43/29. https://undocs.org/A/HRC/43/29. Accessed 21 September 2021.

UN Human Rights Committee (HRC) (1996) CCPR General Comment No. 25: The right to participate in public affairs, voting rights and the right of equal access to public service (Art. 25), CCPR/C/21/Rev.1/Add.7.

van Dijk N, Casiraghi S, Gutwirth S (2021) The "Ethification" of ICT Governance. Artificial Intelligence and Data Protection in the European Union. 43 Computer Law & Security Review 105597.

Verbeek P-P (2005) What Things Do: Philosophical Reflections on Technology, Agency and Design. Pennsylvania State University Press, University Park.

Verbeek P-P (2011) Understanding and Designing the Morality of Things. The Chicago University Press, Chicago/London.

Wagner B (2018) Ethics as an escape from regulation: From "ethics-washing" to ethics-shopping? In: Bayamlioğlu E, Baraliuc I, Janssens LAW, Hildebrandt M (eds) Being Profiled. Amsterdam University Press, Amsterdam.

Weidema FC, Molewijk AC, Widdershoven GAM, Abma TA (2012) Enacting Ethics: Bottom-up Involvement in Implementing Moral Case Deliberation. 20 Health Care Analysis 1.

Wright D, Mordini E (2012) Privacy and Ethical Impact Assessment. In: Wright D, De Hert P (eds) Privacy Impact Assessment. Springer, Dordrecht, pp 397–418.

Chapter 4
Regulating AI

Contents

Abstract Although the debate on AI regulation is still fluid at a global level and the European initiatives are in their early stages, three possible approaches to grounding AI regulation on human rights are emerging. One option is a principles-based approach, comprising guiding principles derived from existing binding and non-binding international human rights instruments, which could provide a comprehensive framework for AI. A different approach focuses more narrowly on the impacts of AI on individual rights and their safeguarding through rights-based risk assessment. This is the path followed by the Council of Europe in its ongoing work on AI regulation. Finally, as outlined in the EU proposal, greater emphasis can be placed on managing high-risk applications by focusing on product safety and conformity assessment. Despite the differences between these three models, they all share a core concern with protecting human rights, recognised as a key issue in all of them. However, in these proposals for AI regulation, the

A. Mantelero, *Beyond Data*, Information Technology and Law Series 36,
https://doi.org/10.1007/978-94-6265-531-7_4

emphasis on risk management is not accompanied by effective models for assessing the impact of AI on human rights. Analysis of the current debate therefore confirms that the HRESIA could not only be an effective response to human-rights oriented AI development that also encompasses societal values, but it could also bridge a gap in the current regulatory proposals.

Keywords Ad hoc Committee on Artificial Intelligence (CAHAI) · AI regulation · Artificial Intelligence Act · Conformity assessment · Co-regulation · Democracy · Technology assessment

4.1 Regulating AI: Three Different Approaches to Regulation

In its early stages, the regulatory debate on AI focused mainly on the ethical dimension of data use and the new challenges posed by data-intensive systems based on Big Data and AI. This approach was supported by several players of the AI industry, probably attracted by the flexibility of a self-regulation based on ethical principles, which is less onerous and easier to align with corporate values.[1]

As in the past, uncertainty about the potential impact of new technology and an existing legal framework not tailored to the new socio-technical scenarios was the main reason for rule makers to turn their gaze towards general principles and common ethical values.

The European Data Protection Supervisor (EDPS) was the first body to emphasise the ethical dimension of data use, pointing out how, in light of recent technological developments, data protection appeared insufficient to address all the challenges, while ethics "allows this return to the spirit of the [data protection] law and offers other insights for conducting an analysis of digital society, such as its collective ethos, its claims to social justice, democracy and personal freedom".[2]

This ethical turn was justified by the broader effects of data-intensive technologies in terms of social and ethical impacts, including the collective dimension of data use.[3] In the same vein, the European Commission set up a high-level group focusing on ethical issues.[4] This ethical wave later resulted in a flourishing of ethical principles, codes and ethical boards in private companies.[5]

---

[1] E.g., Center for Data Innovation 2021.

[2] European Data Protection Supervisor, Ethics Advisory Group 2018, 7. See also European Data Protection Supervisor 2018; European Data Protection Supervisor 2015.

[3] Mantelero 2016. See also Ferguson 2017; Goodman and Powles 2019.

[4] Independent High-Level Expert Group on Artificial Intelligence set up by the European Commission 2019.

[5] See also Taylor and Dencik 2020.

This new focus, which also presented the danger of 'ethics-washing',[6] had the merit of shedding light on basic questions of the social acceptability of highly invasive predictive AI. Such systems may be legally compliant, while at the same time raising crucial questions about the society we want to create, in terms of technological determinism, distribution of power, inclusiveness and equality.

But the ethical debate frequently addressed challenging questions within a rather blurred theoretical framework, with the result that ethical principles were sometimes confused with fundamental rights and freedoms, or principles that were already part of the human rights framework were simply renamed.

A rebalancing of the debate has come from the different approach of the Council of Europe, which has remained focused on its traditional human rights-centred mission,[7] and the change of direction of the European Commission with a new bundle of proposals for AI regulation.[8] These bodies do not marginalise the role of ethics, but see moral and social values as complementary to a strategy based on legal provisions and centred on risk management and human rights.[9]

There are three possible approaches to grounding future AI regulation on human rights, which differ depending on the context in which they are placed – international or EU – and their focus.

The first is the principles-based approach, designed mainly for an international context characterised by a variety of national regulations. Here a set of key principles is clearly needed to provide a common framework for AI regulation at the regional or global level.

The second approach, also designed for the international context, is more focused on risk management and safeguarding individual rights. This approach taken by the Council of Europe, can be complementary to the first one, where the former sets out the key principles and the latter contextualises human rights and freedoms in relation to AI by adding rights-based risk management.

The third approach, embodied by the EU proposal on AI regulation, puts a greater emphasis on (high) risk management in terms of product safety and a conformity assessment. Here the regulatory strategy on AI is centred on a predefined risk classification, a combination of safety and rights protections and standardised processes.

These three models therefore offer a range of options, from a general principles-based approach to a more industry-friendly regulation centred on a

[6] Wagner 2018a.

[7] At its 1353rd meeting on 11 September 2019, the Committee of Ministers of the Council of Europe established an Ad Hoc Committee on Artificial Intelligence (CAHAI) to examine the feasibility and potential elements, on the basis of broad multi-stakeholder consultations, of a legal framework for the development, design and application of artificial intelligence, based on Council of Europe's standards on human rights, democracy and the rule of law.

[8] European Commission 2020d. See also European Commission 2020b.

[9] On the relationship between human right and fundamental rights, see Chap. 1, fn. 90.

conformity assessment of high-risk AI systems. Despite these differences, human rights remain a key element of all of them, though with significant distinctions in emphasis.

All these models also adopt the same co-regulation schema combining hard law provisions with soft-law instruments. This gives the framework flexibility in a field characterised by the rapid evolution of technology and emergence of new issues, while also giving space to sector-specific challenges and bottom-up initiatives.

The HRESIA framework can contribute to all three models by providing a human rights-centred perspective and bridging the two phases of the AI debate by combining a legal framework that takes into account ethical and societal issues with an operational focus that is often absent in the current proposals.

4.2 The Principles-Based Approach

The starting point in identifying the guiding principles that, from a human rights perspective, should underpin future AI regulation is to analyse the existing international legally binding instruments that necessarily represent the general framework in this field. This includes a gap analysis to ascertain the extent to which the current regulatory framework and its values properly address the new issues raised by AI.

Moreover, a principles-based approach focusing on human rights has to consider the state of the art with a view to preserving the harmonisation of the human rights framework, while introducing coherent new AI-specific provisions.

This principles-based approach consists in a targeted intervention, as it focuses on the changes AI will bring to society and not on reshaping every area where AI can be applied. The identification of key principles for AI builds on existing binding instruments and the contextualisation of their guiding principles.

Both the existing binding instruments and the related non-binding implementations – which in some cases already contemplate the new AI scenario – must be considered. This is based on the assumption that the general principles provided by international human rights instruments should underpin all human activities, including AI-based innovation.[10]

Defining key principles for the future regulation of AI through analysis of the existing legal framework requires a deductive methodology, extracting these principles from the range of regulations governing the fields in which AI solutions may be adopted. Two different approaches are possible to achieve this goal: a theoretical rights-focused approach and a field-focused approach based on the provisions set out in existing legal instruments.

In the first case, the various rights enshrined in human rights legal instruments are considered independently and in their abstract notion,[11] looking at how AI

[10] Council of Europe, Committee of Ministers 2020.

[11] Fjeld et al. 2020; Raso et al. 2018.

might affect their exercise. In the second, the focus shifts to the legal instruments themselves and areas they cover, to assess their adequacy in responding to the challenges that AI poses in each sector, from heath to justice.

From a regulatory perspective, and with a view to a future AI regulation, building on a theoretical elaboration of individual rights may be more difficult as it entails a potential overlap with the existing legal instruments and may not properly deal with the sectoral elaboration of such rights. On the other hand, a focus on legal instruments and their implementation can facilitate better harmonisation of new provisions on AI within the context of existing rules and binding instruments.

Once the guiding principles have been identified, they should be contextualised within the scenario transformed by AI, which in many cases requires their adaptation. The principles remain valid, but their implementation must be reconsidered in light of the social and technical changes due to AI.[12] This delivers a more precise and granular application of these principles so that they can provide a concrete contribution to the shape of future AI regulation.

This principles-based approach requires a vertical analysis of the key principles in each of the fields regulated by international instruments, followed by a second phase considering the similarities and common elements across all fields. Ultimately, such an approach should valorise the individual human rights, but departing from the existing legal framework and not from an abstract theoretical notion of each right and freedom.

As the existing international instruments are sector-specific and not rights-based, the focus of the initial analysis is on thematic areas and then a set of guiding principles common to all areas is developed. These shared principles can serve as the cornerstone for a common core of future AI provisions.

A key element in this process is the contextualisation of the guiding principles and legal values, taking advantage of the non-binding instruments which provide granular applications of the principles enshrined in the binding instruments.

AI technologies have an impact on a variety of sectors[13] and raise issues relating to a large body of regulatory instruments. However, from a methodological point of view, a possible principles-based approach to AI regulation can be validated by selecting a few key areas where the impact of AI on individuals and society is particularly marked and the challenges are significant. This is the case for data protection and healthcare.

The intersection between these two realms is interesting in view of future AI regulation, given the large number of AI applications concerning healthcare data

---

[12] This is the case, for example, with freedom of choice using so-called AI black boxes.

[13] See also UNESCO 2019.

and the common ground between the two fields. This is reflected in several provisions of international binding instruments,[14] as well as non-binding instruments.[15] Individual self-determination also plays a central role in both these fields, and the challenges of AI – in terms of the complexity and opacity of medical treatments and data processing operations – are therefore particularly relevant and share common concerns.

4.2.1 Key Principles from Personal Data Regulation

Over the past decade, the international regulatory framework in the field of data protection has seen significant renewal. Legal instruments shaped by principles defined in the 1970s and 1980s no longer responded to the changed socio-technical landscape created by the increasing availability of bandwidth for data transfer, data storage and computational resources (cloud computing), the progressive datafication of large parts of our life and environment (The Internet of Things, IoT), and large-scale and predictive data analysis based on Big Data and Machine Learning.

In Europe the main responses to this change have been the modernised version of Convention 108 (Convention 108+) and the GDPR. A similar redefinition of the regulatory framework has occurred, or is ongoing, in other international contexts – such as the OECD[16] – or in individual countries.

However, given the rapid development of the last wave of AI, these new measures fail to directly address some AI-specific challenges and several non-binding instruments have been adopted to bridge this gap, as well as future regulatory strategies under discussion.[17] This section examines the following data-related international non-binding legal instruments: Council of Europe, Guidelines on Artificial Intelligence and Data Protection [GAI];[18] Council of Europe, Guidelines on the protection of individuals with regard to the processing of personal data in a world of Big Data [GBD];[19] Recommendation CM/Rec(2019)2 of the Committee of Ministers of the Council of Europe to member States on the

---

[14] E.g. the provisions of the Oviedo Convention (Council of Europe, Convention for the Protection of Human Rights and Dignity of the Human Being with regard to the Application of Biology and Medicine: Convention on Human Rights and Biomedicine, Oviedo, 4 April 1997) and Convention 108+ (Modernised Convention for the Protection of Individuals with Regard to the Processing of Personal Data, adopted by the Committee of Ministers of the Council of Europe at its 128th Session of the Committee of Ministers, Elsinore, 18 May 2018).

[15] Council of Europe, Committee of Ministers 2019.

[16] OECD 2013.

[17] European Commission 2020c, d. See also European Commission 2020a.

[18] Consultative Committee of the Convention for the Protection of Individuals with regard to Automatic Processing of Personal Data (Convention 108) 2019.

[19] Council of Europe, Consultative Committee of the Convention for the Protection of Individuals with regard to Automatic Processing of Personal Data (Convention 108) 2017.

protection of health-related data [CM/Rec(2019)2];[20] Recommendation CM/Rec (2010)13 of the Committee of Ministers of the Council of Europe to member States on the protection of individuals with regard to automatic processing of personal data in the context of profiling [CM/Rec(2010)13]; UNESCO, Preliminary Study on a Possible Standard-Setting Instrument on the Ethics of Artificial Intelligence, 2019 [UNESCO 2019];[21] OECD, Recommendation of the Council on Artificial Intelligence, 2019 [OECD];[22] 40th International Conference of Data Protection and Privacy Commissioners, Declaration on Ethics and Data Protection in Artificial Intelligence, 2018 [ICDPPC].[23,24]

These instruments differ in nature: while some instruments define specific requirements and provisions, others are mainly principles-based instruments setting out certain guidelines but without, or only partially, providing more detailed rules.

Based on these instruments and focusing on those provisions that are most pertinent to AI issues,[25] it is possible to identify several general guiding principles which are then contextualised with respect to AI. Several of these principles can be extended to non-personal data, mainly in regard to the impact of its use (e.g. aggregated data) on individual and groups in decision-making processes.

A first group of principles (the primacy of the human being, human control and oversight, participation and democratic oversight) concerns the relationship between humans and technology, granting the former – either as individuals or social groups – control over technological development, in particular regarding AI.

To refine the key requirements enabling human control over AI and support human rights-oriented development, we can identify a second set of principles focussed on the following areas: transparency, risk management, accountability, data quality, the role of experts and algorithm vigilance.

Finally, the binding and non-binding international instruments reveal a further group of more general principles concerning AI development that go beyond data protection. These include rules on interoperability between AI systems,[26] as well as digital literacy, education and professional training.[27]

---

[20] This Recommendation has replaced Council of Europe, Committee of Ministers 1997. See also Council of Europe, Committee of Ministers 2016b and its Explanatory Memorandum.

[21] Despite the reference to ethics only in the title, the purpose of the study UNESCO 2019 is described as follows: "This document contains the preliminary study on the technical and legal aspects of the desirability of a standard-setting instrument on the ethics of artificial intelligence and the comments and observations of the Executive Board thereon".

[22] https://legalinstruments.oecd.org/en/instruments/OECD-LEGAL-0449. Accessed 2 March 2020.

[23] The text of the Declaration is available at https://edps.europa.eu/sites/edp/files/publication/icdppc-40th_ai-declaration_adopted_en_0.pdf. Accessed 2 March 2020.

[24] See also Council of Europe, Committee of Ministers 2020.

[25] For a broader analysis of the issues related to data protection and human rights in general, Council of Europe-Committee of experts on internet intermediaries (MSI-NET) 2018; Mantelero 2018a; Zuiderveen Borgesius 2018. See also Fjeld et al. 2020; Raso et al. 2018.

[26] See also CM/Rec(2019)2, 1, para 14.

[27] ICDPPC, OECD, GAI para III.9, UNESCO 2019, and CM/Rec(2020)1, para 7.

4.2.1.1 Primacy of the Human Being

Although this principle is only explicitly enshrined in the Oviedo Convention and not in the binding international instruments on data protection, such as Convention 108 and 108+, the primacy of the human being is an implicit reference when data is used in the context of innovative technologies.[28] This is reflected in the idea that data processing operations must "serve the data subject".[29] More generally, the primacy of the human being over science is a direct corollary of the principle of respect for human dignity.[30] Dignity is a constitutive element of the European approach to data processing,[31] and of the international approach to civil and political rights in general.[32] Wider reference to human dignity can also be found in the non-binding instruments focused on AI.[33]

In affirming the primacy of the human being within the context of artificial intelligence, AI systems must be designed to serve mankind and the creation, development and use of these systems must fully respect human rights, democracy and the rule of law.

4.2.1.2 Human Control and Oversight

Since the notion of data protection originally rested on the idea of control over use of information in information and communication technology and the first data protection regulations were designed to give individuals some counter-control over the data that was collected,[34] human control plays a central role in this area. It is also related to the importance of self-determination[35] in the general theory of personality rights and the importance of human oversight in automated data processing.

Moreover, in the field of law and technology, human control plays an important role in terms of risk management and liability. Human control over potentially harmful technology applications ensures a degree of safeguard against the possible adverse consequences for human rights and freedoms.

---

28 Council of Europe, Parliamentary Assembly 2017. See also Strand and Kaiser 2015, 6.

29 CM/Rec(2019)2, Preamble.

30 ten Have and Jean 2009, 93.

31 Convention 108+, Preamble. See also Explanatory Report, para 10 ("Human dignity requires that safeguards be put in place when processing personal data, in order for individuals not to be treated as mere objects").

32 International Covenant on Civil and Political Rights, Preamble.

33 GAI, paras I.1 and II.1; UNESCO 2019, para II.3, OECD, para IV.1.2.

34 See Chap. 1, Sect. 1.2.

35 See also ICDPPC, para 1.1; Universal Declaration of Human Rights.

Human control is thus seen as critical from a variety of perspectives – as borne out by both Convention 108+[36] and the non-binding instruments on AI[37] – and it also encompasses human oversight on decision-making processes delegated to AI systems. Several guiding principles for future AI regulation can therefore be discerned in the instruments examined.

By contextualising human control and oversight with regard to AI applications, these applications should allow meaningful[38] control by human beings over their effects on individuals and society. Moreover, AI products and services must be designed in such a way to grant individuals the right not to be subject to a decision which significantly affects them taken solely on the basis of automated data processing, without having their views taken into consideration. In short, Al products and services must allow general human control over them.[39]

Finally, the role of human intervention in AI-based decision-making processes and the freedom of human decision makers not to rely on the result of the recommendations provided using AI should be preserved.[40]

4.2.1.3 Participation and Democratic Oversight on AI Development

Turning to the collective dimension of the use of data in AI,[41] human control and oversight cannot be limited to supervisory entities, data controllers or data subjects. Participatory and democratic oversight procedure should give voice to society at large, including various categories of people, minorities and underrepresented groups.[42] This supports the notion that participation in decision-making serves to

---

[36] Convention 108+, Preamble ("[Considering that it is necessary to secure] personal autonomy based on a person's right to control of his or her personal data and the processing of such data"). See also Explanatory Report, para 10.

[37] Council of Europe, Parliamentary Assembly 2017, para 9.3 ("the need for any machine, any robot or any artificial intelligence artefact to remain under human control") and GAI, para I.6.

[38] The adjective meaningful was discussed in the context of AWS, Moyes 2016. The author explains his preference for the adjective thus: "it is broad, it is general rather than context specific (e.g. appropriate), derives from an overarching principle rather being outcome driven (e.g. effective, sufficient), and it implies human meaning rather than something administrative, technical or bureaucratic". See also Asaro 2016, pp. 384–385. The term has been used to insist that automated tools cannot relegate humans to mere approval mechanisms. The same reasoning underpins human oversight in data processing in Europe, see Article 29 Data Protection Working Party 2018, p. 21 ("To qualify as human involvement, the controller must ensure that any oversight of the decision is meaningful, rather than just a token gesture. It should be carried out by someone who has the authority and competence to change the decision. As part of the analysis, they should consider all the relevant data").

[39] See Convention 108+; GAI, para II.8; ICDPPC; UNESCO 2019.

[40] GAI, para III. 4.

[41] Mantelero 2016.

[42] See also CM/Rec(2020)1, para 5.

advance human rights and is crucially important in bringing specific issues to the attention of the public authorities.[43]

Since human control over potentially hazardous technology entails a risk assessment,[44] this assessment should also adopt a participatory approach. Adopting this approach in the context of AI, participatory forms of risk assessment should be developed with the active engagement of the individuals and groups potentially affected. Individuals, groups, and other stakeholders should therefore be informed and actively involved in the debate on what role AI should play in shaping social dynamics, and in the decision-making processes affecting them.[45]

Derogations may be introduced in the public interest, where proportionate in a democratic society and with adequate safeguards. In this regard, in policing, intelligence, and security, where public oversight is limited, governments should report regularly on their use of AI.[46]

4.2.1.4 Transparency and Intelligibility

Transparency is a challenging[47] and highly debated topic in the context of AI,[48] with several different interpretations, including the studies on 'Explainable AI'. In this sense, it is one of the data protection principles that is stressed most frequently.[49]

But effective transparency is mired by complex analysis processes, non-deterministic models, and the dynamic nature of many algorithms. Furthermore, solutions such as the right to explanation focus on decisions affecting specific persons, while the problems of collective use of AI at group level[50] remain unaddressed.

In any case, none of these points diminishes the argument for the central role of transparency and AI intelligibility in safeguarding individual and collective self-determination. This is truer still in the public sector, where the limited variability of algorithms (ensuring equality of treatment and uniform public procurement procedures) can afford greater transparency levels.

In the AI context, every individual must therefore have the right to be properly informed when interacting directly with an AI system and to receive adequate and

[43] ICDPPC, para 25. See also United Nations, Office of the High Commissioner for Human Rights 2018.

[44] See below in Sect. 4.2.1.5.

[45] GAI, paras II.7 and III.8. See also United Nations, Office of the High Commissioner for Human Rights 2018, para 64.

[46] UNESCO 2019, para 107.K.

[47] Mantelero 2018a, pp. 11–13.

[48] E.g. Selbst and Barocas 2018; Wachter et al. 2017; Selbst and Powles 2017; Edwards and Veale 2017.

[49] Convention 108+, Article 8.

[50] Taylor et al. 2017.

easy-to-understand information on its purpose and effects, including the existence of automated decisions. This information is necessary to enable overall human control over such systems, to verify alignment with individuals' expectations and to enable those adversely affected by an AI system to challenge its outcome.[51] Every individual should also have a right to obtain, on request, knowledge of the reasoning underlying any AI-based decision-making process where the results of such process are applied to him or her.[52]

Finally, to foster transparency and intelligibility, governments should promote scientific research on explainable AI and best practices for transparency and auditability of AI systems.[53]

4.2.1.5 Precautionary Approach and Risk Management

Regarding the potentially adverse consequences of technology in general, it is important to make a distinction between cases in which the outcome is known with a certain probability and those where it is unknown (uncertainty). Since building prediction models for uncertain consequences is difficult, we must assume that "uncertainty and risk are defined as two mutually exclusive concepts".[54]

Where there is scientific uncertainty about the potential outcome, a precautionary approach[55] should be taken, rather than conducting a risk analysis.[56] The same conclusion can be drawn for AI where the potential risks of an AI application are unknown or uncertain.[57] In all other cases, AI developers, manufacturers and service providers should assess and document the possible adverse consequences of their work for human rights and fundamental freedoms, and adopt appropriate risk prevention and mitigation measures from the design phase (human rights by-design approach) and throughout the lifecycle of AI products and services.[58]

The development of AI raises specific forms of risk in the field of data protection. One widely discussed example is that of re-identification,[59] while the risk of de-contextualisation is less well known. In the latter case, data-intensive AI applications may ignore contextual information needed to understand and apply the

---

[51] Convention 108+, Article 8; CM/Rec(2019)2, para 11.3; OECD, para 1.3; UNESCO 2019, Annex I, p. 28. See also ICDPPC, para 3; CM/Rec(2020)1, Appendix, para C.4.1.

[52] Convention 108+, Article 9.1.c; GAI, para II.11.

[53] ICDPPC, para 3.a.

[54] Hansson 2013, p. 12.

[55] See also Peel 2004.

[56] See also Chap. 2, Sect. 2.2. For a broader analysis of risk assessment in the field of AI, see also Mantelero 2018b.

[57] GAI, para II.2. See also Mantelero 2017; ICDPPC ("Highlighting that those risks and challenges may affect individuals and society, and that the extent and nature of potential consequences are currently uncertain"); CM/Rec(2020)1, Appendix, para A.15.

[58] GAI, paras II.2 and II.3; OECD, para 1.4; UNESCO 2019. See also ICDPPC and OECD 2015.

[59] E.g., Narayanan et al. 2016; Ohm 2010.

proposed solution. De-contextualisation can also impact the choice of algorithmic models, re-using them without prior assessment in different contexts and for different purposes, or using models trained on historical data of a different population.[60]

The adverse consequences of AI development and deployment should therefore include those that are due to the use of de-contextualised data and de-contextualised algorithmic models.[61] Suitable measures should also be introduced to guard against the possibility that anonymous and aggregated data may result in the re-identification of the data subjects.[62]

Finally, Convention 108+ (like the GDPR) adopts a two-stage approach to risk: an initial self-assessment is followed by a consultation with the competent supervisory authority if there is residual high risk. A similar model can be extended to AI-related risks.[63] AI developers, manufacturers, and service providers should consult a competent supervisory authority where AI applications have the potential to significantly impact the human rights and fundamental freedoms of individuals.[64]

4.2.1.6 Accountability

The principle of accountability is recognised in Convention 108+[65] and is more generally considered as a key element of risk management policy. In the context of AI,[66] it is important to stress that human accountability cannot be hidden behind the machine. Although AI generates more complicated scenarios,[67] this does not exclude accountability and responsibility of the various human actors involved in the design, development, deployment and use of AI.[68]

From this follows the principle that the automated nature of any decision made by an AI system does not exempt its developers, manufacturers, service providers, owners and managers from responsibility and accountability for the effects and consequences of the decision.

---

[60] Caplan et al. 2018, 7; AI Now Institute 2018.

[61] GAI, para II.5. This principle is also repeated in CM/Rec(2020)1, Appendix, para B3.4.

[62] See also CM/Rec(2010)13, para 8.5.

[63] GAI, para III.5. See also Data Ethics Commission of the Federal Government, Federal Ministry of the Interior Building and Community and Data Ethics Commission 2019, 42, which also suggests the introduction of licensing and oversight procedures.

[64] GAI, para III.4.

[65] Convention 108+, Article 10.1.

[66] OECD para IV.1.5; GAI paras I.2 and III.1.

[67] See also European Commission, Expert Group on Liability 2019.

[68] See also Council of Europe, Parliamentary Assembly 2017, para 9.1.1.

4.2.1.7 Data Minimisation and Data Quality

Data-intensive applications, such as Big Data analytics and AI, require a large amount of data to produce useful results, and this poses significant challenges for the data minimisation principle.[69] Furthermore, the data must be gathered according to effective data quality criteria to prevent potential bias, since the consequences for rights and freedoms can be critical.[70]

In the context of AI, this means that developers are required to assess the nature and amount of data used (data quality) and minimise the presence of redundant or marginal data[71] during the development and training phases, then monitoring the model's accuracy as it is fed with new data.[72]

AI development and deployment should avoid any potential bias, including unintentional or hidden, and critically assess the quality, nature, origin and amount of personal data used, limiting unnecessary, redundant or marginal data, and monitoring the model's accuracy.[73]

4.2.1.8 Role of Experts and Participation

The complex potential impacts of AI solutions on individuals and society demand that AI development process cannot be delegated to technicians alone. The role of experts from various domains was highlighted in the first non-binding document on AI and data protection, suggesting AI developers, manufacturers and service providers set up and consult independent committees of experts from a range of fields, and engage with independent academic institutions, which can help in the design of human rights-based AI applications.[74] Participatory forms of AI development, based on the active engagement of the individuals and groups potentially affected by AI applications, should also been encouraged.[75]

4.2.1.9 Algorithm Vigilance

The existing supervisory authorities (e.g. data protection authorities, communication authorities, antitrust authorities, etc.) and the various stakeholders involved in

---

69 Convention 108+, Article 5.

70 GAI paras II.2 and II.6. See also CM/Rec(2020)1, Appendix, para B.2.2.

71 Synthetic data can make a contribution to this end; see also The Norwegian Data Protection Authority 2018.

72 See also GBD, paras IV.4.2 and IV.4.3.

73 GAI, para II.4; OECD; UNESCO 2019.

74 GAI, para II.6, ICDPPC. See also UNESCO, Declaration on the Human Genome and Human Rights, 11 November 1997, Article 11; CM/Rec(2020)1, Appendix, para B.5.3.

75 GAI, para II.7.

the development and deployment of AI solutions should both adopt forms of algorithm vigilance to react quickly in the event of unexpected and hazardous outcomes.[76]

AI developers, manufacturers, and service providers should therefore implement algorithm vigilance by promoting the accountability of all relevant stakeholders, assessing and documenting the expected impacts on individuals and society in each phase of the AI system lifecycle on a continuous basis, so as to ensure compliance with human rights.[77] Cooperation should be encouraged in this regard between different supervisory authorities having competence for AI.[78]

4.2.2 Key Principles from Biomedicine Regulation

Compared with data protection, international legal instruments on health protection provide a more limited and sector-specific contribution to the draft of future AI regulation. While data is a core component of AI, such that several principles can be derived from international instruments of data protection, healthcare is simply one of many sectors in which AI can be applied. This entails a dual process of contextualisation: (i) some principles stated in the field of data protection can be further elaborated upon with regard to biomedicine; (ii) new principles must be introduced to better address the specific challenges of AI in the sector.

Starting with the Universal Declaration of Human Rights, several international binding instruments include provisions concerning health protection.[79] Among them, the International Covenant on Economic, Social and Cultural Rights, the European Convention on Human Rights, Convention 108+ and the European Social Charter, all lay down several general provisions on health protection and related rights.[80] Provisions and principles already set out in other general instruments have a more sector-specific contextualisation in the Universal Declaration on Bioethics and Human Rights (UNESCO) and the Oviedo Convention[81] (Council of Europe).

---

[76] See also Commission Nationale de l'Informatique et des Libertés – LINC 2017; The Public Voice 2018.

[77] GAI, para II.10; OECD; ICDPPC.

[78] ICDPPC; GAI, para III.6

[79] E.g. Office of the High Commissioner for Human Rights 2000, p. 21; Yamin 2005. At a national and EU level, most of the existing regulation on health focuses on medical treatment, research (including clinical trials) and medical devices/products. AI has a potential impact on all these areas, given its application in precision medicine, diagnosis, and medical devices and services. See also Azencott 2018; Ferryman and Pitcan 2018.

[80] See also the International Covenant on Civil and Political Rights, and the Convention on the Rights of the Child of 20 November 1989.

[81] Convention for the Protection of Human Rights and Dignity of the Human Being with regard to the Application of Biology and Medicine: Convention on Human Rights and Biomedicine, Oviedo, 4 April 1997.

The Oviedo Convention – the only multilateral binding instrument entirely focused on biomedicine – and its additional protocols is the main source to identify the key principles in this field,[82] which require further elaboration to be applied to AI regulation. The Convention is complemented by two non-binding instruments: the Recommendation on health data[83] and the Recommendation on research on biological materials of human origin.[84] The former illustrates the close links between biomedicine (and healthcare more generally) and data processing.

Although the Universal Declaration on Bioethics and Human Rights and the Oviedo Convention – including the related non-binding instruments –, were adopted in a pre-AI era, they provide specific safeguards regarding self-determination, human genome treatments, and research involving human beings, which are unaffected by AI application in this field and require no changes.

However, self-determination in the area of biomedicine faces the same challenges as already discussed for data processing. Notwithstanding the different nature of consent to medical treatment and to data processing, the high degree of complexity and, in several cases, obscurity in AI applications can often undermine the effective exercise of individual autonomy in both cases.[85]

Against this background, the main contribution of the binding international instruments in the field of biomedicine does not concern the sector-specific safeguards they provide, but consists in the important set of general principles and values that can be extrapolated from them to form a building block of future AI regulation.

The key principles can be identified in relation to the following nine areas: primacy of the human being, equitable access, acceptability, the principle of beneficence, private life and right to information, professional standards, non-discrimination, the role of experts, and public debate. This contribution goes beyond biomedicine since several provisions, centred on an appropriate balance between technology and human rights, can be extended to AI in general and contextualised in this field, as explained in the following analysis.[86]

4.2.2.1 Primacy of the Human Being

In a geo-political and economic context characterised by competitive AI development, the primacy of the human being must be affirmed as a key element in the

[82] Andorno 2005; Seatzu 2015.

[83] Council of Europe, Committee of Ministers 2019.

[84] Council of Europe, Committee of Ministers 2016a.

[85] See above Sect. 4.2.1.

[86] Human dignity and informed consent are not included in the table as the first is a value common to the instruments adopted by the Council of Europe in the area of human rights, democracy and the rule of law (see Sect. 3.1) and informed consent is a principle that is also relevant in the context of data processing.

human rights-oriented approach:[87] the drive for better performance and efficiency in AI-based systems cannot override the interests and welfare of human beings.

This principle must apply to both the development and use of AI systems (e.g. ruling out systems that violate human rights and freedoms or that have been developed in violation of them).

4.2.2.2 Equitable Access to Health Care

The principle of equitable access to healthcare,[88] should be extended to the benefits of AI,[89] especially considering the increasing use of AI in the healthcare sector. This means taking appropriate measures to combat the digital divide, discrimination, marginalisation of vulnerable persons or cultural minorities, and limited access to information.

4.2.2.3 Acceptability

Based on Article 12 of the International Covenant on Economic, Social and Cultural Rights, the Committee on Economic, Social and Cultural Rights clarified the notion of acceptability, declaring that all health facilities, goods and services must "be respectful of medical ethics and culturally appropriate".[90] Given the potentially high impact of AI-based solutions on society and groups,[91] acceptability is also a key factor in AI development, as demonstrated by the emphasis on the ethical and cultural dimension found in some non-binding instruments.[92]

4.2.2.4 Principle of Beneficence

Respect for the principle of beneficence in biomedicine and bioethics and human rights[93] should be seen as a requirement where, as mentioned above, the complexity or opacity of AI-based treatments places limitations on individual consent which

---

[87] See also Oviedo Convention, Article 2, and GAI.

[88] Oviedo Convention, Article 3.

[89] See also UNESCO, Universal Declaration on Bioethics and Human Rights, Article 2.f.

[90] Office of the High Commissioner for Human Rights 2000. See also UNESCO, Universal Declaration on Bioethics and Human Rights, Article 12; GBD, paras IV.1 and IV.2.

[91] Taylor et al. 2017.

[92] GAI paras I.4 and II.6; CM/Rec(2020)1.

[93] UNESCO, Universal Declaration on Bioethics and Human Rights, Article 4. See also Oviedo Convention, Article 6 ("an intervention may only be carried out on a person who does not have the capacity to consent, for his or her direct benefit"), and Articles 16 and 17.

cannot therefore be the exclusive basis for intervention. In such cases, the best interest of the person concerned should be the main criterion in the use of AI applications.[94]

4.2.2.5 Private Life and Right to Information

In line with the considerations expressed earlier on data protection, the safeguards concerning self-determination with regard to private life and the right to information already recognised in the field of medicine[95] could be extended to AI regulation.

With specific reference to the bidirectional right to information about health, AI health applications must guarantee the right to information and respect the wishes of individuals not to be informed, unless compliance with an individual's wish not to be informed entails a serious risk to the health of others.[96]

4.2.2.6 Professional Standards

Professional standards are a key factor in biomedicine,[97] given the potential impacts on individual rights and freedoms. Similarly, AI development involves several areas of expertise, each with its own professional obligations and standards, which must be met where the development of AI systems can affect individuals and society.

Professional skills requirements must be based on the current state of the art. Governments should encourage professional training to raise awareness and understanding of AI and its potential effects on individuals and society, as well as supporting research into human rights-oriented AI.

---

[94] See also Beauchamp 1990, p. 153 ("virtually everyone acknowledges-under any model-that a person who is nonautonomous or significantly defective in autonomy is highly dependent on others, does not properly fall under the autonomy model, and therefore should be protected under the beneficence model"); Pellegrino and Thomasma 1987, 42 ("[in the beneficent model] No ethical stance, other than acting for the patient's best interests, is applied beforehand").

[95] Oviedo Convention, Article 10. See also UNESCO, Universal Declaration on Bioethics and Human Rights, Article 10.

[96] See also Council of Europe, Committee of Ministers 2019, para 7.6 "The data subject is entitled to know any information relating to their genetic data, subject to the provisions of principles 11.8 and 12.7. Nevertheless, the data subject may have their own reasons for not wishing to know about certain health aspects and everyone should be aware, prior to any analysis, of the possibility of not being informed of the results, including of unexpected findings. Their wish not to know may, in exceptional circumstances, have to be restricted, as foreseen by law, notably in the data subject's own interest or in light of the doctors' duty to provide care"); UNESCO, Declaration on the Human Genome and Human Rights, 11 November 1997, Article 5.c.

[97] Oviedo Convention, Article 4. See also Council of Europe, Committee of Ministers 2019.

4.2.2.7 Non-discrimination

The principle of non-discrimination[98] and non-stigmatisation in the field of biomedicine and bioethics[99] should be complemented by ruling out any form of discrimination against a person or group based on predictions of future health conditions.[100]

4.2.2.8 Role of Experts

The expertise of ethics committees in the field of biomedicine[101] should be called upon to provide independent, multidisciplinary and pluralist committees of experts in the assessment of AI applications.[102]

4.2.2.9 Public Debate

As with biomedicine,[103] fundamental questions raised by AI development should be exposed to proper public scrutiny as to the crucial social, economic, ethical and legal implications, and their application subject to consultation.

Examination of the above key areas demonstrates that the current legal framework on biomedicine can provide important principles and elements to be extended to future AI regulation, beyond the biomedicine sector. However, four particular shortcomings created by the impact of AI remain unresolved, or only partially addressed, and should be further discussed:

(a) Decision-making Systems

In recent years a growing number of AI applications have been developed for medical diagnosis, using data analytics and ML solutions. Large-scale data pools and predictive analytics are used to try and arrive at clinical solutions based on available knowledge and practices. ML applications in image recognition may provide increased cancer detection capability. Likewise, in precision medicine, large-scale collection and analysis of multiple data sources (medical as well as non-medical data, such as air and housing quality) are used to develop personalised responses to health and disease.

The use of clinical data, medical records and practices, as well as non-medical data, is not in itself new in medicine and public health studies. However, the scale

[98] Oviedo Convention, Article 11.

[99] UNESCO. Universal Declaration on Bioethics and Human Rights, Article 11.

[100] See also Council of Europe, Committee of Ministers 2016a, Article 5.

[101] Oviedo Convention, Article 16. See also UNESCO, Universal Declaration on Bioethics and Human Rights, Article 19.

[102] See Chap. 3. See also GBD.

[103] Oviedo Convention, Article 28.

of data collection, the granularity of the information gathered, the complexity (and in some cases opacity) of data processing, and the predictive nature of the results raise concerns about the potential fragility of decision-making systems. Most of these issues are not limited to the health sector, as potential biases (including lack of diversity and the exclusion of outliers and smaller populations), data quality, de-contextualisation, context-based data labelling and the re-use of data[104] are common to many AI applications and concern data in general. Existing guidance in the field of data protection[105] can therefore be applied here too and the data quality aspects extended to non-personal data.

(b) Self-determination
The opacity of AI applications and the transformative use of data in large-scale data analysis undermine the traditional notion of consent in both data processing[106] and medical treatment. New schemes could be adopted, such as broad[107] or dynamic consent,[108] which however – at the present state of the art – would only partially address this problem.

(c) The Doctor-Patient Relationship
There are several factors in AI-based diagnosis – such as the loss of knowledge that cannot be encoded in data,[109] over-reliance on AI in medical decisions, the effects of local practices on training datasets, and potential deskilling in the healthcare sector[110] – that might affect the doctor-patient relationship[111] and need to be evaluated carefully before adoption.

---

[104] Ferryman and Pitcan 2018, pp. 19–20 ("Because disease labels, such as sepsis, are not clear cut, individual labels may be used to describe very different clinical realities" and "these records were not designed for research, but for billing purposes, which could be a source of systematic error and bias").

[105] GBD and the related preliminary studies: Mantelero 2018a, and Rouvroy 2015.

[106] See Chap. 1; see also Council of Europe, Committee of Ministers 2019.

[107] Sheehan 2011. See also Convention 108+, Explanatory Report, p. 43 ("In the context of scientific research it is often not possible to fully identify the purpose of personal data processing for scientific research purposes at the time of data collection. Therefore, data subjects should be allowed to give their consent to certain areas of scientific research in keeping with recognised ethical standards for scientific research. Data subjects should have the opportunity to give their consent only to certain areas of research or parts of research projects to the extent allowed by the intended purpose") and Council of Europe, Committee of Ministers 2019, 15.6 ("As it is not always possible to determine beforehand the purposes of different research projects at the time of the collection of data, data subjects should be able to express consent for certain areas of research or certain parts of research projects, to the extent allowed by the intended purpose, with due regard for recognised ethical standards").

[108] Kaye et al. 2015.

[109] Caruana et al. 2015.

[110] Cabitza et al. 2017.

[111] See also, UNESCO, Universal Declaration on Bioethics and Human Rights, Article 20; WMA Declaration of Helsinki – Ethical Principles for Medical Research Involving Human Subjects, 9 July 2018. https://www.wma.net/policies-post/wma-declaration-of-helsinki-ethical-principles-for-medical-research-involving-human-subjects/, accessed 6 March 2020.

(d) Risk Management
The medical device industry has already developed risk-based regulatory models, such as Regulation (EU) 2017/745 – based on progressive safeguards according to the class of risk of each device –, which could be generalised for the future AI regulation focusing on the impact on human rights and fundamental freedoms. However, a risk-based classification of AI by law is complicated, given its variety and different fields of application.[112]

4.2.3 A Contribution to a Future Principles-Based Regulation of AI

Based on the analysis of two key areas of AI application, the principles-based approach has revealed how it is possible to define future AI regulation by focusing on a set of guiding principles developed in a way consistent with the existing international human rights framework and reaffirming the central role of human dignity and human rights in AI, where machine-driven solutions risk dehumanising individuals.[113]

The principle-based methodological process, consisting of analysis (mapping and identification of key principles) and contextualisation, has proven its merit in the areas examined, with the development of several key principles. Correlations and a common ground between these principles have been identified facilitating their harmonisation, while other principles represent the unique contributions of each sector to future AI regulation.

The table below (Table 4.1) summarises these findings and the level of harmonisation in these two areas and, notwithstanding the limitations of the scope of this analysis, shows how its results validate the principles-based methodology as a possible scenario for future AI regulation.

---

[112] See in this regard the considerations expressed in Sect. 4.3.2.

[113] See also UNESCO, Declaration on the Human Genome and Human Rights (11 November 1997), Article 2. This may also include the adoption of bans on specific AI technologies developed in a manner inconsistent with human dignity, human rights, democracy and the rule of law. See also UNESCO, Declaration on the Human Genome and Human Rights (11 November 1997), Article 11; Data Ethics Commission of the Federal Government, Federal Ministry of the Interior 2019; Access Now 2019.

Table 4.1 Key principles in Data and Health (AI regulation)

Data	Health
Primacy of human being	Primacy of the human being
Data protection and right to information on data processing	Private life and right to information
Digital literacy, education and professional training Accountability	Professional standards
Transparency and intelligibility	Right to information
Precautionary approach and risk management Algorithm vigilance	Principle of beneficence Non-discrimination Equitable access
Role of experts	Role of experts
Participation and democratic oversight on AI development	Public debate
	Acceptability
Data minimisation and data quality	

Source The author

4.3 From Design to Law – The European Approaches and the Regulatory Paradox

In previous sections we have seen how the future regulation of AI could be based on existing international principles. We can carry out a similar exercise with respect to EU law, where similar principles are recognised, though in the presence of a wider variety of binding instruments, owing to the EU's broader field of action.

Rather than adopt the principles-based methodology described, neither the EU legislator nor the Council of Europe decided to follow this path. Both European legislators abandoned the idea of setting common funding principles for AI development and opted for a different and more minimalist approach with a greater emphasis on risk prevention.

While the focus on risk is crucial and in line with the HRESIA, there is something of a regulatory paradox in Europe's approach to AI. An attempt to provide guiding principles was made through ethical guidelines – such as those drafted by the HLEGAI[114] –, vesting legal principles in ethical requirements. On the other hand, recent regulatory proposals based on binding instruments have preferred not to provide a framework of principles but focus on specific issues such as banning applications, risk management and conformity assessment.

This is a regulatory paradox, where general legal principles are set out in ethical guidelines while the actual legal provisions lack a comprehensive framework. Although this is more pronounced in Brussels than in Strasbourg, concerns at a

[114] See Chap. 3, Sect. 3.1.2.

European level about the impact of AI regulation on competition and the weakness of the AI industry in Europe appear to take precedence over far-reaching regulation.

Such concerns have restricted measures to high-risk applications,[115] leaving aside a broader discussion of the role of AI in society and citizen participation in AI project development. This bears similarities with what we witnessed with the first generation of data protection law in Europe in the 1960's, where the principle concern was risk and the need to provide safeguards against the danger of a database society.[116] Only in later waves of legislation was a more sophisticated framework established with reference to general principles, fundamental rights, and comprehensive regulation of data processing. A similar path could be foreseen for AI and here a principles-based methodology described above might figure in more extensive regulation to resolve the present paradox.

The two European legislators also display further similarities in their approach to co-regulation – combining hard and soft law –, setting red lines on the most harmful AI applications, and oversight procedures.

Finally, neither of the proposals seem oriented towards the creation of a new set of rights specifically tailored to AI. This decision is important since the contextualisation of existing rights and freedoms can often provide adequate safeguards, while some proposals for new generic rights – such as the right to digital identity – rest on notions that are still in their infancy, and not mature enough to be enshrined in a legal instrument.

Against these similarities between the two European initiatives, differences necessarily remain, given the distinct institutional and political remits of the Council of Europe and the European Union: the Council's more variable political and regulatory situation, compared with the EU; the different goals of the two entities, one focused on human rights, democracy and the rule of law, and the other on the internal market and more detailed regulation; the different status of the Council of Europe's international instruments, which are addressed to Member States, and the EU's regulations which are directly applicable in all Member States; and – not least – the business interests and pressures which are inevitably more acute for the European Union given the immediate impact of EU regulation on business.

Having described the key features of Europe's approach, we can go on to discuss the main ways in which it deals with AI risk. After looking at the framing of the relationship between the perceived risks of AI and the safeguarding of human rights in Strasbourg and Brussels, we will examine the possible contribution of the HRESIA model to future regulation.

---

[115] See the subject matter of the European Commission, Proposal for Regulation of the European Parliament and of the Council laying down harmonised rules on Artificial Intelligence (Artificial Intelligence Act) as set in its Article 1: (i) prohibition of certain artificial intelligence practices; (ii) specific requirements for high-risk AI systems; (iii) transparency rules for certain AI systems; (iv) market monitoring and surveillance.

[116] Westin and Baker 1972, p. 346.

4.3.1 *The Council of Europe's Risk-Based Approach Centred on Human Rights, Democracy and Rule of Law*

On 11 September 2019, during its 1353rd meeting, the Committee of Ministers of the Council of Europe set up the Ad hoc Committee on Artificial Intelligence (CAHAI), mandated to examine the feasibility and potential elements of a legal framework for the development, design and application of AI based on the Council of Europe's standards on human rights, democracy and the rule of law.[117] This was the fruit of several ongoing AI initiatives in different branches of the Council of Europe, which had already led to the adoption of important documents in specific sectors.[118]

The CAHAI mandate also confirmed the Council of Europe's focus on legal instruments and its disinclination to regulate AI on the basis of ethical principles.[119] In this sense, the Council of Europe anticipated the EU's turn towards legislation.

After a preliminary study of the most important international and national legal frameworks and ethical guidelines, and an analysis of the risks and opportunities of AI for human rights, democracy and the rule of law,[120] the CAHAI conducted a Feasibility Study on the development of a horizontal cross-cutting regulatory framework[121] on the use and effects of AI (plus policy tools, such as impact

---

[117] This author served as an independent scientific expert to the CAHAI for the preliminary study of the existing legally binding instruments on AI and was a member of the CAHAI as scientific expert to the Council of Europe's Consultative Committee of the Convention for the protection of individuals with regard to automatic processing (Convention 108). The views and opinions expressed in this chapter are those of the author and do not necessarily reflect the Council of Europe's official policy or position. They are based solely on publicly available documents and do not rely on, or refer to, confidential information or internal procedures and exchanges of opinions.

[118] Council of Europe, Committee of Ministers 2020; Council of Europe, Consultative Committee of the Convention for the Protection of Individuals with regard to Automatic Processing of Personal Data (Convention 108) 2019; Council of Europe, Consultative Committee of the Convention for the Protection of Individuals with regard to Automatic Processing of Personal Data (Convention 108) 2021.

[119] This is also evident in Council of Europe, European Commission for the Efficiency of Justice (CEPEJ) 2018 which, despite the reference to ethics, focuses on fundamental rights and the principle of non-discrimination.

[120] Council of Europe 2020.

[121] Council of Europe, Ad hoc Committee on Artificial Intelligence (CAHAI) 2020a, para 76 ("it was noted that ethics guidelines are useful tools to exert some influence on public decision making over AI and to steer its development towards social good. However, it was also underlined that soft law approaches cannot substitute mandatory governance. […] there is a particular risk that self-regulation by private actors can bypass or avoid mandatory governance by (inter)governmental authorities. Soft law instruments and self-regulation initiatives can however play an important role in complementing mandatory governance").

assessment models) which might also include a sectoral approach.[122] The Feasibility Study gives a general overview of the key issues and describes the CAHAI's main directions of travel towards a legal framework and policy instruments.

The approach outlined in the Feasibility Study is based on recognition that the existing human rights legal framework already provides guiding principles and provisions that can be applied to AI.[123] These need to be better contextualised in light of the changes to society brought by AI[124] to fill three perceived gaps in the legal landscape: (i) the need to move from general principles to AI-centred implementation; (ii) the adoption of specific provisions on key aspects of AI (e.g. human control and oversight, transparency, explicability); (iii) the societal impact of AI.[125]

Thus, the Feasibility Study refers to human dignity, the right to non-discrimination, the right to effective remedy and other rights and freedoms enshrined in international human rights law. But it also makes new claims, such as: the right to be informed that one is interacting with an AI system rather than with a human being (especially where there is a risk of confusion which can affect human dignity);[126] the right to challenge decisions informed and/or made by an AI system and demand that such decisions be reviewed by a human being; the right to freely refuse AI-enabled manipulation, individualised profiling and predictions, even in the case of non-personal data processing; the right to interact with a human being

[122] Council of Europe, Ad hoc Committee on Artificial Intelligence (CAHAI) 2020a, para 89, p. 176 ("The study has noted that no international legal instrument specifically tailored to the challenges posed by AI exists, and that there are gaps in the current level of protection provided by existing international and national instruments. The study has identified the principles, rights and obligations which could become the main elements of a future legal framework for the design, development and application of AI, based on Council of Europe standards, which the CAHAI has been entrusted to develop. An appropriate legal framework will likely consist of a combination of binding and non-binding legal instruments, that complement each other"). This approach is in line with the conclusion of the preliminary study on the legal framework, Council of Europe, Ad hoc Committee on Artificial Intelligence (CAHAI) 2020b ("A binding instrument establishing the legal framework for AI, including both general common principles and granular provisions addressing specific issues, could therefore be combined with detailed rules set out in additional non-binding sectoral instruments. This model would provide both a clear regulatory framework and the flexibility required to address technological development.").

[123] Council of Europe, Ad hoc Committee on Artificial Intelligence (CAHAI) 2020a, para 83 ("The CAHAI therefore notes that, while there is no legal vacuum as regards AI regulation, a number of substantive and procedural legal gaps nevertheless exist").

[124] Council of Europe, Ad hoc Committee on Artificial Intelligence (CAHAI) 2020b ("contextualisation of the guiding principles and legal values provides a more refined and elaborate formulation of them, considering the specific nature of AI products and services, and helps better address the challenges arising from AI").

[125] Council of Europe, Ad hoc Committee on Artificial Intelligence (CAHAI) 2020a, paras 84–86.

[126] See also Consultative Committee of the Convention for the protection of individuals with regard to automatic processing of personal data (Convention 108) 2019, para 2.11.

rather than a robot (unless ruled out on legitimate overriding and competing grounds).[127]

In considering these proposals, it is worth noting that the Feasibly Study is not a legal document and uses the language of a policy document rather than the technical language of a legal text like regulation. Many of these rights are not therefore new stand-alone rights, but intended (including through creative interpretation) to complement already existing rights and freedoms, as part of the Council of Europe's contextualisation and concretisation of the law to deal with AI and human rights.

Along with these proposals for the future legal framework, the Feasibility Study also suggests several policy initiatives to be further developed by non-binding instruments or industrial policy, such as those on auditing processes, diversity and gender balance in the AI workforce or environmental-friendly AI development policies.[128]

In line with the CAHAI mandate and the Council of Europe's field of action, the path marked out by the Feasibility Study also includes two sections on democracy and the rule of law.[129] While extension of the proposed rights and obligations to these fields is significantly narrower than those on human rights, this move is atypical in the global scenario of AI regulation, which tends to exclude holistic solutions comprising democracy and the rule of law, or rely on sector-specific guidelines to address these questions.[130]

Regarding democracy, the most important rights with regard to AI are those concerning democratic participation and the electoral process, diverse information, free discourse and access to a plurality of ideas, and good governance. They also entail the adoption of specific policies on public procurement, public sector oversight, access to relevant information on AI systems, and fostering digital literacy and skills.

As for the rule of law, the main risks concern the use of AI in the field of justice. Here the Feasibility Study refers to the right to judicial independence and impartiality, the right to legal assistance, and the right to effective remedy. In policy terms, Member States are encouraged to provide meaningful information to individuals on the AI systems used in justice and law enforcement, and to ensure these systems do not interfere with the judicial independence of the court.[131]

---

[127] These and other proposed rights are discussed in Council of Europe, Ad hoc Committee on Artificial Intelligence (CAHAI) 2020a, Section 7.

[128] Council of Europe, Ad hoc Committee on Artificial Intelligence (CAHAI) 2020a, Section 7.

[129] See also Council of Europe, Ad hoc Committee on Artificial Intelligence (CAHAI) 2020a, Sections 7.8 and 7.9.

[130] E.g. Council of Europe, European Commission for the Efficiency of Justice (CEPEJ) 2018.

[131] Council of Europe, Ad hoc Committee on Artificial Intelligence (CAHAI) 2020a, 42–43. See also Council of Europe, Ad hoc Committee on Artificial Intelligence (CAHAI) 2020b, Section 2.5.1.

The Council of Europe thus takes a risk-based approach to AI[132] including introducing risk assessment criteria, 'red lines' for AI compatibility with human rights, and mechanisms for periodic review and audits.[133]

More specifically, the Feasibility Study considers risk assessment and management as part of the wider human rights due diligence process and as an ongoing assessment process rather than a static exercise.[134] For the future development of its impact assessment approach, the study takes as a reference framework the "factors that are commonly used in risk-impact assessments". It explicitly mentions the following main parameters: (i) the potential extent of the adverse effects on human rights, democracy and the rule of law; (ii) the likelihood that an adverse impact might occur; (iii) the scale and ubiquity of such impact, its geographical reach, its temporal extension; and (iv) the extent to which the potential adverse effects are reversible.[135]

On the basis of this Feasibility Study, the CAHAI created three working groups:[136] the Policy Development Group (CAHAI-PDG) focused on policies for AI development (soft law component); the Consultations and Outreach Group (CAHAI-COG) tasked with developing consultations with various stakeholders on key areas of the Feasibility Study and the CAHAI's ongoing activity; and the Legal Frameworks Group (CAHAI-LFG) centred on drafting proposals for the future legal framework (hard law component). Though from different angles, these three working groups all adopt the Council of Europe's risk-based approach and its implementation through impact assessment tools and provisions.

The main outcomes are expected to come from the CAHAI-LFG, in the form of binding provisions on impact assessment, and the CAHAI-PDG, with the development of an impact assessment model centred on human rights, democracy, and the rule of law. The CAHAI-COG multi-stakeholder consultations found clear expectations of the impact assessment in AI regulation, and stakeholders saw this as the most important mechanism in the Council of Europe's new framework.[137]

---

[132] Council of Europe, Ad hoc Committee on Artificial Intelligence (CAHAI) 2020a, paras 87 ("A comprehensive legal framework for AI systems, guided by a risk-based approach") and 125 ("As noted above, when member States take measures to safeguard the listed principles, rights and requirements in the context of AI, a risk-based approach – complemented with a precautionary approach where needed – is recommended").

[133] Council of Europe, Ad hoc Committee on Artificial Intelligence (CAHAI) 2020a, paras 42, 43, 44 ("A contextual and periodical assessment of the risks arising from the development and use of AI is necessary").

[134] Council of Europe, Ad hoc Committee on Artificial Intelligence (CAHAI) 2020a, para 169.

[135] Council of Europe, Ad hoc Committee on Artificial Intelligence (CAHAI) 2020a, para 126, where the CAHAI also notes that "in specific contexts, 'integrated impact assessments' might be deemed more appropriate to reduce the administrative burden on development teams (bringing together, for example, human rights, data protection, transparency, accountability, competence, and equalities considerations)".

[136] Council of Europe, Ad hoc Committee on Artificial Intelligence (CAHAI) 2020c.

[137] Council of Europe, Ad hoc Committee on Artificial Intelligence (CAHAI) 2021a.

Based on the CAHAI's work, and the more specific contribution of the CAHAI-LFG working group, the Council of Europe's risk-based AI model will introduce an assessment of the impact of AI applications on human rights, democracy, and the rule of law.[138] While the HRIA is not new, as discussed above, the inclusion of democracy and the rule of law is innovative and challenging.

The democratic process, and democracy in its different expressions, covers a range of topics and it is not easy, from a methodological perspective, to assess the impact on it of a technology or its applications, particularly since it is hard to assess the level of democracy itself.

This does not mean that it is impossible to carry out an impact assessment on specific fields of democratic life, such as the right to participation or access to pluralist information, but this remains a HRIA, albeit one centred on civil and political rights.[139] Evaluation of the impact of AI on democracy and its dynamics in general is still quite difficult.[140]

Different considerations regard the rule of law, where the more structured field of justice plus the limited application of AI make it easier to envisage uses and foresee their impact on a more uniform and regulated set of principles and procedures than democracy. Here again however, the specificity of the field and the interests involved may raise some doubts about the need for an integrated risk assessment model – including human rights, democracy, and the rule of law – as opposed to a more circumscribed assessment of the impact of certain AI applications on the rule of law.

The HUDERIA (HUman rights, DEmocracy and the Rule of law Impact Assessment)[141] proposed by the CAHAI therefore seems much more challenging in its transition from theoretical formulation to concrete implementation than the HRESIA, given the latter's modular structure and its distinction between human rights assessment (entrusted to the customised HRIA) and the social and ethical assessment (entrusted to committees of experts). The HUDERIA's difficulties

[138] Council of Europe, Ad hoc Committee on Artificial Intelligence (CAHAI) 2021b, p. 2.

[139] Council of Europe – Ad hoc Committee on Artificial Intelligence (CAHAI) 2021c, p. 3 seems to be aware of this challenge when it "agreed to use human rights as proxies to democracy and the rule of law. The idea is to explore if the magnitude of certain individual human rights violations closely linked to the good functioning of democratic institutions and processes, as well as rule of law core elements, could undermine democracy and the rule of law". However, using human rights as proxies for democracy and the rule of law means that the proposed model is *de facto* a HRIA.

[140] This is the case with the overall impact of AI-based solutions for smart cities. The case study discussed in Chap. 2 shows that the use of AI in a smart city can foster citizen engagement and interaction, public interest data sharing etc. But at the same time this environment can be captured by big private players and result in a shift in powers traditional exercised by public bodies, on the basis of democratic rules, towards private companies who can privatise and contractualise public tasks and interaction with citizens. It is difficult therefore to define overall impact on democracy as a stand-alone item of the impact assessment. A more feasible solution might be to perform a HRIA but consider the results for the democratic process as an issue for discussion and analysis (see Chap. 3).

[141] Council of Europe, Ad hoc Committee on Artificial Intelligence (CAHAI) 2021c.

appear to be confirmed by the slower progress of the CAHAI-PDG's work on this model compared with the rest of the CAHAI's activities.

Looking at the criteria proposed by the CAHAI-LFG for the impact assessment, they are largely those commonly used in impact assessment theory, i.e. likelihood and severity. Several factors are considered in relation to the severity of the impact (gravity, number of people affected, characteristics of impacted groups, geographical and demographical reach, territorial extension, extent of adverse effects and their reversibility, cumulative impact, likelihood of exacerbating existing biases, stereotypes, discrimination and inequalities). The assessment model should also consider further concurring factors, such as AI-specific risk increasing factors, the context and purpose of AI use, possible mitigation measures, and the dependence of potentially affected persons on decisions based on AI.[142]

The model envisaged is based on the traditional five risk levels (no risk, low, medium, high, extreme). The proposed provisions also leave room for the precautionary principle when it is impossible to assess the envisaged negative impact.

Finally, the level of transparency of the results of the assessment – in terms of their publicly availability –, accountability, auditability and transparency of the process are also considered in the CAHAI-LFG proposal.

At the time of writing, the proposed HUDERIA model adopts a four-stage iterative and participatory model – identification of relevant rights, assessment of the impact on those rights, governance mechanisms, continuous evaluation – which are common to all impact assessments. Its distinguishing feature is "that it includes specific analysis of impact on fundamental rights proxies which are directed towards the Rule of Law and Democracy".[143] In this the CAHAI documents do not limit the impact assessment obligations to specific AI applications in certain fields, a (high) level of risk or the nature and purpose of the technology adopted.

4.3.2 *The European Commission's Proposal (AIA) and Its Conformity-Oriented Approach*

After an initial approach centred on ethics[144] and the White Paper on Artificial Intelligence,[145] in April 2021 the European Commission proposed an EU regulation

---

[142] See also Council of Europe – Ad hoc Committee on Artificial Intelligence (CAHAI) 2021d, p. 3 ("the CAHAI-LFG has considered, besides the likelihood and severity of the negative impact, also contextual factors, such as the sector and area of use; the complexity of the AI-system and the level of automation; the quality, type and nature of data used, or the level of compliance with regulation in other fields").

[143] Council of Europe – Ad hoc Committee on Artificial Intelligence (CAHAI) 2021e.

[144] See also Chap. 2, Sect. 2.1.

[145] European Commission 2020d.

on AI (hereinafter the AIA Proposal).[146] This proposal introduces two new elements: the departure from more uncertain ethical grounds towards the adoption of a hard law instrument, albeit within the familiar framework of co-regulation;[147] the adoption of a regulation in the absence of national laws on AI or differing approaches among EU Member States.

The latter aspect highlights the EU legislator's concerns about the rapid development of AI, the EU's limited competitive power in this area in terms of market share, and the need to address the public's increasing worries about AI which might hamper its development.[148] The typical harmonisation goal of EU regulations – not applicable here in the absence of national laws on AI – is therefore replaced by a clear industrial strategy objective embodying a stronger and more centralised regulatory approach by the Commission which is reflected in the AIA Proposal.

As in the case of data protection, the EU proposal therefore stands within the framework of internal market interests, while protecting fundamental rights.[149] This focus on the market and competition appears to be the main rationale behind regulating an as yet unregulated field, designed to encourage AI investment in the EU.[150] It also emerged clearly from the four objectives of the proposed regulation: (i) ensure that AI systems marketed and used in the Union are safe and respect existing law on fundamental rights and Union values; (ii) guarantee legal certainty to facilitate investment and innovation in AI; (iii) enhance governance and effective enforcement of existing law on fundamental rights and safety requirements applicable to AI systems; (iv) facilitate the development of a single market for lawful, safe and trustworthy AI applications and prevent market fragmentation.[151]

In this context a central role is necessarily played by risk regulation, as in the first generation of data protection law where citizens were concerned about the potential misuse of their data and public and (some) private entities were aware of

---

[146] European Commission, Proposal for Regulation of the European Parliament and of the Council laying down harmonised rules on Artificial Intelligence (Artificial Intelligence Act) and amending legislative acts, COM(2021) 206 final, Brussels, 21 April 2021.

[147] European Commission, Proposal for Regulation of the European Parliament and of the Council laying down harmonised rules on Artificial Intelligence (Artificial Intelligence Act) and amending legislative acts, COM(2021) 206 final, Brussels, 21 April 2021, Explanatory Memorandum (hereinafter AIA Explanatory Memorandum), 9.

[148] European Commission, AIA Explanatory Memorandum, 6 ("This proposal constitutes a core part of the EU digital single market strategy. The primary objective of this proposal is to ensure the proper functioning of the internal market by setting harmonised rules in particular on the development, placing on the Union market and the use of products and services making use of AI technologies or provided as stand-alone AI systems").

[149] This is clearly evident in Article 1 (Subject matter) of the Proposal where there is no explicit or direct reference to the safeguarding of fundamental rights and freedoms and AI's potential impact on them, but only general references to "certain artificial intelligence practices" and "high-risk AI systems". For a different approach, see Article 1 of the General Data Protection Regulation.

[150] European Commission, AIA Explanatory Memorandum. ("It is in the Union interest to preserve the EU's technological leadership"). See also Recital No. 6 AIA Proposal.

[151] European Commission, AIA Explanatory Memorandum, p. 3.

the value of personal data in enabling them to carry out their work. For this reason, the EU proposal wishes to limit itself to the "minimum necessary requirements to address the risks and problems linked to AI, without unduly constraining or hindering technological development or otherwise disproportionately increasing the cost of placing AI solutions on the market".[152]

These goals and the framing of the risk-based approach reveal how the EU differs from the Council of Europe, which places greater emphasis on the safeguarding of human rights and fundamental freedoms. This inevitably impacts on the risk management solutions outlined in the AIA Proposal.

The European Commission's 'proportionate'[153] risk-based approach addresses four level of risks: (i) extreme risk applications, which are prohibited;[154] (ii) high risk applications, dealt with by a conformity assessment (where HRIA is only one of its components); (iii) a limited number of applications that have a significant potential to manipulate persons, which must comply with certain transparency obligations; (iv) no high-risk uses, dealt with by codes of conduct designed to foster compliance with AIA main requirements.[155] Of these, the most important from a human rights impact assessment perspective are the provisions on high risk applications.

The first aspect emerging from these provisions is the combination, under the category of high-risk applications, of AI solutions impacting on two different categories of protected interests: physical integrity, where AI systems are safety components of products/systems or are themselves products/systems regulated under the New Legislative Framework legislation (e.g. machinery, toys, medical devices, etc.),[156] and human rights in the case of so-called stand-alone AI systems.[157]

Safety and human rights are two distinct realms. An AI-equipped toy may raise concerns around its safety, but have no or only limited impact on human rights (e.g. partially automated children's cars). Meanwhile another may raise concerns largely in relation to human rights (e.g. the smart doll discussed in Chap. 2). AI may have a negative impact and entail new risks for both safety and human rights, but the fields, and related risks, are separate and require different remedies. This does not mean that an integrated model is impossible or even undesirable, but that different assessments and specific requirements are essential.

---

[152] European Commission, AIA Explanatory Memorandum, p. 3.

[153] European Commission, AIA Explanatory Memorandum, p. 3.

[154] AIA Proposal, Article 5, and AIA Explanatory Memorandum, para 5.2.2, which refers to unacceptable risks (prohibited practices) as "contravening Union values, for instance by violating fundamental rights".

[155] AIA Proposal, Article 69.

[156] AIA Proposal, Annex II. The AIA Proposal is not applicable to products/systems regulated under the Old Approach legislation (e.g. aviation, cars), see AIA Proposal, Article 2.2.

[157] AIA Proposal, Annex III; see also rec. 64 ("different nature of risks involved").

Looking at the risk model outlined by the AIA Proposal, its structure is based on Article 9. The chief obligations on providers of high-risk AI systems,[158] as set out in Article 16, regard the performance of a conformity assessment (Articles 19 and 43, Annexes VI and VII) and the adoption of a quality management system (Article 17). The conformity assessment – except for the AI regime for biometric identification and the categorisation of natural persons[159] and the AI applications regulated under the New Legislative Framework (NLF) legislation – is an internal self-assessment process based on the requirements set out in Annex VI. This Annex requires an established quality management system in compliance with Article 17 whose main components include the risk management system referred to in Article 9.[160]

In this rather convoluted structure of the AIA Proposal, Article 9 and its risk management system is the key component of a combined conformity assessment and quality management system. Indeed, the quality management system comprises a range of elements which play a complementary role in risk management. However, the risk assessment and management model defined by Article 9 is based on three traditional stages: risk identification, estimation/evaluation, and mitigation.

The peculiarity of the AIA model consists in the fact that the risk assessment is performed in situations that are already classified by the AIA as high-risk cases. In the EU's proposal, the risk-based approach consists mainly of risk mitigation rather than risk estimation.

The proposal makes a distinction between use of AI in products already regulated under safety provisions, with some significant exceptions,[161] and the rest. In the first group, AI is either a safety component of these products[162] or itself a product in this category. The second group consists of stand-alone AI systems not covered by the safety regulations but which, according to the European Commission, carry a high-risk.

This classification emphasises the importance of the high-risk evaluation set out in the AIA Proposal. With regulated safety applications, risk analysis is only broadened from safety to the HRIA.[163] For stand-alone AI systems, on the other hand, it introduces the completely new regulation based on a comprehensive conformity assessment, which includes the impact on fundamental rights.

---

[158] An AI provider is "a natural or legal person, public authority, agency or other body that develops an AI system or that has an AI system developed with a view to placing it on the market or putting it into service under its own name or trademark, whether for payment or free of charge". See AIA Proposal, Article 3.2.

[159] AIA Proposal, Article 43.1.

[160] AIA Proposal, Article 17.1.g.

[161] AIA Proposal, Article 2.2.

[162] On the notion of safety component of a product or system, AIA Proposal, Article 2, No. 14 ("a component of a product or of a system which fulfils a safety function for that product or system or the failure or malfunctioning of which endangers the health and safety of persons or property").

[163] But AIA Proposal, rec. 31.

However, the approach adopted raises questions concerning the following issues: (i) a top-down and more rigid system of high-risk assessment; (ii) a critical barrier between high risk and lower risk; (iii) opaque regulation of technology assessment (Annex III) and risk assessment carried out by providers (Article 9); (iv) use of the notion of acceptability; (v) marginalisation of the role of AI system users. These elements, discussed below, all reveal the distinction between the AIA Proposal's complicated model of risk management and the HRIA's cleaner model based on a general risk assessment.[164]

Given the variety of fields of application of AI and the level of innovation in this area, dividing high-risk applications into eight categories and several sub-fields seems to underestimate the evolving complexity of the technology scenario.

Considering how rapidly AI technology is evolving and the unexpected discoveries regarding its abilities,[165] a closed list of typical high-risk applications may not be easy to keep up-to-date properly or promptly.[166] In addition, the decision to delegate such a key aspect to the Commission, the EU's executive body,[167] is likely to raise concerns in terms of power allocation.

A closed list approach (albeit using broad definitions and open to updating) appears to be reactive rather than preventive in anticipating technology development. By contrast, a general obligation of an AI impact assessment (HRIA) does not suffer from this shortcoming and can act more swiftly in detecting critical new applications. Moreover, a general risk assessment removes the burden of rapidly updating the list of stand-alone high-risk applications, which can remain an open list of presumed high-risk cases, as in Article 35.3 of the GDPR.

The focus on a list of high-risk cases also introduces a barrier between them and the rest where risks are lower. This sharp dichotomy contrasts with the more nuanced consideration of risk and its variability depending on the different technology solutions, contexts, etc. Furthermore, a rigid classification of high-risk applications leaves room for operators wishing to circumvent the regulation by denying that their system falls into one of the listed categories.[168]

---

[164] A similar general risk assessment, not based on a predefined close list of high-risk cases, was also adopted by the GDPR. See GDPR, Article 35.

[165] E.g., Simonite 2021.

[166] The Commission can add new cases, but on the basis of those listed as a benchmark, AIA Proposal, Article 7.2 ("an AI system poses a risk of harm to the health and safety or a risk of adverse impact on fundamental rights that is equivalent to or greater than the risk of harm posed by the high-risk AI systems already referred to in Annex III").

[167] Regarding the power of the Commission to update the list in Annex III with the addition of new high-risk AI systems, it was also pointed out that "it remains nebulous when the threshold of high-risk, as defined in Article 7(2), will be reached, i.e., when a system's risk count[s] as 'equivalent to or greater' than those of other systems already on the list", AlgorithmWatch 2021.

[168] AlgorithmWatch 2021, p. 3.

Finally, as pointed out in Chap. 2, this cumulative quantification of the level of risk of a given application (described as a high-risk use of AI) contradicts the necessarily multifaced impact of AI applications, which usually concerns different rights and freedoms. The impact may therefore be high with respect to some rights and medium or law with respect to others. The different nature of the impacted rights does not make it possible to define an overall risk level.

The only possible conclusion is that if there is a high risk of a negative impact on even one right or freedom, the overall risk of AI application is high. This is in line with the idea that all human rights must be protected and the indivisible, interdependent and interrelated nature of human rights.

The categories of high-risk application set out in Annex III are defined on the basis of a technology assessment resting on four key elements: (i) AI system characteristics (purpose of the system and extent of its use or likely use); (ii) harm/impact (caused or foreseen harm to health and safety or adverse impacts on fundamental rights; potential extent of such harm or such adverse impacts; reversibility); (iii) condition of affected people (dependency or vulnerability); (iv) legal protection (measures of redress[169] or to prevent or substantially minimise those risks).

This is necessarily an abstract exercise by the legislator (and in future by the Commission) which uses a future scenario approach or, when referring to existing practices, generalises or aggregates several cases. The assessment required by Article 9 on the other hand is a context-specific evaluation based on the nature of the particular case of AI application. These different types of assessment suggest that the applications listed in Annex III, in their context-specific use, may not entail the high level of risk presumed by the Regulation.

In addition, the Proposal fails to explain how and on the basis of which parameters, and method of evaluation, these risks should be assessed in relation to specific AI applications, according to Article 9. Nor, with regard to the general technology assessment used for the Annex III list, does the Commission's Proposal provide transparency on the methodology and criteria adopted.[170]

Another aspect that requires attention is the relationship between high-risk, residual risk and acceptability.[171] Risk assessment and mitigation measures should act in such a way that the risk "associated with each hazard as well as the overall residual risk of the high-risk AI systems is judged acceptable". But the AIA Proposal fails to provide a definition of acceptable risk.

---

[169] It is worth emphasising that these measures are not directly related to risk assessment.

[170] European Center for Not-for-Profit Law 2021, 9 ("there is currently no provision nor clearly identified procedure allowing for adding new categories to annex III related to the list of high-risk uses of AI systems"). Another major shortcoming is the lack of public debate on the cases listed, AlgorithmWatch 2021 ("many of these sensitive applications have not yet been the object of public debate. Before they are put to use, citizens should have the opportunity to discuss whether there are limits to what decisions should be automated in the first place").

[171] AIA Proposal, Article 9.4.

The notion of acceptable risk comes from product safety regulation, while in the field of fundamental rights the main risk factor is proportionality. While acceptability is largely a social criterion,[172] Article 2(b) of Directive 2001/95/EC on general product safety define a safe product as one that "does not present any risk or only the minimum risks compatible with the product's use, considered to be acceptable". Here acceptability results from an absence of risk or "minimum risks", which is necessarily context-dependent[173] and suggests a case-specific application of the criteria set out in Article 7.2 of the AIA Proposal. What is more, these criteria – like the focus on the product characteristics, the categories of consumers at risk and the measures to prevent or substantially minimise the risks – are coherent with those considered by Article 2(b) of Directive 2001/95/EC.

If we accept this interpretation, acceptability is incompatible with AI's high risk of adverse impacts on fundamental rights and any impact assessment based on a quantification of risk levels will play a crucial part in risk management.

Finally, the AIA Proposal marginalises the role of the AI users. They play no part in the risk management process and have no obligations in this regard, even though AI providers market solutions that are customisable by users. AI users[174] may independently increase or alter the risks of harm to health and safety by their particular use of the systems, especially in terms of impact on individual and collective rights, given their variety and context dependence.

For example, an AI company can offer a platform for participatory democracy, but its implementation can be affected by exclusion biases depending on the user's choice of settings and the specific context. AI providers cannot fully take into account such contextual variables or foresee the potentially affected categories, so

[172] Nordlander et al. 2010, pp. 241–42 ("Determining the acceptable level of risk is not the function of the risk assessment itself, which simply attempts to identify the ranges of risk. The decision as to what constitutes acceptable risk is a socio-political, not a scientific, decision"); Whipple 1988, 85–86. See also Muhlbauer 2004, p. 335 ("In general, society decides what is an acceptable level of risk for any particular endeavor"); Bergkamp 2015.

[173] See also Commission Implementing Decision (EU) 2019/417 of 8 November 2018 laying down guidelines for the management of the European Union Rapid Information System 'RAPEX' established under Article 12 of Directive 2001/95/EC on general product safety and its notification system (notified under document C(2018) 7334) 2019 (OJ L), p. 171 ("Taking action to counteract a risk may also depend on the product itself and the 'minimum risks compatible with the product's use, considered to be acceptable and consistent with a high level of protection'. This minimum risk will probably be much lower for toys, where children are involved, than for a chain-saw, which is known to be so high-risk that solid protective equipment is required to keep the risk at a manageable level") and 183 ("Any injury harm that could easily have been avoided will be difficult to accept for a consumer").

[174] An AI user is "'any natural or legal person, public authority, agency or other body using an AI system under its authority, except where the AI system is used in the course of a personal non-professional activity", AIA Proposal, Article 3.4.

their adoption of a general mitigation strategy will have only a limited effect.[175] Risk management and risk assessment duties should therefore also apply to AI users in proportion to their role in system design and deployment.

In line with risk management theory and practice, a circular iterative approach is adopted by the AIA Proposal, including post-market monitoring.[176] This is crucial since lifelong monitoring, learning and re-assessment are essential elements in an evolving technology scenario where risk levels may change over time.[177]

Considering the AIA Proposal as a whole, the legislator's rationale is to largely exempt AI users (i.e. entities using AI systems under their own authority) from risk management duties and to avoid creating extensive obligations for the AI producers, limiting the regulatory impact only to specific sectors, characterised by potential new AI-related risks or the use of AI in already regulated product safety areas.

While this is effective in terms of policy impact and acceptability, it is a weak form of risk prevention. The Proposal makes a quite rigid distinction between high-level risk and the rest, providing no methodology to assess the former, and largely exempting the latter from any mitigation (with the limited exception of transparency obligations in certain cases).

In addition, two large elements are missing from the EU's Proposal: integration between law and ethical/societal issues and the role of participation. As for the first, following several years of discussion of the ethical dimension of AI, the prevailing vision seems to be to delegate ethical issues to other initiatives[178] not integrated with the legal assessment. In the same way that focusing exclusively on ethics was critical,[179] this lack of integration between the legal and societal impacts of AI is problematic. An integrated assessment model, like the HRESIA, could overcome this limitation in line with the proposed risk-based model.

Equally, introducing a participatory dimension to the assessment model, covering both legal and societal issues, would bridge the second gap, related to the lack of participation, and align the AIA proposal with the emphasis on civic engagement of other EU initiatives and a vision of AI use for the benefit of citizens.[180]

---

[175] In addition, different AI systems can be combined by the user to achieve a specific goal.

[176] AIA Proposal, Article 61. See also Consultative Committee of the Convention for the Protection of Individuals with regard to Automatic Processing of Personal Data (Convention 108) 2019, Section 2.10.

[177] AIA Proposal, Recital No. 66 ("as regards AI systems which continue to 'learn' after being placed on the market or put into service (i.e. they automatically adapt how functions are carried out), it is necessary to provide rules establishing that changes to the algorithm and its performance that have been pre-determined by the provider and assessed at the moment of the conformity assessment should not constitute a substantial modification").

[178] E.g. Independent High-Level Expert Group on Artificial Intelligence set up by the European Commission 2020.

[179] See Chap. 3.

[180] See also European Center for Not-for-Profit Law 2021, pp. 11 and 15–16.

4.4 The HRESIA Model's Contribution to the Different Approaches

Looking at the three approaches to AI regulation described at the beginning of this chapter, neither the Council of Europe nor the European Commission decided to adopt a principles-based approach. This, even though several of the key principles enshrined in binding and non-binding human rights instruments can be valuable – with due contextualisation – to AI regulation and are also partially reflected in the proposals of both bodies.

The predominant focus on risk and accountability is probably due to the reductive and incremental approach of this first stage of AI regulation, as was the case with data protection in the 1970s or with regard to product safety in the first phase of industrial mass production.[181] As with the early data protection regulations, the priority is to establish specific procedural, technical and organisational safeguards against the most serious risks rather than building a clear and complete set of governing principles.

The EU's closed list of high-risk systems, and the Council of Europe's key guiding principles for AI development and use reflect the fact that these proposals represent the first generation of AI regulation.

As with data protection,[182] further regulation will probably follow, broader in scope and establishing a stronger set of guiding principles. In regard to the EU initiative, a fuller consideration of the potential widespread impact of non-high-risk applications and the challenges of rigid pre-determined risk evaluation systems could provide more effective protection of individual rights and collective interests.

Both proposals are also characterised by a focus on the legal dimension at the expense of a more holistic approach covering ethical and societal issues, which are either ignored or delegated to non-legal instruments.

This gap could be bridged by a hybrid model, such as the HRESIA, combining human rights and ethical and societal assessments to give a more complete view of the consequences of AI applications and affect their design. This is even more important in the case of large-scale projects or those with significant effects on social communities.

In addition, the key notion of acceptability in the AIA Proposal,[183] discussed in the previous section, necessarily implies the value of the HRIA to assess the impact on fundamental rights covered by Article 9. But it would also benefit from the broader HRESIA model given the societal dimension of acceptability[184] which should be paid greater attention with regard to each context-specific AI application and addressed by expert committees, as described in Chap. 3.

---

[181] Gregory 1951, p. 385; Traynor 1965; McMahon 1968; Oliphant 2005.

[182] Mayer-Schönberger 1997.

[183] AIA Proposal, Article 9.

[184] See above fn. 172.

Regarding the costs and resources involved in extending the HRESIA, we should recall the considerations expressed above about the model's modularity and scalability.[185] Based on a HRIA and adopting internal advisors for the societal issues, the burdens are proportional to the impact of the technology and minimum or negligible in the case of low risk. Moreover, the experience gained by the HRESIA experts would further reduce the costs in relation to the frequency of the assessments.

Both the Council of Europe and the European Commission suggest a self-assessment procedure in line with the HRESIA model. The latter also includes a layer of participation, which is mentioned by the Council of Europe[186] and one of the recognised shortcomings of the AIA Proposal.

The EU Proposal limits the obligation to perform an impact assessment to AI providers, in line with the thinking behind product safety regulation. However, a more nuanced approach is required, given the part played by providers and users in the development, deployment and use of AI applications, and the potential impacts of each stage on human rights and freedoms.

It is worth remembering that AI differs from data protection in the greater role that AI providers play in the complicated and often obscure AI processing operations.[187] This makes it inappropriate to recreate the controller/provider distinction, albeit with different nuances,[188] regardless of the criticisms expressed about the distinction itself.[189] Still, the effective role played by AI users[190] in system design and deployment should be addressed by their involvement in risk management and assessment duties.

This can be achieved for most of the AI systems in use, excepting those cases where the user has little ability to customise or train the system for a specific context, and a HRESIA should be performed by all entities that use third-party AI services for their own purposes. This does not mean that the HRESIA cannot be used by producers in the design of their systems. but suggests a model – already

---

[185] See Chap. 2.

[186] Council of Europe, Ad hoc Committee on Artificial Intelligence (CAHAI) 2021f, pp. 26–27.

[187] Mantelero 2018b.

[188] Microsoft Corporation 2021, 5 ("we recommend creating a new designation of "deployer," defined as the entity that takes the specific decision to implement an AI system for one of the high-risk scenarios detailed in Annex III. We also recommend that this entity be responsible for ensuring that any such Annex III deployment satisfies the requirements set out in Article 16. This approach has the virtue of ensuring that regulatory responsibilities fall in the first instance on the entity that has the greatest control over, and visibility into, the operation of the specific deployment that brings it within scope of Annex III (and thus subject to the requirements of Articles 9–17). It is, however, contingent on "technology suppliers" also assuming responsibilities that they are well-placed to bear, as described below.)").

[189] de Hert and Papakonstantinou 2016, p. 184.

[190] AIA Proposal, Article 3(4) ("'user' means any natural or legal person, public authority, agency or other body using an AI system under its authority, except where the AI system is used in the course of a personal non-professional activity").

proposed in data protection regulation[191] –, in which the providers perform the HRESIA on their products, but AI users perform their own HRESIA with regard to specific implementation.

Finally, both the Council of Europe and the European Commission base their approaches on risk assessment and a series of variables to be considered but fail to specify a method of assessing the level of risk, making them difficult to put into practice.[192] In contrast, the HRESIA not only identifies the assessment criteria but also explains a how to go about defining the risk levels and evaluating the systems.

With its nature, scope, and methodology the HRESIA model not only responds to AI impact assessment requirements of the European proposals, but it could also address the shortcomings of the proposed provisions and serve as a model that is as yet absent in the ongoing work of these regulatory bodies.

4.5 Summary

The ongoing debate on AI in Europe has been characterised by a shift in focus, from the identification of guiding ethical principles to a first generation of legal obligations on AI providers.

Although the debate on AI regulation is still fluid at a global level and the European initiatives are in their early stages, three possible approaches are emerging to ground AI regulation on human rights.

One option is a principles-based approach, comprising guiding principles derived from existing international binding and non-binding human rights instruments, which could provide a comprehensive framework for AI, in line with previous models such as Convention 108 or the Oviedo Convention.

A different approach focuses more narrowly on the impacts of AI on individual rights and their safeguarding through rights-based risk assessment. This is the path followed by the Council of Europe in its ongoing work on AI regulation.

Finally, as outlined in the EU proposal, greater emphasis can be placed on managing high-risk applications focusing on product safety and conformity assessment, combining safety and rights protection with a predefined risk classification.

---

[191] Article 29 Data Protection Working Party 2017, 8 ("A DPIA can also be useful for assessing the data protection impact of a technology product, for example a piece of hardware or software, where this is likely to be used by different data controllers to carry out different processing operations. Of course, the data controller deploying the product remains obliged to carry out its own DPIA with regard to the specific implementation, but this can be informed by a DPIA prepared by the product provider, if appropriate").

[192] As demonstrated in the field of Corporate Social Responsibility, the lack or vagueness of specific operational implementation of general law requirements can hamper the effectiveness of value-oriented regulations; Wagner 2018b.

Despite the differences between these three models, they each share a core concern with protecting human rights, recognised as a key issue in all of them. Moreover, while this first generation of AI regulation reveals a pragmatic approach with a focus on risk management at the expense of a framework of guiding principles and a broader consideration of the role of AI in society, this does not rule out a greater emphasis on these aspects in future regulation, as happened with data protection.

Identifying a common core of principles can be of help for this second stage of AI regulation. In the end, therefore, all three approaches can contribute in different ways and probably with different timescales to posing the building blocks of AI regulation.

In these early proposals for AI regulation, the emphasis on risk management is not accompanied by effective models to assess the impact of AI on human rights. Following the turn from ethical guidelines to legal provisions, there are no specific instruments to assess not just the legal compliance of AI solutions, but their social acceptability, including a participatory evaluation of their coherence with the values of the target communities.

Analysis of the current debate confirms that the HRESIA may not only be an effective response to human-rights oriented AI development which also encompasses societal values, but it may also bridge a gap in the present regulatory proposals. Furthermore, a general risk assessment methodology is better suited to the variety of AI and technology developments than regulatory models based on a predefined list of high-risk applications or, at any rate, might represent a better guide to rule-makers in their definition.

References

40th International Conference of Data Protection and Privacy Commissioners, Declaration on Ethics and Data Protection in Artificial Intelligence, 2018.

Access Now (2019) The European Human Rights Agenda in the Digital Age. https://www.accessnow.org/access-now_the-european-human-rights-agenda-in-the-digital-age_final1/. Accessed 4 July 2020.

AI Now Institute (2018) Litigating Algorithms: Challenging Government Use of Algorithmic Decision Systems. https://ainowinstitute.org/litigatingalgorithms.pdf. Accessed 5 February 2020.

AlgorithmWatch (2021) Draft AI Act: EU Needs to Live up to Its Own Ambitions in Terms of Governance and Enforcement. https://algorithmwatch.org/en/wp-content/uploads/2021/08/EU-AI-Act-Consultation-Submission-by-AlgorithmWatch-August-2021.pdf. Accessed 6 August 2021.

Andorno R (2005) The Oviedo Convention: A European Legal Framework at the Intersection of Human Rights and Health Law. Journal of International Biotechnology Law 2(1):133–143.

Article 29 Data Protection Working Party (2017) Guidelines on Data Protection Impact Assessment (DPIA) and determining whether processing is "likely to result in a high risk" for the purposes of Regulation 2016/679', WP 248 rev.01.

Article 29 Data Protection Working Party (2018) Guidelines on Automated individual decision-making and Profiling for the purposes of Regulation 2016/679.

Asaro P (2016) Jus Nascendi, Robotic Weapons and the Martens Clause. In: Calo R, Froomkin A, Kerr I (eds) Robot Law. Edward Elgar Publishing, Cheltenham, pp 367–386.

Azencott CA (2018) Machine Learning and Genomics: Precision Medicine versus Patient Privacy. Phil. Trans. R. Soc. A 376:20170350.

Beauchamp TL (1990) Promise of the Beneficence Model for Medical Ethics. J. Contemp. Health L. & Pol'y 6:145–155.

Bergkamp L (2015) Is There a Defect in the European Court's Defect Test? Musings about Acceptable Risk. European Journal of Risk Regulation 6:309–322.

Cabitza F, Rasoini R, Gensini GF (2017) Unintended Consequences of Machine Learning in Medicine. JAMA 318:517–518.

Caplan R, Donovan J, Hanson L, Matthews J (2018) Algorithmic Accountability: A Primer. https://datasociety.net/output/algorithmic-accountability-a-primer/. Accessed 24 May 2019.

Caruana R, Lou Y, Gehrke J, Koch P, Sturm M, Elhadad N (2015) Intelligible models for healthcare: Predicting pneumonia risk and hospital 30-day readmission. In: Proceedings of the 21st Annual SIGKDD International Conference on Knowledge Discovery and Data Mining, 1721–1730. http://people.dbmi.columbia.edu/noemie/papers/15kdd.pdf. Accessed 14 January 2020.

Center for Data Innovation (2021) How Much Will the Artificial Intelligence Act Cost Europe? https://www2.datainnovation.org/2021-aia-costs.pdf. Accessed 16 August 2021.

Commission Nationale de l'Informatique et des Libertés – LINC (2017) La Plateforme d'une Ville Les Données Personnelles Au Cœur de La Fabrique de La Smart City. https://www.cnil.fr/sites/default/files/atoms/files/cnil_cahiers_ip5.pdf. Accessed 18 November 2019.

Council of Europe (2020) Towards regulation for AI systems. Global perspectives on the development of a legal framework on Artificial Intelligence systems based on the Council of Europe's standards on human rights, democracy and the rule of law, Compilation of contributions prepared by the CAHAI Secretariat, DGI (2020)16. https://rm.coe.int/prems-107320-gbr-2018-compli-cahai-couv-texte-a4-bat-web/1680a0c17a. Accessed 5 January 2021.

Council of Europe, Ad hoc Committee on Artificial Intelligence (CAHAI) (2020a) Feasibility Study, CAHAI(2020)23. https://rm.coe.int/cahai-2020-23-final-eng-feasibility-study-/1680a0c6da. Accessed 29 July 2021.

Council of Europe, Ad hoc Committee on Artificial Intelligence (CAHAI) (2020b) Elaboration of the feasibility study. Analysis of the International legally binding instruments. Final report. Paper prepared by Alessandro Mantelero, CAHAI(2020)08-fin. https://rm.coe.int/cahai-2020-08-fin-mantelero-binding-instruments-report-2020-def/16809eca33. Accessed 29 July 2021.

Council of Europe, Ad hoc Committee on Artificial Intelligence (CAHAI) (2020c) Working methods of the CAHAI: functioning of the working groups, CAHAI(2020)10 ADD REV1. https://rm.coe.int/cahai-2020-10-add-rev1-en/16809ee918. Accessed 2nd August 2021.

Council of Europe, Ad hoc Committee on Artificial Intelligence (CAHAI) (2021a) Analysis of the Multi-Stakeholder Consultation, Strasbourg, CAHAI(2021)07. https://rm.coe.int/cahai-2021-07-analysis-msc-23-06-21-2749-8656-4611-v-1/1680a2f228. Accessed 4 August 2021.

Council of Europe, Ad hoc Committee on Artificial Intelligence (CAHAI) (2021b) 5th meeting. Strasbourg, 5–7 July 2021. Abridged meeting report and list of decisions, CAHAI(2021)10. https://rm.coe.int/cahai-2021-10-5th-plenary-abridged-report-2776-1003-8532-v-2/1680a31d48. Accessed 5 August 2021.

Council of Europe, Ad hoc Committee on Artificial Intelligence (CAHAI) (2021c) Progress Report by the Co-Chairs of the CAHAI-PDG, CAHAI(2021)09. https://rm.coe.int/cahai-2021-09-pdg-progress-report-2784-0682-4452-v-1/1680a2fd49. Accessed 4 August 2021.

Council of Europe, Ad hoc Committee on Artificial Intelligence (CAHAI) (2021d) Progress Report by the Co-Chairs of the CAHAI-LFG, CAHAI(2021)08. https://rm.coe.int/cahai-2021-08-eng-cahai-lfg-progress-report-june-2021-2770-4668-9539-v/1680a2f5cc. Accessed 5 August 2021.

Council of Europe, Ad hoc Committee on Artificial Intelligence (CAHAI) (2021e) Human Rights, Democracy and Rule of Law Impact. Assessment of AI systems, CAHAI-PDG(2021)05.

https://rm.coe.int/cahai-pdg-2021-05-2768-0229-3507-v-1/1680a291a3. Accessed 5 August 2021.
Council of Europe, Ad hoc Committee on Artificial Intelligence (CAHAI) (2021f) – Policy development Group (CAHAI-PDG) Human Rights, Democracy and Rule of Law Impact. Assessment of AI systems, CAHAI-PDG(2021)05.
Council of Europe-Committee of experts on internet intermediaries (MSI-NET) (2018) Study on the Human Rights Dimensions of Automated Data Processing Techniques (in Particular Algorithms) and Possible Regulatory Implications. https://rm.coe.int/algorithms-and-human-rights-en-rev/16807956b5. Accessed 10 March 2020.
Council of Europe, Committee of Ministers (1997) Recommendation No. R(97)5 of the Committee of Ministers to member States on the protection of medical data.
Council of Europe, Committee of Ministers (2010) Recommendation CM/Rec(2010)13 of the Committee of Ministers of the Council of Europe to member States on the protection of individuals with regard to automatic processing of personal data in the context of profiling.
Council of Europe, Committee of Ministers (2016a) Recommendation CM/Rec(2016)6 of the Committee of Ministers to member States on research on biological materials of human origin.
Council of Europe, Committee of Ministers (2016b) Recommendation CM/Rec(2016)8 on the processing of personal health-related data for insurance purposes, including data resulting from genetic tests and its Explanatory Memorandum.
Council of Europe, Committee of Ministers (2019) Recommendation CM/Rec(2019)2 of the Committee of Ministers to member States on the protection of health-related data.
Council of Europe, Committee of Ministers (2020) Recommendation CM/Rec(2020)1 of the Committee of Ministers to member States on the human rights impacts of algorithmic systems. https://search.coe.int/cm/pages/result_details.aspx?objectid=09000016809e1154. Accessed 10 March 2020.
Council of Europe, Consultative Committee of the Convention for the Protection of Individuals with regard to Automatic Processing of Personal Data (Convention 108) (2017) Guidelines on the Protection of Individuals with Regard to the Processing of Personal Data in a World of Big Data, T-PD(2017)01. https://rm.coe.int/t-pd-2017-1-bigdataguidelines-en/16806f06d0. Accessed 15 April 2020.
Council of Europe, Consultative Committee of the Convention for the Protection of Individuals with regard to Automatic Processing of Personal Data (Convention 108) (2019) Guidelines on Artificial Intelligence and Data Protection, T-PD(2019)01. https://rm.coe.int/guidelines-on-artificial-intelligence-and-data-protection/168091f9d8. Accessed 15 April 2020.
Council of Europe, Consultative Committee of the Convention for the protection of individuals with regard to automatic processing of personal data (Convention 108) (2021) Guidelines on Facial Recognition, 28 January 2021, T-PD(2020)03rev4.
Council of Europe, European Commission for the Efficiency of Justice (CEPEJ) (2018) European Ethical Charter on the Use of Artificial Intelligence in Judicial Systems and their environment. https://www.coe.int/en/web/cepej/cepej-european-ethical-charter-on-the-use-of-artificial-intelligence-ai-in-judicial-systems-and-their-environment. Accessed 4 March 2019.
Council of Europe, Parliamentary Assembly (2017) Recommendation 2102 (2017)1 Technological Convergence, Artificial Intelligence and Human Rights.
Data Ethics Commission of the Federal Government, Federal Ministry of the Interior Building and Community and Data Ethics Commission (2019) Opinion of the Data Ethics Commission. https://www.bmjv.de/DE/Themen/FokusThemen/Datenethikkommission/Datenethikkommission_EN_node.html. Accessed 16 June 2020.
De Hert P, Papakonstantinou V (2016) The New General Data Protection Regulation: Still a Sound System for the Protection of Individuals? Computer Law & Security Review 32(2):179–194.
Edwards L, Veale M (2017) Slave to the Algorithm? Why a 'Right to an Explanation' Is Probably Not the Remedy You Are Looking For. Duke Law & Technology Review 16(1):18–84.
European Center for Not-for-Profit Law (2021) ECNL Position Statement on the EU AI Act. https://ecnl.org/sites/default/files/2021-07/ECNL%20EU%20AI%20Act%20Position%20Paper.pdf. Accessed 7 August 2021.

European Commission (2020a) A European strategy for data, COM(2020) 66 final. https://ec.europa.eu/info/sites/default/files/communication-european-strategy-data-19feb2020_en.pdf. Accessed 15 March 2020.
European Commission (2020b) Report from the Commission to the European Parliament, the Council and the European Economic and Social Committee, COM/2020/64 final. https://ec.europa.eu/info/files/commission-report-safety-and-liability-implications-ai-internet-things-and-robotics_en. Accessed 12 March 2020.
European Commission (2020c) Report on the Safety and Liability Implications of Artificial Intelligence, the Internet of Things and Robotics, COM/2020/64 final. https://ec.europa.eu/info/files/commission-report-safety-and-liability-implications-ai-internet-things-and-robotics_en. Accessed 12 March 2020.
European Commission (2020d) White Paper on Artificial Intelligence – A European Approach to Excellence and Trust, COM(2020) 65 final. https://ec.europa.eu/info/files/white-paper-artificial-intelligence-european-approach-excellence-and-trust_en. Accessed 12 March 2020.
European Commission, Expert Group on Liability (2019) Liability for Artificial Intelligence and Other Emerging Digital Technologies. https://www.europarl.europa.eu/meetdocs/2014_2019/plmrep/COMMITTEES/JURI/DV/2020/01-09/AI-report_EN.pdf. Accessed 13 January 2020.
European Data Protection Supervisor (2015) Towards a new digital ethics: Data, Dignity and Technology. https://edps.europa.eu/data-protection/our-work/publications/opinions/towards-new-digital-ethics-data-dignity-and_en. Accessed 4 October 2021.
European Data Protection Supervisor (2018) Public Consultation on Digital Ethics. Summary of Outcomes. https://edps.europa.eu/sites/edp/files/publication/18-09-25_edps_publicconsultation-digitalethicssummary_en.pdf. Accessed 12 March 2020.
European Data Protection Supervisor, Ethics Advisory Group (2018) Towards a Digital Ethics. https://edps.europa.eu/sites/edp/files/publication/18-01-25_eag_report_en.pdf. Accessed 12 March 2020.
Ferguson AG (2017) The Rise of Big Data Policing: Surveillance, Race, and the Future of Law Enforcement. New York University Press, New York.
Ferryman K, Pitcan M (2018) Fairness in Precision Medicine. Data & Society. https://datasociety.net/wp-content/uploads/2018/02/Data.Society.Fairness.In_.Precision.Medicine.Feb2018.FINAL-2.26.18.pdf. Accessed 25 June 2020.
Fjeld J, Achten N, Hilligoss H, Nagy A, Srikumar M (2020) Principled Artificial Intelligence: Mapping Consensus in Ethical and Rights-Based Approaches to Principles for AI. Berkman Klein Center for Internet & Society, Cambridge, MA, https://papers.ssrn.com/abstract=3518482. Accessed 12 April 2020.
Goodman EP, Powles J (2019) Urbanism Under Google: Lessons from Sidewalk Toronto. Fordham L. Rev. 88(2):457–498.
Gregory CO (1951) Trespass to Negligence to Absolute Liability. Virginia Law Review 37 (3):359–397.
Hansson SO (2013) The Ethics of Risk. Palgrave Macmillan, New York.
https://www.sciencedirect.com/science/article/pii/B9780750675796500182. Accessed 5 August 2021.
Independent High-Level Expert Group on Artificial Intelligence set up by the European Commission (2019) Ethics Guidelines for Trustworthy AI. https://ec.europa.eu/futurium/en/ai-alliance-consultation.1.html. Accessed 12 March 2020.
Independent High-Level Expert Group on Artificial Intelligence set up by the European Commission (2020) The Assessment List For Trustworthy Artificial Intelligence (ALTAI) for Self-Assessment. https://digital-strategy.ec.europa.eu/en/library/assessment-list-trustworthy-artificial-intelligence-altai-self-assessment. Accessed 17 September 2021.
Kaye J, Whitley EA, Lund D, Morrison M, Teare H, Melham K (2015) Dynamic Consent: A Patient Interface for Twenty-first Century Research Networks. European Journal of Human Genetics 23(2):141–146.

Mantelero A (2016) Personal Data for Decisional Purposes in the Age of Analytics: From an Individual to a Collective Dimension of Data Protection. Computer Law & Sec. 32(2):238–255.

Mantelero A (2017) Regulating Big Data. The Guidelines of the Council of Europe in the Context of the European Data Protection Framework. Computer Law & Security Rev. 33(5):584–602.

Mantelero A (2018a) Artificial Intelligence and Data Protection: Challenges and Possible Remedies. Report on Artificial Intelligence, T-PD(2018)09Rev, Consultative Committee of the Convention for the Protection of Individuals with Regard to Automatic Processing of personal data: Strasbourg, 2019. https://rm.coe.int/artificial-intelligence-and-data-protection-challenges-and-possible-re/168091f8a6. Accessed 20 July 2020.

Mantelero A (2018b) AI and Big Data: A Blueprint for a Human Rights, Social and Ethical Impact Assessment. Computer Law & Sec. Rev. 34(4):754–772.

Mayer-Schönberger V (1997) Generational Development of Data Protection in Europe. In: Agre PE, Rotenberg M (eds) Technology and Privacy: The New Landscape. The MIT Press, Cambridge, pp 219–241.

McMahon BME (1968) The Reactions of Tortious Liability to Industrial Revolution: A Comparison: I. Irish Jurist 3(1):18–32.

Microsoft Corporation (2021) Feedback from: Microsoft Corporation [to the European Commission's Proposal for a Regulation on Artificial Intelligence (AI) Systems]. https://ec.europa.eu/info/law/better-regulation/have-your-say/initiatives/12527-Artificial-intelligence-ethical-and-legal-requirements/F2665556_en. Accessed 9 August 2021.

Moyes R (2016) Key Elements of Meaningful Human Control. Background Paper to Comments. Convention on Certain Conventional Weapons (CCW) Meeting of Experts on Lethal Autonomous Weapons Systems (LAWS) Geneva, 11–15 April 2016. Article 36. https://article36.org/wp-content/uploads/2016/04/MHC-2016-FINAL.pdf. Accessed 24 May 2021.

Muhlbauer WK (2004) Risk Management. In: Muhlbauer WK (ed) Pipeline Risk Management Manual. Gulf Professional Publishing, Amsterdam, pp 331–355.

Narayanan A, Huey J, Felten EW (2016) A Precautionary Approach to Big Data Privacy. In: Gutwirth S, Leenes R, De Hert P (eds) Data Protection on the Move. Springer, Dordrecht, pp 357–385.

Nordlander K, Simon C-M, Pearson H (2010) Hazard v. Risk in EU Chemicals Regulation. European Journal of Risk Regulation 1 (3):239 239–250.

OECD (2013) Recommendation of the Council concerning Guidelines governing the Protection of Privacy and Transborder Flows of Personal Data, C(80)58/FINAL, as amended on 11 July 2013 by C(2013)79.

OECD (2015) Recommendation of the Council on Digital Security Risk Management for Economic and Social Prosperity. https://www.oecd-ilibrary.org/science-and-technology/digital-security-risk-management-for-economic-and-social-prosperity/recommendation-of-the-council-on-digital-security-risk-management-for-economic-and-social-prosperity_9789264245471-1-en. Accessed 18 March 2019.

OECD (2019) Recommendation of the Council on Artificial Intelligence. https://legalinstruments.oecd.org/en/instruments/OECD-LEGAL-0449. Accessed 29 July 2019.

Office of the High Commissioner for Human Rights (2000) CESCR General Comment No. 14: The Right to the Highest Attainable Standard of Health (Art. 12) Adopted at the Twenty-Second Session of the Committee on Economic, Social and Cultural Rights, on 11 August 2000 (Contained in Document E/C.12/2000/4).

Ohm P (2010) Broken Promises of Privacy: Responding to the Surprising Failure of Anonymization. UCLA L. Rev. 57:1701–1777.

Oliphant K (2005) Rylands v Fletcher and the Emergence of Enterprise Liability in the Common Law. In: Koziol H, Steininger BC (eds) European Tort Law, Vol. 2004. Tort and Insurance Law Yearbook. New York, Springer, pp 81–120.

Peel J (2004) Precaution – A Matter of Principle, Approach or Process? Melb. J. Int. Law 5 (2):483–501.

Pellegrino ED, Thomasma DC (1987) The Conflict between Autonomy and Beneficence in Medical Ethics: Proposal for a Resolution. The Journal of Contemporary Health Law and Policy 3:23–46.

Raso F, Hilligoss H, Krishnamurthy V, Bavitz C, Kim L (2018) Artificial Intelligence & Human Rights Opportunities & Risks. Berkman Klein Center for Internet & Society. https://cyber.harvard.edu/sites/default/files/2018-09/2018-09_AIHumanRightsSmall.pdf?subscribe=Download+the+Report. Accessed 12 April 2020.

Rouvroy A (2015) "Of Data and Men" – Fundamental rights and freedoms in a world of Big Data. Consultative Committee of the Convention for the Protection of Individuals with Regard to Automatic Processing of personal data, T-PD-BUR(2015)09Rev. http://rm.coe.int/CoERMPublicCommonSearchServices/DisplayDCTMContent?documentId=09000016806a6020. Accessed 24 June 2020.

Seatzu F (2015) The Experience of the European Court of Human Rights with the European Convention on Human Rights and Biomedicine. Utrecht Journal of International and European Law 31(81):5–16.

Selbst AD, Barocas S (2018) The Intuitive Appeal of Explainable Machines. Fordham L. Rev. 87:1085–1139.

Selbst AD, Powles J (2017) Meaningful Information and the Right to Explanation. International Data Privacy Law 7(4):233–242.

Sheehan M (2011) Can Broad Consent be Informed Consent? Public Health Ethics 3:226–235.

Simonite T (2021) These Algorithms Look at X-Rays—and Somehow Detect Your Race. Wired, May 5. https://www.wired.com/story/these-algorithms-look-x-rays-detect-your-race/. Accessed 7 August 2021.

Strand R, Kaiser M (2015) Report on Ethical Issues Raised by Emerging Sciences and Technologies. Council of Europe, Committee on Bioethics, Strasbourg. https://www.coe.int/T/DG3/Healthbioethic/Activities/12_Emerging%20technologies/BergenStudy%20e.pdf. Accessed 12 May 2020.

Taylor L, Dencik L (2020) Constructing Commercial Data Ethics. Technology and Regulation. https://techreg.org/index.php/techreg/article/view/35/9. Accessed 14 April 2020.

Taylor L, Floridi L, van der Sloot B (eds) (2017) Group Privacy New Challenges of Data Technologies. Springer International Publishing, Cham.

ten Have HAMJ, Jean MS (2009) The UNESCO Universal Declaration on Bioethics and Human Rights: Background, Principles and Application. UNESCO, Paris.

The Norwegian Data Protection Authority (2018) Artificial Intelligence and Privacy Report. https://www.datatilsynet.no/globalassets/global/english/ai-and-privacy.pdf. Accessed 15 July 2019.

The Public Voice (2018) Universal Guidelines for Artificial Intelligence. https://thepublicvoice.org/AI-universal-guidelines/. Accessed 5 May 2019.

Traynor RJ (1965) The Ways and Meanings of Defective Products And Strict Liability. Tenn. L. Rev. 32(3):363–376.

UNESCO (2019) Preliminary Study on a Possible Standard-Setting Instrument on the Ethics of Artificial Intelligence. https://unesdoc.unesco.org/ark:/48223/pf0000369455. Accessed 8 March 2020.

United Nations, Office of the High Commissioner for Human Rights (2018) Guidelines for States on the Effective Implementation of the Right to Participate in Public Affairs. https://www.ohchr.org/EN/Issues/Pages/DraftGuidelinesRighttoParticipationPublicAffairs.aspx. Accessed 20 November 2019.

Wachter S, Mittelstadt B, Floridi L (2017) Why a right to explanation of automated decision – making does not exist in the General Data Protection Regulation. International Data Privacy Law 7(2):76–99.

Wagner B (2018a) Ethics as an Escape from Regulation: From Ethics. In: Bayamlioğlu E, Baraliuc I, Janssens LAW, Hildebrandt M (eds) Being Profiling. Cogitas Ergo Sum. Amsterdam University Press, Amsterdam, pp 84–89.

Wagner CZ (2018b) Evolving Norms of Corporate Social Responsibility: Lessons Learned from the European Union Directive On Non-Financial Reporting. Transactions: The Tennessee Journal of Business Law 19:619–708.

Westin AF, Baker MA (1972) Databanks in a Free Society. Computers, Record-Keeping and Privacy. Quadrangle/The New York Time Book Co., New York.

Whipple C (1988) Acceptable Risk. In: Travis CC (ed) Carcinogen Risk Assessment. Springer, Boston, pp 157–170.

Yamin AE (2005) The Right to Health Under International Law and Its Relevance to the United States. American Journal of Public Health 95(7):1156–1161.

Zuiderveen Borgesius F (2018) Discrimination, Artificial Intelligence, and Algorithmic Decision-Making. Anti-discrimination department of the Council of Europe. https://rm.coe.int/discrimination-artificial-intelligence-and-algorithmic-decision-making/1680925d73. Accessed 16 May 2020.

Chapter 5
Open Issues and Conclusions

Contents

Abstract Having discussed in previous chapters the valuable contribution that an assessment model encompassing human rights, ethical and societal issues can provide to the development and regulation of AI, these concluding remarks address some of the challenges we face in implementing this approach in tangible reality. The focus on future global regulatory scenarios in the field of AI shows how the holistic HRESIA model, which includes the contextualisation of human rights and socio-ethical values in a given area, could be an effective answer for both the countries which have a human rights-based AI regulation and those who do not. In addition, holistic assessment and values-oriented design procedures can build trust in the development of AI, addressing the increasing public concern for invasive and pervasive AI applications, as well as the growing attention of policy makers to the side effects of AI use in the presence of concentration of power in digital services.

Keywords AI regulation · Data protection · Digital ecosystems · Human rights · Risk assessment · Trust

A. Mantelero, *Beyond Data*, Information Technology and Law Series 36,
https://doi.org/10.1007/978-94-6265-531-7_5

5.1 Addressing the Challenges of AI

For more than fifty years the progressive digitalisation and datafication of our societies and their impact on individuals have been largely managed by legislators through data protection laws. In a world concerned about the use (and misuse) of personal information, data protection became the key component in the response at individual and social level.

Since its origins, data protection has been seen as an enabling right to tackle potential risks concerning discrimination, undemocratic social control, invasion of private life, and limitations on several freedoms, such as freedom of thought, expression, and association.

However, this link between data protection and human rights (fundamental rights in the EU) has not been explored in the cases decided by the data protection authorities or in the literature.[1] Although the relationship between data protection and other competing rights has been considered in court decisions, the theory and practice of data protection remain largely remote from human rights doctrine and the attention of human rights experts. This also reflects the different backgrounds of the main scientific communities in these fields. Privacy scholars traditionally come from private, constitutional or administrative law, while human rights scholars have an international law background and are more focused on prejudice to human rights other than privacy and data protection.

This barrier between the two areas has collapsed under the blows of the latest wave of AI development, since the last decade of the twentieth century to the present day. Pervasive datafication together with the use of AI for a variety of activities impacting on society, from medicine to crime prevention, has raised serious concerns about the potentially harmful effects of data-intensive AI systems. This has led legislators and policymakers to look beyond data and data protection to consider the different ways in which AI might interfere with human organisations and behaviour, from automated decision-making process to behavioural targeting.

The breadth of the questions raised by AI and the relationship between machines (and those who determine their underlying values) and humans, the struggle of traditional data protection principles to fully address these new and broader issues,[2] and the limited discussion of human rights in AI led business and regulators to look to ethics for answers to these challenges.

However, the variety of ethical approaches stood in contrast to the need for a common framework in a world of global players and the same models replicated in different countries. This has led AI regulators to the current debate on a future legal framework, where human rights represent a key component in addressing the potential risks of AI.

Having briefly summarised the trajectory and after highlighting the valuable contribution that an assessment model encompassing human rights, ethical and

[1] Mantelero and Esposito 2021, para 4.

[2] See Chap. 1.

societal issues can provide, the big challenge that still faces us is how to implement this approach in tangible reality. Two different scenarios have to be taken into account: (i) AI development and use in countries where human rights are protected by national law and where compliance is therefore mandatory on business and the public sector, and (ii) AI development and use, by companies and their subsidiaries and suppliers, in countries where those rights are not fully protected, or not protected at all, despite the ratification of international human rights treaties. In any case, it has to be remembered that, in both cases, ethical and social issues remain largely outside the legal discourse and an awareness of AI's impact in these spheres remains lacking.

While in the first scenario HRESIA can be more easily implemented, where business is conducted in the absence of national human rights safeguards, the United Nations' Guiding Principles on Business and Human Rights may be of help.[3] These Principles, and specifically Section II on corporate responsibility to respect human rights, enshrine several key HRIA requirements (stakeholder consultation, regular assessment, transparency, role of experts, etc.).[4] While this is not a legally binding instrument, it does represent an influential global model in addressing the relationship between human rights and business.[5]

However, despite the presence of this authoritative framework, the impact of these principles is still limited, perhaps because of their focus on the entire value chain, which normally demands an extensive effort in all directions.[6] The ongoing debate on the Guiding Principles on Business and Human Rights and the challenges their application raises may point the way to narrower product-focused human rights assessments, such as the HRESIA, which spotlights the design of each product or service, rather than targeting the entire business.[7]

If the lack of legal safeguards for human rights at a national level is problematic, the situation is much more complicated when we consider the ethical and societal values underpinning AI development and use. Here, even proposed human rights-oriented regulations do not specifically address the societal acceptability of AI, and its compatibility with societal values is not fully reflected in the law.[8]

---

[3] See also United Nations High Commissioner for Human Rights 2021.

[4] United Nations 2011; Council of Europe, Committee of Ministers 2016. On the distinction between the approach adopted in UN Guiding Principles and Corporate Social Responsibility (CSR), and on the limitations of the latter, see Wettstein 2020.

[5] See also European Commission 2020, pp. 48–49. But see Deva 2013, who also points out the limits of transplanting international human rights instruments designed for state in a corporate business context.

[6] European Commission 2020, p. 41. But see United Nations 2011, Commentary to Principle 17, on product/service due diligence for adverse impacts on human rights where companies have a large number of entities in their value chains making it difficult to conduct an impacts assessment of all of them.

[7] For a broader approach, see Sect. 5.3.

[8] See Chap. 3.

Rather than try to arrive at improbable universal ethical and social values or, on the contrary, shape codes of ethics to fit corporate values, the best solution is probably to use experts to understand the context. Experts can help identify underlying societal values and also make for greater accuracy and inclusion through active dialogue with shareholders and participation.[9]

5.2 The Global Dimension of AI

As in the case of data processing, the global use of AI technologies is making regulation a pressing challenge. Although only a few proposals for AI regulation are available and as yet in their early stages, we can envisage what might happen in the future in terms of global regulatory competition and fragmentation.

On the one hand, Europe might build on its front runner status in data protection, to reproduce for AI the so-called Brussels effect,[10] as well as the Strasbourg effect,[11] exporting its regulatory model and risk-based approach including attention to human/fundamental rights.

On the other, it is worth recalling the limits of the universal human rights position[12] and European legislators' dependence on the European Court of Human Rights and the European Court of Justice, making it hard to export the European models to different legal contexts.[13]

In addition, regulatory fragmentation at a regional level may ensue from state policies targeting digital sovereignty, either with the intention to bolster human rights or on the contrary in countries wishing to limit these individual rights and freedoms.

This scenario is not new and was seen already with respect to data protection. Data localisation obligations and restrictions on transborder data flows were introduced by European countries under Convention 108 or the GDPR to provide their citizens with a greater level of protection than third countries with weaker data protection regimes, or to safeguard competing interests (national security, defence, public safety, etc.).[14] Meanwhile, some countries have introduced rules on transborder data flows and data localisation for foreign service providers, not to safeguard human rights, but as a means to secure governmental control over their citizens' online behaviour.

---

[9] See Chap. 3.

[10] Bradford 2020.

[11] Bygrave 2021.

[12] See Chap. 3, Sect. 3.1.1.

[13] Pauletto 2021.

[14] Convention 108+, Article 14, and GDPR, Chapter IV.

Replicating European progress in data protection[15] in the regulation of AI around the world therefore looks unlikely. Despite the worldwide interest in the EU and Council of Europe AI initiatives, we must remember that Convention 108 dates back to 1981 and the GDPR was built on a 1995 Directive. While we might envisage a Brussels/Strasbourg effect for AI, even conceding a faster international harmonisation in response to the globalisation of services, needs and trends, it is unrealistic to expect a common legal framework on AI to be realised any time soon. This is partly due to the difficulties of exporting the European models noted above, but also to the varying regulatory approaches of some states, in particular with respect to recognising human rights.

This means that at present a holistic assessment model, which includes the contextualisation of human rights and socio-ethical values in a given area, could be an effective answer for both the countries which have human rights-based AI regulation and those who do not. For the former, the HRESIA could be integrated into proposed AI risk assessment procedures,[16] while in the latter it would help companies and other bodies develop a new approach, recognising the impact of AI applications on society in line with human rights-oriented business practices.

Indeed, assessment models like the HRESIA do not need to be mandatory but could be voluntarily included in business and public sector best practices when dealing with legal and societal needs. Of course, the mandatory or voluntary obligation to carry out the assessment would impact its adoption and the achievement of its goals.

The absence of a mandatory obligation would only reinforce concerns already expressed about the self-assessment of AI risks,[17] pointing to the conflicting interests of AI manufacturers and users. Further, while the danger of unfair risk assessment exists, both the mandatory and voluntary schemes are open to manipulation, and internal mitigation measures could be taken to combat this.[18]

Moreover, the new notion of trustworthy AI, though based on a non-legal and uncertain frame of reference (trust), highlights the importance of the relationship between AI providers/users and end-users. A wider adoption of impact assessments by providers/users can certainly play a part in boosting confidence among AI end-users.

Given the increasing public concern for invasive and pervasive data-intensive applications,[19] plus the growing attention of policy makers for the side effects of their use in the presence of concentration of power in digital services, building trust has become a major goal for AI providers and users. Though a variety of strategies (including marketing) can be used to achieve this, implementation of a risk

---

[15] Greenleaf 2021.

[16] See Chap. 4.

[17] E.g., AlgorithmWatch 2021, p. 5.

[18] The HRESIA model includes several features to reduce this risk, see Chap. 2.

[19] E.g., Veliz 2021; Zuboff 2020; O'Neil 2017.

assessment model with its transparent outcomes and practices can be an effective way to develop genuinely trustworthy AI.

Adopting holistic assessment and values-oriented design procedures such as the HRESIA could therefore replicate in AI the experience and results achieved in other sectors with regard to human rights and ethical practice, including the repercussions for business reputation[20] and consumer/investor choices[21] (e.g. fair trade labels).[22] The implementation might even be certified. Here, the effect on the biggest AI adopters (e.g. municipalities) would be even more significant if they were accountable to AI end-users.

Besides, a greater focus on these requirements by the big players and in public procurement[23] could also help override the scarce interest in these issues of many AI start-ups and SMEs. A bottom-up demand for responsible AI, supported by appropriate assessment models, could counter the lack of focus on societal and human rights questions due to an absence of competence or attention to aspects that are not immediately related to business profits.[24]

On the other hand, following the European model in introducing a mandatory AI human rights impact assessment[25]– hopefully extended to non-legal societal issues – would undoubtedly foster a quicker diffusion of this practice.[26] But this option has its own implications that need to be thought through.

In the first place, a universal mandatory assessment might provoke adverse reactions from businesses complaining of additional burdens and costs. While these are proportional to the complexity of the AI and risks in question, legislators could be induced (see the EU proposal) to restrict mandatory assessments to certain categories of applications. This could result in a dual situation, with some areas fully secured and monitored (or even over-scrutinised, given the broad categories in the AIA proposal, potentially including non high-risk applications) while other widespread AI uses go largely unregulated despite their not insignificant risks.

Second, the history of data protection reveals the difference between the ambitions of the law and its concrete implementation. Underfunded and understaffed supervisory authorities, pervasive adoption of data-intensive solutions, obscurity of processing operations, foreign providers, interplay between AI developers and

---

[20] See also Spiekermann 2016, pp. 184–85.

[21] European Commission 2020, pp. 89–90.

[22] E.g., Castaldo et al. 2009; Bartels et al. 2020.

[23] Consultative Committee of the Convention for the protection of individuals with regard to automatic processing of personal data (Convention 108) 2019, para 3.2. See also Wylie 2020; United Nations 2011, p. 6.

[24] Powell 2021.

[25] See also European Parliament 2021.

[26] Wagner 2018, who highlights that, in the field of Corporate Social Responsibility, the development of non-financial reporting practices "is an evolutionary process that may take years to accomplish as countries adapt to new and changing circumstances pertaining to such reporting", even when supported by specific law provisions.

governments, are all factors that may reduce the enforcement of mandatory solutions, as happened with data protection.[27]

Very likely in coming years both mandatory and non-mandatory AI risk assessment models will coexist and may include the adoption of technical standards. A middle way based on ex post assessment is also possible, in response to concerns by some supervisory authorities. Here the dual dimension of the HRESIA model, in its universal and local treatment of human rights and societal values, might also make it a useful tool for supervisory authorities.

Finally, the global scenario in which AI should be seen also highlights the value of a risk-based approach from the perspective of the historical development of system use. Particularly in the public sector, the lack of attention to human rights and societal impact can encourage a sort of development bias, which sees only the positive results of AI and disregards or underestimates potential misuse. As recently demonstrated by the use of data-intensive biometric systems in Afghanistan[28] (as well as some contact-tracing applications during the Covid-19 pandemic[29]), the lack of a holistic assessment of the potential consequences of AI-based systems can be damaging. It also fails to give voice to minorities, affected groups and stakeholders, leading to technology-driven solutions whose efficiency is not accompanied by an absence of risks when operating conditions or the system controllers change.

5.3 Future Scenarios

A thread running through this book has been the idea of looking beyond data protection to tackle the challenges of AI and avoid a split between the focus on human rights and ethics in the broader sense. While today a growing number of voices are calling for a human rights assessment, this option was largely unexplored at the start of this research, and the question of how to put a human rights-based approach to AI into practice remains little examined.

The first chapter pointed out the reason for this change of focus in the regulation of AI data-intensive systems from data protection to human rights and highlighted the role that assessment methodologies can play in this change.

A workable methodology that responds to the new paradigm can also help to bridge the gap between the ethical guidelines and practices developed in the last few years and the more recent hard law approach. Here the regulatory turn missed an opportunity to combine these two realms, both of which are significant when AI applications are used in a social context and have an impact on individuals and groups.

[27] See also Schilling-Vacaflor 2021.

[28] Privacy International 2021.

[29] United Nations et al. 2020; Council of Europe 2020.

Shaping AI on the basis a paradigm that rests on legal and societal values through risk assessment procedures does not mean simply crafting a questionnaire with separate blocks of questions for legal issues, ethical values and social impact. Such a simplistic approach tends to overestimate the value of the questionnaire-based self-assessment[30] and ignores the challenges associated with the idea that AI developers/users can fully perform this evaluation as if it were a mere checklist.

Chapters 2 and 3 therefore outline a more elaborate model, the HRESIA (Human Rights, Ethical and Social Impact Assessment), which combines different tools ranging from self-assessment, expert panels, to participation. The biggest distinction to be made here is between the Human Rights Impact Assessment (HRIA) module of the HRESIA and the complete evaluation of ethical and societal values. While the first is based on questionnaires and risk models, the second is characterised by a greater role for experts and participation in identifying the values to be embedded in AI solutions. Furthermore, the HRIA component, though based on lengthy experience in human rights assessment, has reshaped the traditional model to make it better suited to AI applications and an increasingly popular regulatory approach based on risk thresholds and prior assessment.

This interplay between risk assessment and AI regulation led to an examination of the major current proposals, presented by the European Commission and the Council of Europe. Chapter 4 emphasised their limitations compared with the HRESIA model, by not including ethical and social issues and (in the EU case) restricting risk assessment to predefined high-risk categories. It should be noted however that the Council of Europe's proposal does broaden the assessment to include democracy and the rule of law, in line with its mandate, but at the same time making it more complicated to envisage a feasible assessment model that properly covers all these issues without reducing them to a mere list of questions.

As regards the social and ethical components in the design and operation of AI systems and assessing their coherence with contextual values, Chap. 3 explored the practices of ethics committees considering both committees set up by companies and committees in the field of medical ethics and research. Their experience, and their shortcomings, were used to highlight the role of experts in the HRESIA in identifying key societal values and also to outline how these committees might work, including with the participation of major stakeholders and groups potentially affected by AI applications.

Comparison of the HRESIA with its various components and the ongoing proposals for AI regulation show how the HRESIA can represent a better implementation of the risk-based approach adopted by European legislators and, in a global perspective, encourage a focus on the holistic consequences for society in countries where there are no regulations.

Notwithstanding the positive outcomes that a better understanding of human rights and societal values can bring to AI design, development and use, the longer

[30] Sarfaty 2013.

term poses further questions that are not fully addressed by the HRESIA and it may be that we have to raise the bar of human rights expectations with respect to an AI-based society. Three main issues will dominate discussion and analysis over the coming years: (i) partial reconsideration of the traditional theoretical framework of human rights; (ii) extension of the requirements concerning human rights safeguards, but also compliance with ethical and social values, to the entire AI supply chain; (iii) a broader reflection on digital ecosystems.

As for the first issue, there is an ongoing debate on the collective dimension of human rights which is leading us to reconsider the traditional view taken in this field.[31] The classification of the world by AI and its consequent decision-making processes, irrespective of the identity of the targeted persons and based merely on their belonging to a certain group, suggests we need a broader discussion of the largely individual nature of human rights.

Similarly, the traditional approach to non-discrimination should be reconsidered. Here intersectional studies and other theories can contribute to providing a legal framework more responsive to the new AI scenario.[32] Nevertheless, the variety of criteria used by business to discriminate in AI and their lack of a link to protected grounds suggests more research called for into the blurred confines between unfair discrimination and unfair commercial practices.[33]

Moving from the theoretical framework to impact assessment implementation, this book has focused on the impact of AI-based solutions on their potential social targets, looking forward to the effects of AI use. But we need to extend the same attention to the upstream stage of this process, namely compliance with human rights and ethical values, as well as the social acceptability of manufacturing practices and the AI products/services supply chain.[34]

---

[31] Newman 2004; Mitnick 2018, p. 6; Hartney 1991.

[32] Mann and Matzner 2019; Hoffmann 2019. See also Wachter et al. 2021.

[33] Ebers 2021; Galli 2020.

[34] European Commission 2020, p. 16 ("Just over one-third of business respondents indicated that their companies undertake due diligence which takes into account all human rights and environmental impacts, and a further one-third undertake due diligence limited to certain areas. However, the majority of business respondents which are undertaking due diligence include first tier suppliers only. Due diligence practices beyond the first tier and for the downstream value chain were significantly lower. The vast majority of business stakeholders cover environmental impacts, including climate change, in their due diligence, although the term 'climate change due diligence' for a self-standing process is currently rarely used, and human rights and climate change processes often take place in 'silos'. The most frequently used due diligence actions include contractual clauses, codes of conduct and audits.").

New studies are emerging in this field,[35] but it remains largely unexplored, especially with regard to the possible solutions in terms of policies and regulation. Aspects such as labour exploitation or the environment impact of AI solutions need to be examined not only for the benefit of AI adoption and development, but also of competition. Existing and proposed barriers to market entry are based on legal requirements and standards on product safety and the human rights impact of AI use, but ignore human rights violations in the production of AI.

While some personal data protection is possible when data subjects belong to countries with robust data protection regulations,[36] in other cases rights and freedoms are more difficult to protect. This is particularly true when the legal systems of AI producer countries lack effective human rights protection or enforcement. The UN Guiding Principles on Business and Human Rights can serve as a guide in these cases.

Barriers to market access,[37] but also mandatory obligations on human rights and fundamental freedoms as well as due diligence[38] for subcontractors can be an important step forward in extending human rights to upstream AI manufacturing, in part following the experience of data protection, but also the EU's ethical rules on biomedicine and research. This would contribute to an improved AI ecosystem where respect for human rights and ethical and social values are widely accepted as a condition for doing business, in the same way ethical and legal compliance is a requirement of the pharma industry.

Reference to the AI ecosystem brings us to a final forward-looking scenario regarding the ability to outline an ecology for the digital environment, including AI-based applications which will increasingly become its dominant components.

Despite the limited investigation of this topic, we urgently need to revise the approach to digital technology adopted in the wake of the computer revolution in the 1950s. The increasing availability of new, more powerful and cheaper solutions led to the pervasive presence of digital technologies with their limitless appetite for data and the escalating reliance on them by decision makers. The result is a world that is seen more and more through the lens of algorithms and the social values and

---

[35] Crawford 2021. See also Crawford and Joler 2018.

[36] E.g., European Data Protection Board (2021). Swedish DPA: Police unlawfully used facial recognition app https://edpb.europa.eu/news/national-news/2021/swedish-dpa-police-unlawfully-used-facial-recognition-app_en. Accessed 28 March 2021. The decision of the Swedish SA is available (in Swedish) at https://www.imy.se/globalassets/dokument/beslut/beslut-tillsyn-polismyndigheten-cvai.pdf. Accessed 28 March 2021.

[37] See also European Parliament 2021, n. 10.

[38] United Nations 2011, p. 15, on the notion of due diligence, ("A human rights due diligence process to identify, prevent, mitigate and account for how they [rights, business enterprises] address their impacts on human rights"). This position is also reflected in the ILO Tripartite declaration of principles concerning multinational enterprises and social policy (MNE Declaration) revised in 2017, and in the UN Global Compact. But see the critical observations, about the use of this notion in the human rights context, made by Deva 2013, pp. 98–101.

standpoints of their developers, often without questioning the real need for such systems.[39]

Just as industrial consumer societies are raising questions about the ecological sustainability of the apparently endless abundance of goods and services, the digital society must also question the need for, and acceptability of, a society increasingly governed by pervasive AI. This includes critical questions about the lack of democratic participation and oversight in shaping and adopting AI solutions.

The starting point should not be to see technological evolution as an inevitability that society must adapt to, but to question the desirability of a society based on microtargeting, profiling, social mapping, etc. where the trade-offs for democracy, human rights and freedoms are not necessarily positive, except in the rhetoric of service providers and decision makers who place cost reductions and efficiency at the top of their scale of values.

References

AlgorithmWatch (2021) Draft AI Act: EU Needs to Live up to Its Own Ambitions in Terms of Governance and Enforcement. https://algorithmwatch.org/en/wp-content/uploads/2021/08/EU-AI-Act-Consultation-Submission-by-AlgorithmWatch-August-2021.pdf. Accessed 6 August 2021.

Bartels J, Reinders MJ, Broersen C, Hendriks S (2020) Communicating the Fair Trade Message: The Roles of Reputation and Fit. International Journal of Advertising 39(4): 523–547.

Bradford A (2020) Brussels Effect: how the European Union rules the world. Oxford University Press, New York.

Bygrave LA (2021) The 'Strasbourg Effect' on data protection in light of the 'Brussels Effect': Logic, mechanics and prospects. Computer Law & Security Review 40, https://doi.org/10.1016/j.clsr.2020.105460.

Castaldo S, Perrini F, Misani N, Tencati A (2009) The missing link between corporate social responsibility and consumer trust: The case of fair trade products. Journal of Business Ethics 84:1–15.

Consultative Committee of the Convention for the protection of individuals with regard to automatic processing of personal data (Convention 108) (2019) Guidelines on Artificial Intelligence and data protection, T-PD(2019)01. https://rm.coe.int/guidelines-on-artificial-intelligence-and-data-protection/168091f9d8. Accessed 15 April 2020.

Council of Europe (2020) Joint Statement on Digital Contact Tracing by Alessandra Pierucci, Chair of the Committee of Convention 108 and Jean-Philippe Walter, Data Protection Commissioner of the Council of Europe. https://rm.coe.int/covid19-joint-statement-28-april/16809e3fd7 Accessed 8 May 2020.

Council of Europe, Committee of Ministers (2016) Recommendation CM/Rec(2016)3 of the Committee of Ministers to member States on human rights and business.

Crawford K (2021) Atlas of AI : Power, Politics, and the Planetary Costs of Artificial Intelligence : Power, Politics, and the Planetary Costs of Artificial Intelligence. Yale University Press, New Haven.

[39] See the Sidewalk Toronto case in Chap. 2.

Crawford K, Joler V (2018) Anatomy of an AI System: The Amazon Echo As An Anatomical Map of Human Labor, Data and Planetary Resources. AI Now Institute and Share Lab. http://www.anatomyof.ai. Accessed 27 December 2019.

Deva S (2013) Treating Human Rights Lightly: A Critique of the Consensus Rhetoric and the Language Employed by the Guiding Principles. In: Bilchitz D, Deva S (eds) Human Rights Obligations of Business: Beyond the Corporate Responsibility to Respect? Cambridge University Press, Cambridge, pp 78–104.

Ebers M (2021) Liability for Artificial Intelligence and EU Consumer Law. JIPITEC 12:204-220.

European Commission (2020) Study on Due Diligence Requirements through the Supply Chain: Final Report. https://doi.org/10.2838/39830. Accessed 11 July 2021.

European Parliament (2021) Report with Recommendations to the Commission on Corporate Due Diligence and Corporate Accountability. https://www.europarl.europa.eu/doceo/document/A-9-2021-0018_EN.pdf. Accessed 11 July 2021.

Galli F (2020) Online Behavioural Advertising and Unfair Manipulation Between the GDPR and the UCPD. In: Ebers M, Cantero Gamito M (eds) Algorithmic Governance and Governance of Algorithms. Springer, Cham, pp 109–135.

Greenleaf G (2021) Global Data Privacy Laws 2021: Despite COVID Delays, 145 Laws Show GDPR Dominance 169 Privacy Laws & Business International Report 1. https://papers.ssrn.com/abstract=3836348. Accessed 30 September 2021.

Hartney M (1991) Some Confusions Concerning Collective Rights. Canadian Journal of Law & Jurisprudence 4(2):293–314.

Hoffmann AL (2019) Where Fairness Fails: Data, Algorithms, and the Limits of Antidiscrimination Discourse. Information, Communication & Society 22(7):900–915.

Mann M, Matzner T (2019) Challenging Algorithmic Profiling: The Limits of Data Protection and Anti-Discrimination in Responding to Emergent Discrimination. Big Data & Society 6, https://doi.org/10.1177/2053951719895805.

Mantelero A, Esposito MS (2021) An Evidence-Based Methodology for Human Rights Impact Assessment (HRIA) in the Development of AI Data-Intensive Systems. Computer Law & Sec. Rev. 41 https://doi.org/10.1016/j.clsr.2021.105561.

Mitnick EJ (2018) Rights, Groups, and Self-Invention : Group-Differentiated Rights in Liberal Theory. Routledge, New York.

Newman DG (2004) Collective Interests and Collective Rights. American Journal of Jurisprudence 49(1):127–163.

O'Neil C (2017) Weapons of math destruction : how big data increases inequality and threatens democracy. Broadway Books, New York.

Pauletto C (2021) Options towards a global standard for the protection of individuals with regard to the processing of personal data. Computer Law & Sec. Rev. 40, https://doi.org/10.1016/j.clsr.2020.105433.

Powell AB (2021) Undoing optimization: civic action in smart cities. Yale University Press, New Haven.

Privacy International (2021) Afghanistan: What Now After Two Decades of Building Data-Intensive Systems? http://privacyinternational.org/news-analysis/4615/afghanistan-what-now-after-two-decades-building-data-intensive-systems. Accessed 30 September 2021.

Sarfaty GA (2013) Regulating Through Numbers: A Case Study of Corporate Sustainability Reporting. Va J Int'l L 53(3):575–621.

Schilling-Vacaflor A (2021) Putting the French Duty of Vigilance Law in Context: Towards Corporate Accountability for Human Rights Violations in the Global South? Human Rights Review 22:109–127.

Spiekermann S (2016) Ethical IT innovation : a value-based system design approach. CRC Press, Boca Raton.

United Nations (2011) Guiding Principles on Business and Human Rights. https://www.ohchr.org/Documents/Publications/GuidingPrinciplesBusinessHR_EN.pdf. Accessed 8 December 2020.

United Nations, IOM, ITU, OCHA, OHCHR, UNDP, UNEP, UNESCO, UNHCR, UNICEF, UNOPS, UPU, UN Volunteers, UN Women, WFP, WHO (2020) Joint Statement on Data

Protection and Privacy in the COVID-19 Response. https://www.who.int/news/item/19-11-2020-joint-statement-on-data-protection-and-privacy-in-the-covid-19-response. Accessed 26 November 2020.

United Nations High Commissioner for Human Rights (2021) The Right to Privacy in the Digital Age. Report of the United Nations High Commissioner for Human Rights. https://www.ohchr.org/EN/Issues/DigitalAge/Pages/cfi-digital-age.aspx. Accessed 15 September 2021.

Veliz C (2021) Privacy is Power. Why and How You Should Take Back Control of Your Data. Corgi Books, London.

Wachter S, Mittelstadt B, Russell C (2021) Why Fairness Cannot Be Automated: Bridging the Gap between EU Non-Discrimination Law and AI. Computer Law & Security Review 41, https://doi.org/10.1016/j.clsr.2021.105567.

Wagner CZ (2018) Evolving Norms of Corporate Social Responsibility: Lessons Learned from the European Union Directive On Non-Financial Reporting. Transactions: The Tennessee Journal of Business Law 19:619–708.

Wettstein F (2020) The History of Business and Human Rights and Its Relationship with Corporate Social Responsibility. In: Deva S, Birchall D (eds) Research Handbook on Human Rights and Business. Edward Elgar Publishing, Cheltenham/Northampton, MA, pp 23–45.

Wylie B (2020) In Toronto, Google's Attempt to Privatize Government Fails—For Now. Boston Review. https://bostonreview.net/politics/bianca-wylie-no-google-yes-democracy-toronto. Accessed 2 June 2020.

Zuboff S (2020) The age of surveillance capitalism: the fight for a human future at the new frontier of power. PublicAffairs, New York.

Index

A. Mantelero, *Beyond Data*, Information Technology and Law Series 36,
https://doi.org/10.1007/978-94-6265-531-7

The manufacturer's authorised representative in the EU is Springer Nature Customer Service Centre GmbH, Europaplatz 3, 69115 Heidelberg, Germany. If you have any concerns regarding our products, please contact ProductSafety@springernature.com

Printed and bound by CPI Group (UK) Ltd, Croydon, CR0 4YY
22/09/2026
02221055-0004